BUSINESS/SCIENCE/TECHNOLOGY DIVISION
CHICAGO PUBLIC LIBRARY
400 SOUTH STATE STREET
CHICAGO, ILLINOIS 60605

D0919800

Chicago Public Library

C
P L

REFERENCE

Form 178 rev. 11-00

DISCARD

Management, Work and Welfare in Western Europe

For Joan, Kerry, Michael and Hilary. With many thanks to Steve Anelay for help in preparing this book.

Management, Work and Welfare in Western Europe

A Historical and Contemporary Analysis

Mick Carpenter

Reader in Social Policy, University of Warwick, UK

Steve Jefferys

Professor of European Employment Studies, University of North London, UK

REF HC 240 .C345 2000
Carpenter, Mick.
Management, work, and
 welfare in Western Europe

Edward Elgar
Cheltenham, UK • Northampton, MA, USA

© Mick Carpenter and Steve Jefferys 2000

All rights reserved. No part of this publication may be reproduced, stored in a retrieval system or transmitted in any form or by any means, electronic, mechanical or photocopying, recording, or otherwise without the prior permission of the publisher.

Published by
Edward Elgar Publishing Limited
Glensanda House
Montpellier Parade
Cheltenham
Glos GL50 1UA
UK

Edward Elgar Publishing, Inc.
136 West Street
Suite 202
Northampton
Massachusetts 01060
USA

A catalogue record for this book
is available from the British Library

Library of Congress Cataloguing in Publication Data

Carpenter, Mick.
    Management, work and welfare in Western Europe : a historical and
contemporary analysis / Mick Carpenter, Steve Jefferys.
    Includes index.
    1. Europe, Western—Economic conditions—1945–. 2. Europe,
Western—Social conditions. 3. Europe, Western—Politics and
government—20th century. 4. Management—Europe, Western.
    5. Labor—Europe, Western. 6. Public welfare—Europe, Western.
    I. Jefferys, Steve.

HC240.C345 2001
306.3'6'094—dc21   00–046644

ISBN 1 85898 281 2

Printed and bound in Great Britain by MPG Books Ltd, Bodmin, Cornwall

R02016 29613

BUSINESS/SCIENCE/TECHNOLOGY DIVISION
CHICAGO PUBLIC LIBRARY
400 SOUTH STATE STREET
CHICAGO, ILLINOIS 60605

Contents

v

List of Figures

List of Tables

1. A Western European Tradition in Management, Work and Welfare

This book develops an historically grounded perspective towards the challenges which now face the distinctive patterns of Western European management, work and welfare which were the product of the exceptional 30 year period of low unemployment and high economic growth after 1945. While processes of management, work relations and social policy are often considered separately, our approach stresses the interconnections between them. It is true that recent policy shifts such as 'welfare to work', and the privatization and managerial restructuring of the welfare state are making these linkages clearer. However, we take the long view to show that these three areas of social life have always been closely connected, even if it is has not always been quite so apparent. We seek above all to show that they are themselves woven into the fabric of broader social and *political-economic* transformations. We use italics to signal our belief that political and ideological influences have shaped the nature of changing capitalist forms, rather than being simply a 'reflection' of them; but we also insist that these 'political' influences cannot be analysed separately from the capitalist totalities in which they are embedded.

Western Europe itself is an uncertain and shifting concept. Although conventionally defined as the 7% of the world's land mass situated to the West of the Urals the distinctions between north and south, east and west are, as Braudel (1993) insisted, 'as much the result of history as of geography'. Europe is also a changing 'idea' or 'imaginary community' as well as a real place (Wilson and van der Dussen 1995) The contemporary profile of Western Europe that we focus on was constructed by the Cold War although the roots of the division with the 'East' lie much further back. For the purposes of this book Western Europe broadly covers the 15 current European Union members together with Switzerland and Norway, and references to Germany between 1945 and 1990 mean West Germany.

1.1 A SUMMARY OF THE ARGUMENT

However defined, we argue that with significant local variations, and with

1

the important exception of the countries of its southern flank (Greece, Portugal and Spain), Western Europe's 'social' approach in the decades after 1945 was a distinct 'model' which attempted to combine liberal democracy and advanced capitalism with high levels of collectivist intervention in social and economic life. It was a more constrained form of capitalism structured by traditions of collectivism and interventionism than that which emerged in the USA. To varying degrees, and excluding Britain (apart from the period 1960 to 1979), European societies were also associated with pronounced tendencies to 'corporatism', a system of governance which formally involves and sometimes delegates state responsibilities to producer groups of capital and labour, and sometimes also to religious groupings. Though it operated within a wide range of forms of state governance that led to significant differences between them, Western European capitalism nevertheless characteristically exhibited:

- An interventionist state accepting that governments should plan the economy, organise public enterprises, and provide employment at a living wage for all adult males and increasingly for women too.

- Socially restrained and collectively coordinated management, in which a plurality of management values and practices coexisted, and where quality of life and social status competed as management goals with profitability.

- Work experiences in which subordination was mitigated by industrial relations 'pluralism', involving rights for workers to join trade unions to press for higher wages and challenge the exercise of employer powers, combined with many legally enforceable employment rights.

- A comprehensive range of 'social citizenship' rights in welfare that guaranteed access to a minimum income at times of enforced social dependency, and to a range of 'public goods' such as education, health and social services.

We see these Western European traditions as attempts to run unequal societies with more accountability to and recognition of a public responsibility for meeting the human 'needs' of subordinated social groups, than those which preceded them. Whatever their limitations, these tendencies made the capitalist societies in this part of the globe less unequal and more deeply democratic than elsewhere, embracing however partially a 'social' democracy that extended beyond formal civil and political rights.

In explaining these developments our account disputes reformist assumptions that they emerged primarily from a European consensus on core values between all social groups at the end of the Second World War.

Rather most European employers and right-wing parties and governments went along with these developments for pragmatic reasons and in response to historically embedded pressures. We also question the extent to which they were fuctionally necessary responses to the 'needs' of large-scale 'organized' capitalism. While capitalist interaction has always required a certain amount of regulation, this could have taken different forms. The crisis of economic and political liberalism in the interwar period gave rise to two even more 'organized' rivals, Soviet communism and German fascism. While the latter was militarily defeated, the former emerged as a strengthened force at the end of the Second World War, albeit contained by the military advance of the Allied forces. The example of the USA shows that a more 'liberal' model of capitalism, significantly different from European forms, continued to be viable in the postwar world.

Our account therefore emphasizes the political influences upon the creation of postwar social democracy in Europe. The first, not to be overlooked, is the fact that it took place under an American military and political economic 'umbrella'. After 1945, under American guidance, the two immediate tasks for Western European governments were to renew liberal capitalism by integrating it within an expansionary world economy safeguarded by the strength of the US dollar, and to deal with the popular shift to the left in ways that secured the loyalty of the mass of the people to the Western side of the emerging Cold War. Although there is a danger of painting too rosy a picture of the so-called 'Golden Age', by the 1960s it appeared that Western Europe's 'welfare capitalist' states had permanently accomplished both tasks, steering their economies away from the slumps that had devastated the capitalist world in the 1920s and 1930s, and meeting some of the aspirations for mass consumption and improved welfare provision within the existing society. The growth of Western European institutions embodying an interventionist state, managerial pluralism, employment rights and welfare states were not simply by-products of this economic success story, but among its prime causes. To this extent, then, they 'functioned' well. However, the varying European 'corporatist' arrangements between capital, labour and the state would not have become embedded in this period except for labour mobilization in the context of a perceived communist threat, as demonstrated by the much weaker restraints on capitalism established in the USA where the organized working class was a less politically independent and effective force. Although the resulting 'settlements' were subsequently adapted to the purposes of Western Europe's ruling groups, diluting their radical force, they would not have happened in quite the same way without significant pressures from below. These grew out of wartime resistance movements, trade unions and left political parties, which produced urgent agendas for reform and mounted pressures for change that could not be ignored if postwar Europe was to be politically stabilized and then socially reinvigorated.

The most important influences upon these developments were Social and Christian Democracy which became the dominant domestic political influences, eclipsing for the most part both communist and liberal (i.e. 'free market') parties. There is a need for a balanced view of these political forces, as there is a danger in exaggerating the extent to which Social Democracy was left and Christian Democracy right wing (e.g. Esping-Anderson 1990). In the immediate postwar period both reached similar zeniths of radicalism, while with the onset of the Cold War both moved to the right, but Christian Democracy more so. The general shape of the Western European 'model' was shaped by the rise and partial retreat from postwar radicalism, while the precise nature of domestic settlements around management, work and welfare were mainly affected by national traditions and the extent to which either Social or Christian Democracy were uppermost. In some instances this contest was also affected by divided working class support for communist and socialist parties, notably in France and Italy, which largely benefited Christian Democracy.

Yet while from the end of the 1940s there was a partial recovery of conservatism which was sustained into the 1950s, the 1960s and the first half of the 1970s witnessed a significant extension of European postwar settlements, triggered by further mobilizations from below. This renewed shift to the left in Europe was magnified by the expectations generated by the end of colonialism in the Third World, and the faltering of American power at home and abroad. Renewed demands for greater equality and extension of social rights were made which went beyond the aspirations of the 1940s. There was a revival of labour militancy which sometimes spilled outside formal corporatist frameworks, most dramatically in France and Italy in 1968 and 1969. Collective organization and pursuit of grievances spread also to 'new middle class' layers of white collar workers and students, and 'new' egalitarian social movements emerged involving women, black people, environmentalists and others. The initial response by Europe's ruling groups was to seek to contain this renewed challenge from below through neo-corporatist pacts of various kinds which met some of the new demands. However, as the economic situation worsened by the late 1970s with the collapse of the US dollar standard, the oil shocks and attendant recessions, Western Europe's social frameworks came under considerable strain. The tried and familiar Keynesian medicine no longer seemed to revive distressed economies.

European welfare capitalism did not, however, immediately give way. Although many countries witnessed political shifts to the right in the 1980s, in Scandinavia left governments survived, while in France and the former dictatorships of Southern Europe, the reformist left came to power for the first time in the early 1980s. Equally, where the right did reassert power, this was often through a 'traditional' conservatism, as in Germany, which sought to trim the wings of neo-corporatism and welfare capitalism rather than fundamentally undermine it. Only in Britain, aided by the Westminster electoral system, did neo-liberalism become the ascendant political force following the election of the Thatcher government in 1979. Yet although European welfare capitalism survived the tests of the early 1980s, by the end of the decade it was coming under renewed pressure. There was no single cause, but the effect was the rising influence of capital as a social force and a weakening of labour's collective influence. This included growing competition in the world economy arising from the strength of Japanese capitalism, the greater international mobility of finance capital and the considerable influence of multinational corporations, in a context where right-wing governments in the USA were steering the international economy in a neo-liberal direction. In the face of these forces and rising unemployment, there were mounting difficulties in mobilizing from below, which was also linked to social shifts in European societies themselves. There was a continuing shift from manufacturing to services, and a substantial growth in the numbers of 'managers'. This led to a growing separation between those who appeared to benefit from the freeing of market forces, and those adversely affected by them, which tended to corrode alliances between manual and professional groups. The need for ruling groups to respond to the needs of the latter to ensure social cohesion also diminished considerably after 1989, with the disappearance of the threat of communism.

These combined internal and external pressures led to a growing reassertion of management's 'right to manage', a growing individualization of employment contracts, and the erosion of much job security and employment rights, a retreat of the state from parts of the political economy via privatizations and curbs on public social expenditure, and the imposition of harsher conditions on welfare recipients. The new political environment led unevenly towards declining trade union membership and activity in Western Europe and challenged many well-embedded social democratic traditions. As the 1980s and 1990s proceeded governments of the left adjusted to this new environment. Beginning in Spain and France, Western Europe's governing social democratic parties turned with greater or lesser zeal towards a 'new realism', defined variously as the 'social market' or 'third way'. The abandonment of the goal of socialist *transformation* had already occurred by the 1950s although a renewed challenge did emerge at the end of the 1960s. The turn in the 1980s and 1990s implied shying away from the *reform* of capitalist social relations. Market social relations, operating as a set of disciplinary forces through a complex set of intermediary institutions such as transnational companies and processes of European integration and monetary union established by the 1992 Maastricht Treaty, began to erode the nationally established restrictions to which capital had been subject since 1945.

This unleashing of market forces since the 1990s is neither an inevitable nor a desirable response to intense global pressures and secular social changes. It is better understood as a politically constructed shift towards a more powerful 'American' model of market relationships in management, work and welfare. If the period from the 1940s to the 1970s can be seen as a compromise between European and American visions of how best to organize capitalist societies, the 1980s and especially the 1990s saw the resurgence of the American market vision of the future that 'one size fits all'. This was constructed partly on ideological premises, the undoubted renewal of American capitalism in the 1990s through strategies of deregulation, cutbacks and shift to disciplinary welfare, compared to Western Europe's relatively 'sclerotic' economies and high unemployment. However, rather than suggesting that this constitutes a new 'consensus' we would emphasize how political process has played a significant role in both pushing this agenda forward as a project adopted increasingly adopted by Europe's elites (including centre-left politicians), but which generates unease and even active opposition outside these circles. Thus we stress the role of mobilization, conflict and compromise in both the making and unmaking of Western Europe's relations of management, work and welfare. Neither the emergence or demise of European models of welfare capitalism can therefore be regarded as predetermined. Though they are under great pressure, it is still possible to preserve, adapt and develop the best elements of Western European traditions of pluralist management, employment rights, and extensive welfare protection.

At both national and European levels, then, a battle is ensuing between European social and American market traditions, in which the outcomes are as yet uncertain, though the direction is clear. We believe that the vision of a 'social Europe', despite its limited nature to date, has much to offer a world beset by turmoil as a result of the unravelling of the neo-liberal globalization project from the late 1990s and the rise of popular opposition to its effects. The election of centre-left governments throughout much of Europe by 1998 were indications of widespread popular doubts about the validity of the neo-liberal experiment of the past 20 years. However there were also other worrying signs of a revival in far right politics. Unless there is a renewal of social democratic traditions, other concerted challenges to neo-liberalism based on national protectionism and overt racism may well be mounted.

1.2   COMBINING AGENCY AND STRUCTURE IN THE RISE AND DECLINE OF THE EUROPEAN TRADITION

The above outline argument, in emphasizing the role of political choices and mobilizations around management, work and welfare, in the context of broader pressures associated with industrial capitalism, emphasizes social 'agency' while acknowledging the pull of 'structuralist' currents.

An emphasis on agency alone, for example, might see European patterns of management, work and welfare as institutionalized political expressions of dominant social values. Likewise, recent changes could be seen as caused by a shift away from European values of collectivism, state regulation, and egalitarianism and towards American values of individualism, laissez-faire and celebration of economic success. However, social values themselves are shaped by underlying pressures and identities, and do not always reliably predict how institutions which are mediated by power relations actually behave. Thus Navarro (1989) has pointed out that American public opinion is more collectivist than is commonly presumed, with strong support for a national health service, which makes little headway in a political system so strongly influenced by dominant groups. Similarly, in Europe today, while evidence points to majority ambivalence or even opposition to the erosion of established employment relations and systems of welfare, this does not necessarily protect them.

Yet while an over-emphasis on values is by itself insufficient, structuralist forms of explanation can end up being excessively deterministic, as was the case with the orthodox Marxism and American functionalist sociology that was designed to win converts to respective sides of the Cold War. Orthodox Marxism sought to resolve ambiguities in the writings of Marx and Engels in favour of a deterministic base-superstructure model, the reading that was the official sociology of twentieth-century communist parties under the influence of Stalinist ideology or 'Soviet Marxism' (see Marcuse 1961). This portrayed Soviet state socialism as the form of society which had overcome the contradictions between an increasingly social 'base' and a private capitalist superstructure, and showed the path down which all others must follow. American functionalist theories of 'industrial society' provided a similarly deterministic prediction that technological imperatives of mass production would draw virtually all societies down a similar path to that followed by the USA, leading to a similar 'pluralistic' industrial society to its own constructed around a consensual capitalist ideology. The shift to large-scale industry, Clark Kerr *et al.* (1973) argued, created corps of professional managers and mass labour whose dealings were or would come to be governed by networks of bureaucratic rules and collective bargaining, most probably overseen by a liberal democratic state. The state would intervene through Keynesian economic measures to facilitate full employment, to sustain demand for industry's products, and to ensure the social reproduction of the workforce, but industry itself would necessarily be granted substantial operating autonomy. Functionalist social policy, in drawing on these more general theories, argued that state welfare emerged as a response to societal 'needs' to invest in the quality of labour through education, health and other forms of social provision (Rimlinger 1971). Or else it might be characterized as ways of dealing with the harmful but correctable side-effects of industrial capitalist societies: to regulate the problems of health and order involved in the shift to urban living: to cater for those too young, old or otherwise incapacitated for market labour; and to satisfy the aspirations of the masses for a share in the spoils of economic growth (Wilensky and Lebeaux 1965). The underlying argument was thus that state welfare contributed both to the economic efficiency of industrial society and its political stabilization. The independent role of political institutions and mobilizations was downplayed by such theories.

Both of these rival approaches came under challenge when the pictures they portrayed were shown to be at variance with reality. Deterministic Marxism became increasingly discredited as the political and economic deficiencies of the Soviet 'model' became apparent in the 1950s and 1960s. American functionalism faltered when the US global project ran into the sands of the Vietnam War, and radicalized movements of labour, students, poor people, blacks and women challenged the established power structures of Western capitalist societies. When Western societies also faltered economically in the 1970s, it was apparent that unexpected problems of economic and social management had emerged.

Social science also started to reflect and interpret these social shifts. One consequence was a renewed emphasis on the role of agency in social life, both as an explanation and as a 'humanistic' reaction against the technocratic tendencies in both Soviet Marxism and American functionalism. For example, Giddens's (1984) concept of 'social structuration' attempted to develop a model of the social world that was created by agents, but who are then constrained by it. There was a growing recognition that social contradictions could be politically managed in a variety of ways which could not be predicted in advance. The emergence of the new right as an intellectual and political force also emerged out of the same 'critical' climate. Espousing an individualist rather than social conception of agency it saw 'managed' capitalism as inherently dysfunctional and suggested its contradictions can only be resolved by a restoration of market capitalism.

We do not have any ready-made solutions to the structure-process debate, but seek instead to construct a political-economic and historically grounded account of the rise and relative decline of European welfare capitalism in the post-1945 period. We do concur with the Marxian position that modern societies have an embedded requirement to realize profit, necessitating continuous expansion and periodic transformations of the means of production to realize new means of extracting surplus value. Linked to this, we see the requirements of the capitalist labour process as not just 'technical' but necessarily socially configured in order to extract labour from workers to service a system in which they are not the chief beneficiaries (Braverman 1974). These requirements in turn constrain many of the political and cultural features of modern societies, including work and management relations, and patterns of state welfare. However we recognize that this as an inherently uncertain process, which can lead to a wide variety of social forms and power relations, influenced by factors such as national traditions and institutions, and the strength and direction of social mobilizations from below.

In pursuing our task, we take inspiration from Edward Thompson's (1968: 9) insistence that 'class is a relationship, and not a thing' that only becomes manifest as concrete historical processes unfold. This underpins our empirical and historical approach, except that we would add that classes are themselves differentiated, and relations of gender, and 'race' and ethnicity, are also significant in social life (Bradley 1996). We also associate ourselves with the work of Raymond Williams (1973) who disputed the deterministic dichotomy between base and superstructure and placed a central emphasis on the role of 'culture' in social life, which included highlighting the 'keywords' which emerged and became socially influential in the shift to capitalist modernity (Williams 1976). He thus anticipated the now fashionable emphasis on language and 'discourse' as an influence on social life, but without ascribing it the prime role. He thus provided a balanced approach to 'culture' and ideology which we seek to maintain against the voluntaristic tendencies associated with postmodern theorizing.

We also seek to steer a course away from the other fashionable tendency in social science, a revived form of neo-functionalism which seems rather reminiscent of earlier base-superstructure models. This tends to picture contemporary social change, particularly the form of the state, as largely the result of shifts in capitalist technological 'requirements' from above, from those of 'Fordism' and the nationally based mass production society described by Kerr, to globally organized post-industrial and post-Fordist or 'flexible production' social forms driven by new technology. These strongly imply that European welfare capitalisms and their associated forms of management, work and welfare relations have become 'dysfunctional' to the conditions of 'new times' (see Hall and Jacques 1989). Whereas mass production technologies based on national markets necessitated Keynesian regulation of the national economy to ensure high demand, full employment and welfare states based on principles of citizenship, the profitability of these technologies has been exhausted and the system of state regulation outmoded. In the shift to new technology competitive capitalism has been renewed and led to 'lean' production, full employment has collapsed and the position of national states eroded by 'globalization'. The state has sought to respond by emulating lean productive processes by decentralization and privatization, and shifting increasingly from citizenship or consumptionist welfare to production-oriented 'workfare' (Jessop 1990, 1994).

The evidence for such shifts will be assessed at appropriate points in the narrative. We would, however, dispute the implication that the European traditions of regulated capitalism established after 1945 were largely expressions of technological imperatives and capitalist interests. We view the restraints on market social relations as the result of both long-evolving institutional traditions and democratic gains from below, the best elements of which can and should be preserved. Our approach to management, work and welfare, and the role of the state in relation to them, therefore seeks to combine both the 'new institutionalism' and group or class mobilization analysis (see John 1998). Neither are capitalist interests always as unified or easy to decipher in advance as productivist theories tend to imply. In Britain for example many commentators have pointed to deep conflicts of interest between finance and industrial capital (Gamble 1988; Hutton 1995).

Nevertheless, despite our emphasis on state traditions and mobilization from below, there is strong evidence for structural pressures generated by periodic capitalist transformations initiated from above, even if their outcome is not predetermined. Thus Perry Anderson (1980) argues that Thompson's narrative of a working class 'making itself' underplays the extent to which they were brought together by capitalist entrepreneurs. The existence of 'long waves', first identified by the Russian economist Kondratieff, can be shown to be linked to major shifts in capitalist activity and organization in an expanding world system, though what drives them is an unresolved issue. They are often depicted in reductionist terms as attempts by capitalism to renew itself through 'creative destruction' by shifting to more technologically efficient forms of production as profit rates fall: initially cotton and coal, then railways and engineering, and later mass production utilizing oil and electrical power (Schumpeter 1943). Thus the changes since the 1970s can be pictured as the next stage, leading necessarily to 'flexible production' based on computerization and information technology.

Sophisticated accounts have sought to show how such waves have been associated with particular forms of political regulation, without which tendencies to 'crisis' could not be managed, a preoccupation of the French 'regulation' school which has filtered into much contemporary theorizing (Aglietta 1979; Lipietz 1987). Another influential account sees the earlier waves as associated with an advancing liberalism in economics and politics, necessarily giving way to forms of 'organized capitalism' from the end of the nineteenth century, which reached its most developed form in the post-Second World War period. This is claimed to be now giving way to a globalized and increasingly 'disorganized' capitalism (Lash and Urry 1987). While such attempts to identify general phases in the development of capitalism have merits, there are also dangers inherent in theorizing politics from productive relationships, and in 'over-periodization'. Although theories derived from the regulation paradigm are often quite sophisticated, they still exhibit tendencies towards the economic reductionism and technological determinism associated with earlier structuralist theories. To acknowledge the 'relative autonomy' of the political is not sufficient, as the political has always been an integral element in constituting the economic. In the run-up to the modern period and since, nation states, and the institutions and actors associated with them were prerequisites for, and not just servants of, emerging capitalist economies. Symbiotic but problematic power relations grew up between capitalists and politicians that in an era of mass democracy and large-scale industry became particularly difficult to resolve (Tilly 1992). The increasingly interventionist forms of capitalism adopted since the late nineteenth century were as much a response to these tensions and the shocks of popular challenges as to technological advances. Periodization is also fraught with dangers, not least because the old may not be completely erased by the new. There have undoubtedly been significant social, economic and political changes since the 1970s, but acknowledging this is quite different from asserting the overthrow of an old era and the arrival of a new one. Theories may themselves become 'self-fulfilling prophecies', for example if theories of globalization and the demise of the nation state influence people's actions and choices (Hirst and Thompson, 1996). They have certainly become the staple discourse of political elites, though across Europe there appears to be a stronger commitment to retaining the 'social model' of capitalism in these changed circumstances than in Britain.

1.3   BOOK STRUCTURE

Central to our argument, then, is that contemporary patterns of management, work and welfare associated with European welfare capitalism were not newly created out of the ashes of war in 1945, even though this was a crucial political moment. They have deep roots in the European past and this necessitates a 'long' historical approach to our subject in order to set the context for contemporary analysis. Thus the book first briefly reviews management, work and welfare in the pre-industrial period, and the transformations that occurred with the industrial and political 'revolutions' of the late eighteenth and nineteenth centuries (Chapter 2). We then outline how patterns of management, work and welfare began to be shaped by the emergence of a pan-European industrial capitalism of liberal nation states from the end of the nineteenth century to the Treaty of Versailles in 1918, but which then become overtaken by economic depression and Nazi conquest by 1940 (Chapter 3). Close attention is then given to the political economic developments and interrelated patterns of management, work and welfare that emerged after 1945 in most countries of Western Europe, when industrial capitalism and a liberal democracy of nation states was successfully restored, and the first steps towards European integration were taken, with American help. We then show how the resulting postwar 'settlements' came under intense pressure by the 1970s (Chapters 4 and 5). The book then gives central attention to developments in the 1980s and 1990s, when Western Europe's traditions of welfare capitalism have come under increasing strain, in a European and global political economy increasingly dominated by the American neo-liberal model of 'individual contract' capitalism. After setting the scene by outlining the changing political-economic contexts of the 1980s and 1990s, including renewed moves to European integration (Chapter 6), subsequent chapters assess the impact in turn on management (Chapter 7), work (Chapter 8) and welfare (Chapter 9). Finally, Chapter 10 assesses whether a 'European' rather than an 'American' future remains a viable option.

2. The Historical Roots of Western European Management, Work and Welfare

This chapter reviews a long historical period, from the turn of the first millennium to around 1850, by when the 'two revolutions', industrial and political, had been launched across Europe (Hobsbawm 1975). The account is therefore inevitably superficial and compressed. However, we have taken a long approach to show how the roots of nineteenth-century European capitalism lie further back than the conventional 'take off' date of the late eighteenth century, and also how features of the European past have been carried forward into the modern era. While bearing in mind our own concerns about the hazards of periodization, two main phases of pre-modern European development can be identified within which developments in work, management and welfare may be situated: (1) the 'high' and later Middle Ages from around 1000 to 1500 associated with the 'urban' revolution and the beginnings of the spread of market relations within a predominantly closed Europe, and (2) the 'early modern' period from 1500 to around 1750 which was increasingly 'proto-industrial', and the period when Western European states became the hub of a global trading system. The concluding section of the chapter then outlines the accelerated transformations that took place from the mid-eighteenth to the mid-nineteenth century, the one hundred years during which, once all the necessary qualifications have been made, a fundamental threshold in European and world history was crossed.

2.1 CONTINUITY AND CHANGE IN EUROPEAN SOCIETY DURING THE MEDIAEVAL PERIOD 1000-1500

Feudal Europe from the tenth century was a hierarchical, locally structured and static society, but also a world where social and geographical escape routes began to open up, establishing liberties that mark the beginnings of modern civil and political rights (Braudel 1993). Although these were mainly enjoyed by privileged classes, even among the peasantry there were 'degrees of unfreedom' (Heer 1962). As well as being dynamic and expanding economically, mediaeval Europe was increasingly rent by tensions and dissent.

Before 1500 society was strongly layered. Ancient seigniorial obligations between peasant and landlord overlay a social order based on an uneasy and, ultimately, unstable alliance between the theocratic and military power imposed after the disintegration of the Roman Empire (Bloch 1962; Duby 1980). Fledgling states emerged which granted substantial rights to local lords to run their own 'fiefs' on condition that they fight to maintain the integrity of the larger territory against external threat. The peasant or villein received protection, but at the cost of subordination and exploitation. The church played a key role in cementing feudalism as a pan-European system around a cohesive authority radiating from Rome so that, despite variations of climate and geography, there was a broadly similar religious and secular culture. Agriculture, as the common occupation of the vast majority, also promoted uniformity, though in the long term differences in soil and climate would be one factor projecting north and south along different trajectories.

Feudalism has appropriately been described as 'hereditary juridical servitude' based on the local manor (Hilton 1969). The manorial farm constituted the demesne, and those working it formed part of the squire's household. Outside the demesne peasants tilled their own strips or fields but were obliged to yield a part of the produce to the lord, and to work the demesne at busy times of the year such as ploughing or harvesting (Kranzberg and Gies 1975). Work was physically exhausting, but peasants were normally autonomous on a day-to-day basis as feudalism exacted a tribute on labour rather than seeking directly to organize it. However peasants were also regularly organized collectively in 'managed' forms of work such as building castles, roads and bridges. It was, however, the activities of the church and the organization of frequent wars that demanded the most sophisticated organizational and management skills.

The crusades of the late eleventh century onwards represented a major shift in mediaeval society. They relieved the social tensions generated by growing poverty and refocused them outwards, laying foundations for the subsequent capitalist and imperialist expansion of Europe. The growth of towns particularly upset the orderly division of feudal society. Modest improvements in agricultural productivity enabled the population to grow for most of the later mediaeval period, and a market economy for commodities started to emerge in the expanding cities who won charters granting them 'liberties' outside feudal constraints. For Cippola (1976) the 'urban revolution' of this period represents a key turning point not just in European, but also in world history. The shift was spearheaded initially by the city states of Northern Italy. Towns like Venice, Genoa and Pisa which had supplied the Western armies during the crusades, became the hub of an expansionist European economy, stretching across the Alps to cities in northern Europe such as Paris, London and Brussels, that by the fourteenth century became the Hanseatic League. Alongside it, merchant or finance capital emerged, or 'making money with money' as Marx called it (cited in Braudel 1982: 257), and new forms of business organization flourished, such as partnerships and joint ventures. The powerful Medicis of Florence were an example of the former in which one man or family was dominant, whereas joint ventures involved a more genuine pooling of risks and sharing of profits. Both depended on the development of cost accounting skills and double entry bookkeeping, which were in use by Genovese bankers as early as 1340 and were popularized in 1490 by Luca Pacioli (George 1972). From the fifteenth century onwards, however, the locus of economic activity shifted from Italy to Northern European centres of cloth production in the Netherlands and England.

The regulation of different crafts through guilds was the chief form of work organization in mediaeval towns, but the rising merchant capitalists increasingly sought to undermine them in favour of the more 'rational' system of wage labour, initiating a struggle that would persist for centuries. The guilds emerged across urban Europe on the crest of the economic upswing, and in their heyday even controlled some cities. They defended their trades by training apprentices, licensing journeymen, setting prices and regulating standards, but they often also had important social and political functions, such as providing the means of access to voting rights. Foreigners were typically excluded from their privileges, and membership became increasingly a hereditary male preserve. Almost from the outset 'guild schisms' occurred on the back of emerging class divisions between artisans, masters and merchants. Class struggle between journeymen and merchants, with the masters increasingly caught in the middle, broke out in the wool towns of Flanders in the late thirteenth century, where workers' actions included strikes for higher wages. The guilds were complex institutions, which often sought to mobilize collectively to maximize workers' advantages in the expanding market economy, and it is claimed that modern trade unions are descended from them (Lis *et al.* 1994). However, capitalism as a system of capitalist ownership of the means of production that necessarily entailed worker subordination had scarcely begun to emerge.

The social position of women in pre-modern Europe was shaped by their subordinated patriarchal status as a 'separate category of being', primarily through their relationship as a daughter, wife, widow, or mother to a man (Anderson and Zinsser 1988). The vast majority of women led lives bound by the cycles of the seasons and by childbearing and family responsibilities. They were 'free' to marry the man of their choice, and the dowry in theory sustained women in widowhood (Mundy 1991). However women commonly paid death duties to the landlord (heriot), and had to surrender the land when the son and heir came of age, so widows swelled the growing ranks of the wandering poor. Women were a significant part of urban workforces, and in some cities, like Cologne in the twelfth century, 'brothers and sisters' had equal rights in guilds, while in Paris some women became Masters in woollen guilds. While active in banking and commerce, they were excluded from the learned professions as the new mediaeval universities were a male preserve (Mundy 1991). For Cippola (1976) the separation of professions such as law and medicine from the trades was a major shift in social structure which has impacted on the modern era, delineating enduring differences between 'intellectual' and 'manual' labour.

In the early mediaeval period, social welfare was integrated into the communal and paternalistic aspects of village and manorial life. Food sharing occurred in times of famine, and women helped each other at childbirth. The first formal forms of assistance were provided by the monasteries, who extended the support initially given their sick and disabled to pilgrims in 'hospices'. This monopoly on the formal care of the poor was lost when a revival of religious feeling saw an upsurge in lay and religious assistance for the urban poor. New orders appeared, such as the Dominicans and Franciscans who actively sought out the poor rather than waiting for them to apply at the monastery gate (Mollat 1986). The guilds, too, often became an important source of collective aid, financed from subscriptions. The most developed were the Italian city guilds which organized assistance through co-fraternities linked to the church, placing particular emphasis on access to a decent Christian burial.

The growth of a wealthy class, and the Church's own growing wealth, created dilemmas for a social order that celebrated Christ's poverty and condemned profit as 'usury'. The rich could, however, ensure that they left the world poor by divesting themselves of their wealth and endowing foundations to care for the poor, sick and old, where grateful recipients would then pray for their benefactors' souls. The hospitals of the later Middle Ages emerged from these twelfth-century roots initially assisting all the poor, not just the sick (Carlin 1989). The emergence of the mediaeval medical profession itself was associated with the rivalry between the guilds and the newly founded universities which split the artisanal apothecaries and surgeons from the elite physicians who became university-trained 'professionals'. The most developed forms of health provision occurred in the commercially advanced city states of Italy (Park 1992).

In mediaeval society the poor were thus able to exploit Christian theology to find a social niche. However, official opinion increasingly saw the wandering poor as both social and health threats, an attitude foreshadowed in the exclusionary and punitive treatment of lepers (Watts 1997). From the fourteenth century onwards, as agriculture became more capitalistic, many peasants were transformed into day labourers to whom the lord owed less responsibility of protection. As the countryside became gradually sucked into the urban market economy a surplus population emerged that was pulled towards Western Europe's expanding cities, hungry for labour because of their high death rates (Lis and Soly 1979). Wealthy burghers established charitable reception centres to provide temporary material and spiritual assistance to travellers, becoming formalized into Tables of the Holy Ghost (*Mensae Spiritus Sanctus*). Thus early social policy often sought to aid the mobility of labour.

The greatest shock to mediaeval society was the Black Death. By 1300 Europe's population had expanded to around 80 million, but in the three years from 1348-51 some 25 million people died (Cippola 1976: 150). This deprived farms and particularly urban elites of desperately needed labour. In Western Europe, where traditions of village autonomy and urban independence were strong, it enhanced popular power and accelerated the decline of feudalism, stimulating fierce struggles and rebellions, whereas in Eastern Europe the powerful landlords ruthlessly reinforced feudal servitude (Lis and Soly 1979). In Western Europe a flurry of both labour and social legislation were primarily responses to the sudden improvement in the bargaining power of common people. In England Edward III proclaimed an Ordinance of Labourers in 1349 that with later amendments enforced the duty to work, set maximum rates of pay on pain of prosecution, and prohibited the giving of alms to 'sturdy' beggars. Other countries such as Spain, France and Portugal followed suit and for the first time an explicit distinction was made between 'deserving' and 'undeserving' poor. The Black Death thus hastened a shift from the religious to the secular supervision of the poor by the state (Woolf 1986; Lis and Soly 1979).

2.2   CAPITAL AND COERCION IN THE RISE OF MODERN EUROPEAN STATES, 1500-1750

The Black Death checked but did not halt the economic and political development of Europe which from around 1500 onwards accelerated again. The most striking emergent feature of this period was what Arrighi (1994) calls the 'unique fusion of capital and the state' at national and international levels. Business activities of giant merchant capitalists were underwritten and authorized through monopolies granted to such ventures as the Dutch

and British East India Companies which spread European influence across
the globe. The emergence of this alliance undermined feudalism both as a
transnational system of unified religious authority under the Catholic church
(compounding the blow struck by the Reformation), and as a system of
decentralized 'independent' cities. They lost out in the shift to secularized
nation states directed by a single 'sovereign', which were forged through an
alliance between military and economic power or 'capital and coercion'
(Tilly 1992). Gunpowder offered big advantages to large mobile armies,
making all cities and castles pregnable, and gradually but decisively shifted
the balance of power towards the nation state and modern capitalism. The
fragmented Italian city states could not emulate the economies of military
scale available to the emerging Northern Atlantic-based nations (Tilly 1992;
Braudel 1993).

Ever since the sixteenth-century voyages of discovery Western Europe
experienced increasing mechanization of production processes, the
commodification of factors of production, including labour, and the
growing proletarianization of the expanding population, which rose from an
estimated 69 million in 1500 to 188 million by 1800 (Hamerow 1983: 59).
The growth of the nation state and concentration of economic power were
in the main associated with the reassertion of authority in social life and the
curbing of the freedoms that city dwellers had won for themselves.
However, there were oppositional currents that emphasized 'freedoms', as
the demands for 'citizenship' associated with the mediaeval urban
revolution, were increasingly transferred to the national level. The balance
between the two, and the emerging political shape of European societies,
became increasingly affected by whether merchant capitalists or political
rulers, often drawn from feudal groups, had the upper hand. In England
after the 1688 Glorious Revolution the power of the sovereign was finally
curbed and a party system began to emerge which made the political class
relatively accountable to the dominant capitalist groups in civil society. In
the United Provinces of Holland too the commercial and trading classes
were able to establish a degree of political independence from traditional
ruling groups. By contrast in much of continental Europe, and particularly
in France, the feudal class united behind the sovereign to maintain
absolutist *ancien régimes* (Anderson 1979). Rokkan (1972) suggests that
this process was shaped by the proximity of countries to the Church's
authority, with those on the distant Atlantic seaboard (France excepted)
more able to break free by subordinating churches to nations during the
Reformation. The countries of southern Europe were more likely to give
rise to *ancien régimes* after the Counter Reformation in which Church and
aristocratic classes predominated. Germany and Austria were *ancien régime*
empires in which nationalism was, with the exception of the more distant

Prussia, inhibited (Braudel 1993). These different state traditions, represented by Britain and Holland on the one hand, and former *ancien régimes* on the other, were to have enduring effects which are still felt today. They typically led to strong central executives and state bureaucracies, particularly in the latter. The French post-revolutionary state provided one influential model for this, influencing not just other national states but creating an institutional inheritance which has also shaped the modern day institutions of the European Union.

The decay of the guilds and the restructuring of social policy after 1500 were elements in this evolving process. The spread of the domestic 'putting out' system was the chief factor undermining the guilds. The merchant or *Verleger* began to stand between the urban artisan and the market, controlling access to raw materials and the market for finished products. The artisan, sometimes through the master craftsman, was provided with raw materials and a part wage, the remainder to be paid on completion. Merchants started to reduce costs by shifting production to the countryside, where poverty and growing unemployment reduced landless workers' bargaining power, often utilizing women and children at low wages which were often commandeered by men (Berg 1983). In consequence the guilds everywhere found themselves in increasing economic competition with growing numbers of rural craft workers, and became victims of their own exclusiveness. By the eighteenth century the spread of this 'proto-industrialization' had largely undermined the guild system except in a few countries like Germany where it was deeply embedded, and states everywhere started to dismantle their controls on industry.

Emerging welfare was closely allied to changing work requirements, through the 'reorganization of relief' that took place across Europe after 1500. This sought to reinforce labour discipline and patriarchal responsibility: the poor should work rather than seek alms, and the male breadwinner and other family members must provide for each other. It also increasingly used state institutions to contain, discipline and even set the poor to work. Both of these features of poor law policy were set in place in the early modern period after 1500 when sharp distinctions between the 'deserving' and the 'undeserving' poor overturned the mediaeval notion of the virtue of poverty. Most initial attempts to control the migratory poor were made by town authorities, who were often influenced by numerous tracts disseminated via the new printing presses. Thus in England in 1577 William Harrison defined three types of poverty, first by 'impotency' such as a 'fatherlesse child', second by 'casualty' such as a 'wounded souldier' or 'decaied householder', and third as 'thriftless', including 'the vagabund that will abide nowhere' and 'the rog[u]e and strumpet'. In this and similar propaganda, the able-bodied poor were often defined as wilfully idle and not deserving of public help (Jütte 1994). In 1523 Martin Luther helped to establish a centralized 'common box' in the Saxon town of Leisnig, insisting that the poor should only receive help at bare subsistence level. Following his lead, similar schemes were initiated in cities across Western Europe (Lis and Soly 1979). Emerging Protestant nation states, such as England, where under Henry VIII the sacking of the monasteries had created a crisis in relief, increasingly intervened to impose such responsibilities on parishes and municipalities (Jütte 1994).

Some of these measures, like the Elizabethan Poor Law of 1601, have been seen prefiguring 'citizenship' entitlements to welfare associated with modern welfare states. However, they normally sought to enforce work obligations in the emerging market society, which became more prominent from the seventeenth century with repeated attempts to exercise the power of the central state, especially in the *ancien régimes*. As well as attempts to draw up lists and drive unwanted beggars away, there were increasing efforts to confine poor people in institutions such as workhouses, hospitals and prisons, a process Foucault (1967) dubbed 'the Great Confinement'. Such institutions were often tied into emerging forms of economic discipline, either producing for the market - they were among the first factories - or seeking to 'train' new forms of behaviour appropriate to market discipline. This was part of a wider trend towards more severe punishment of the poor which, alongside paternalistic philanthropy, was a feature of public policy in many countries during the eighteenth century.

Women were particularly targeted by the emerging nation states. Inflation and demographic shifts were creating larger numbers of poor widows, more of whom were forced to join the ranks of the vagrant poor. While our image of the pre-industrial past is often a rosy one of extended families offering support to all its members across the generations, there is some evidence of a Northern European norm of nuclear-type families and inter-generational households elsewhere (Anderson 1980). More important however in the proto-industrial period was the tendency towards increasing numbers of landless wage labourers who were less able to provide support for members, compared to peasant and subsistence households. Women and children, who commanded lower wages, were particularly vulnerable to these trends. Nevertheless the family unit remained the most important source of welfare assistance, especially since poor law allowances were below subsistence level. These emerging trends were much less pronounced in Southern Europe where the dowry system and Church charities also mediated family-economy relations (Henderson and Wall 1994). Women were at risk also from the hardening of attitudes towards prostitutes in the wake of the increase in venereal disease, who became one of the prime targets of 'the great confinement' (Norberg 1993). The persecution, torture and execution of witches, reached a peak in the sixteenth and seventeenth centuries and perhaps 100,000 people, 80% of them women, were executed for the crime. It has been recently argued that the rise and fall of witchcraft prosecutions was partly associated with the attempt to assert state power over all deviant behaviour, declining as this power was consolidated in the eighteenth century (Sallmann 1993; Weisner 1993).

Hesitatingly, the mercantilist nation states born out of the seventeenth-century sought to harness the insights of the seventeenth century scientific revolution and the inquiring approach of the eighteenth-century philosophical Enlightenment to projects of partial modernization and national advance. Enlightenment values stressed the 'autonomy of reason' in face of the bigotry, intolerance, superstition and fanaticism that dogged European Christianity after the Reformation, as a means of understanding and improving the world. Thus eighteenth-century mercantilist economic theory, developed most systematically by the Physiocrats, supported the development of an 'enlightened despotism' which increasingly leant itself to state intervention in social policies of an 'improving' kind such as elementary education to stimulate commerce, growth in population, taxes and the numbers of conscripts. Prussia under Frederick II, the powerhouse of what would by 1871 become a unified German state, provided one notable example. Repressive measures were thus combined uneasily with state-sponsored attempts at social improvement to expand the population and control epidemic disease. However state intervention was not motivated by enlightened reason alone. Fear of the poor was a powerful motivating force. By the eighteenth-century their numbers were huge: something like 30% of British people depended on poor relief, while in France around 40% of the population lived in poverty. Hunger was rife, squalor widespread and infant mortality rates were high. The poor were also increasingly restive. In the face of the decline of crafts and the attack on the guilds, even journeymen became prone to take strike action and other forms of protest. The political economic shifts in this period exacerbated divisions between rich and poor, while the rise in prices associated with the expansion of overseas European trade and plunder increased profits but heightened the exploitation of labour (Kamen 1984).

2.3 A CENTURY OF INDUSTRIAL AND POLITICAL CHANGE 1750-1850

The concept of 'the industrial revolution' is now regarded as problematic. Many changes were cumulative rather than the result of an abrupt rupture at the end of the eighteenth century, and not everything changed overnight.

However, looked at across a longer span, the hundred-year time-span from roughly 1750 to the mid-nineteenth century decisively directed European societies and the world along a major productive shift in the lives of human beings towards urban, industrial societies of mass scale.

Another objection to the notion of an 'industrial' revolution is that the changes were as much ideological and political as technological in origin. Modernity gave rise to the spread of a new 'mentality' or outlook, rational and future-oriented, the most dramatic result of which was the demand arising from the 1789 French Revolution that the sovereignty of nation states should be transferred from the shoulders of 'the prince' to the social collectivity. Although this arose primarily from the struggle of the rising middle classes who were obliged to mobilize the masses in order to wrest power away from the feudal aristocracy, it proved difficult to maintain that the logic of 'popular sovereignty' should be restricted to men of property alone, or that adult women should be excluded from it. The French Revolution itself gave way to a Napoleonic dictatorship and 'statist' liberal economy, which sought to impose this as an imperialist model on the rest of Europe. As well as serving as an early demonstration of the destructive side to European nationalistic modernism, it did help to establish, through the Code Napoleon a common legal and regulatory framework. Following Napoleon's defeat, the 1815 Treaty of Vienna, political conservatism reasserted established dynasties and empires, until the next wave of revolutions swept Europe in 1848.

The shift to more 'liberal' economies based on urban industrial capitalism proceeded at a faster pace. The first country to go down this road was Britain where the middle class had won the most freedom to act, where the 'common' law protected the 'rights' of property, and the peasantry had been most systematically dispossessed. Even so the pace of transformation was not so rapid and as completely achieved as standard accounts often imply (Samuel 1977). Nevertheless there is no doubt that the shift to factory production, though not entirely novel, was a major social innovation, in which middle-men capitalists assumed direct responsibility for production through their ownership of the means of production. The emerging factory system not only cheapened processes, it also enabled closer supervision of workers and regulation of their effort. Factory discipline therefore involved a temporal and spatial shift from a work regime largely structured from below by 'custom', with cycles of high effort interspersed by periodic rest, to a regime in which continuous labour at a high tempo was organized according to formal, 'rational' rules laid down by the capitalist (Thompson 1967). Subordination, the division of labour and acceptance of time discipline were often preconditions of capitalist economic growth and preceded mechanization and steam power (Marglin 1976). Thus the first clocking-in system was introduced in Josiah Wedgwood's Etruria porcelain works before any significant technological innovation (Rule 1986).

Several pioneering capitalists developed labour control practices that were later written up in the first management texts such as Charles Babbage's *On the Economy of Machinery and Manufactures* in 1832 (George 1972). While there was agreement on the objectives of 'handling' men and women employees to secure the maximum profits, there were two contrasting views as to how this should best be achieved. The most influential notion of the early nineteenth century, advocated by urban industrialists like Richard Arkwright, was that wage labour was an anathema to human beings and that people had to be 'broken' like horses to accept it. Robert Owen, on the other hand, believed in treating his 'human machinery' well by providing amenities such as housing and schools for child workers. He sought to coax people by incentives to voluntarily take on the 'work ethic' and other appropriate traits. This stance was more often adopted by paternalistic rural continental European employers, in factory villages or company towns, and by British Quaker manufacturers who felt a 'corporate' responsibility for their workpeople (Pollard 1965). Because the process of industrialization occurred over a prolonged period from below in Britain, the 'family firm' became a particularly enduring institution.

This emphasis upon alternative managerial strategies to the capitalist labour process partly qualifies the 'technical progress' thesis that technological innovation was dictated overwhelmingly by considerations of technical efficiency and reduction in costs (e.g. Landes 1969). The organization of production varied considerably according to the nature of the firm, and the business culture in which it operated. In small firms owner-entrepreneurs were more likely to trust family members and to rely upon personal loyalty from employees than to develop formal procedures and hierarchies for controlling the business. Sometimes the production process itself affected whether work was organized on factory lines, which even before the nineteenth century was typical of mines, potteries, and glass. After it, capitalist expansion often fostered artisan production in workshops, as in the metal trades. Although the factory spread rapidly during the nineteenth century spearheaded by the cotton industry which drew in large numbers of women and child labourers, it coexisted with other forms of economic exploitation, notably the sweated labour of women in the garment trade, as an alternative means of lowering labour costs. The rising wealth of the middle classes also led to an expansion of domestic service particularly for women. These forms of exploitation of female and child labour also built on the traditions established in the early modern period (Goodman and Honeyman 1988).

The requirements of state production also had a major impact on the capitalist labour process. Even before the modern era the state was a major pioneer of industrial enterprise, the largest in Europe being the Venice Arsenal, where artisans worked for a wage (often resentfully) under the supervision of foremen (George 1972). In other countries, state-organized or sponsored ordinances or shipyards were the largest enterprises. The requirements of war had a more pervasive effect in that nation states demanded precision military equipment and large orders of standardized products, which stimulated technological change and mass organization and discipline of labour. Cost was in fact a secondary consideration. As a result a corps of large firms were created which later became significant in the civil economy: Krupps in Germany, Schneider in France and Vickers in Britain (Goodman and Honeyman 1988; McNeill 1983).

Labour legislation and social policy were important aspects of the socially constructed liberal economy, often working together hand-in-glove. The approach varied: while many guild controls and associated forms of regulation of wages and master-servant relations had been eliminated by the market aided by local justices in Britain, in France the Le Chapelier law of 1791 formally abolished the guilds and outlawed trade unions. Only in Germany were guilds allowed to continue into the modern age. Everywhere workers became nominally free but their rights to organize collectively or to take strike action were often outlawed as restraints on trade. Although these restrictions on labour were later accompanied by legislation on factory owners limiting the hours worked by children over eight years old, these laws were generally ineffective. In this early nineteenth-century context Britain established the first truly national system of poor law relief. This reinforced the requirement for able-bodied adult males to seek waged work, and confirmed women's dependency and secondary status in the labour market. The 1834 New Poor Law did not go so far as abolishing relief, as called for by some free market liberals, but it did impose harsh and stigmatizing conditions for obtaining it, permitting whole families to be incarcerated in the workhouse. The abolition of the earlier discretionary right to outdoor relief based on cost of living and family size helped to drive the workers off the land and into the expanding cities (Fraser 1973). The harsh and patriarchal principles of early modern relief were thus reinforced rather than 'reformed' in a Europe whose population grew rapidly from around 187 to 266 million between 1800 and 1850 (Armengaud 1973).

2.4   CONCLUSION: TOWARDS EUROPEAN CAPITALIST MODERNITY

This chapter has sketched out the changing forms of social hierarchy, work regulations and social policy within the broader currents of political economic change in the long run up to the modern era. The foundations for modern European forms of management, work and welfare can be traced initially to the urban transformation of the late Middle Ages, which set in train processes that accelerated during the early modern period, when national economies emerged centred particularly upon the countries of northern Europe. However the tense alliances struck between mercantile capital and the state as it emerged from the late mediaeval period etched themselves differently onto the institutions, ideologies and cultures that formed modern Europe, with absolutism characterizing France, bourgeois freedoms Britain and Holland, and aristocratic fragmentation Germany. While the French revolution set the political agenda for the coming century, the British productive changes based on coal, iron and cotton drove forward the material foundations of the new form of society. These birth pangs of modernity all sprung out of old societies, which inevitably constrained their development. Across the Atlantic, however, a new society was emerging as a fledgling of the European political and industrial revolutions which was not subject to the same contraints. Its ruling groups did not have to confront or bargain with a feudal aristocracy, and set about eliminating the native societies which stood in the way of their realizing a 'pure' vision of modernity. However not until the 1860s, when the industrial and bourgeois north defeated the plantation slavocracy of the south, would it be able to pursue these goals with full vigour.

Meanwhile, after the defeat of Napoleon, it seemed that much reverted to normality as traditional hierarchies were restored to prominence with the 1814-15 Congress of Vienna. However beneath this constitutional edifice European society was changing rapidly. By the mid-1840s the growing economic and political integration of Europe was signalled first by the spread of a continent-wide recession and second by the political revolutions of 1848 that followed in its wake. Industrial capitalism had spread outwards from its initial British base, around the core industries of cotton, railways and shipping, and the foundations had been laid for European domination of the globe. At this stage this was mainly carried forward by 'free trade imperialism' which flooded foreign markets with cheap manufactured goods, particularly textiles, forcing most non-European countries to specialize in primary products (Goodman and Honeyman 1988). Europe's century, the century of the industrial and commerical middle classes, had truly begun.

The next chapter shows how the larger-scale industrial forms of industrial capitalism that developed from the late nineteenth century transformed European work, management and welfare. The key social questions became the viability of political and industrial relations between the middle and the working classes, in the context of the extension of overt imperialist domination across much of the world. Even at this moment of triumph, discordant notes of uncertainty sounded as European ruling groups began to feel threatened by conflict from within, the emergence of non-European industrial powers in Japan and the USA, and the rise of potentially destructive national rivalries among themselves.

3. Management, Work and Welfare before 1940: 'Logics' of Organization and Citzenship?

This chapter outlines the emergence of a European-wide industrial capitalism from the mid-century and the recognizably 'modern' patterns of management, work and welfare that began to accompany it. While focusing particularly on how these pressures had unfolded by the First World War it also gives some attention to the interwar period, a time when West European capitalism started to be influenced not only by its internal dynamics, but also by American capitalist and Russian communist challenges to its ascendancy, still more central questions after 1945. The chapter accepts that growth of large-scale production for national and international markets, and increasing concentration of people in large cities, created pressures favourable to mass democracy, a political and industrial challenge of labour, the beginnings of an erosion of patriarchy, and state intervention in welfare. However, notions of inherent evolutionary imperatives towards a particular dominant form of industrial capitalism, that finally came into its own after 1945, are disputed.

While it is true that some of the foundations for post-1945 organized patterns of management and work, and collectivist forms of welfare, were laid during this period, their selection and further development was crucially affected by the outcome of the 1939-45 war and onset of the Cold War. By the end of the interwar period a variety of shifts or adaptations from a failed liberal capitalism had occurred. At the fringes of Europe the Russian revolution of 1917 represented one route out of underdevelopment, while the Swedish reformist socialism of the 1930s offered an organized capitalist route of the Great Depression. In the USA Roosevelt's New Deal sought to rescue America's liberal form of capitalism through large doses of state intervention, while Britain, typically, adapted by a process of 'muddling through'. However throughout most of Western Europe by 1940 authoritarian and Nazi forms of capitalism had triumphed domestically in Iberia, Italy and Germany and spread by conquest to engulf their neighbours. This diversity provides a caution against viewing late nineteenth-century developments as the result of a 'second industrial revolution' whose 'new' industries 'inevitably' dictated organizational and political shifts, as this is prone to the technological determinism which we criticize throughout this book. Thus Lash and Urry (1987) see technology as one of the prime elements in a set of social changes at national and international levels which necessarily leads to the decline of the 'liberal capitalism' associated with the British 'industrial revolution', giving rise to a new 'organized' capitalist regime type more appropriately attuned to the twentieth-century productive capacities.

In what follows, then, considerable emphasis is placed on political-cultural influences. Though technological changes associated with production for scale in large markets were clearly significant developments, the social forms of modern life were shaped by historical and institutional legacies, especially unresolved conflicts between aristocratic and bourgeois class forces within each nation, and the increasingly pressing political need to respond to the challenge of labour. This analysis is a necessary prelude to the argument in Chapter 4 that post-1945 state-regulated and state-constrained capitalisms cannot be seen simply as a 'natural' evolution from trends established in the late nineteenth century, but were particularly the product of the far from inevitable defeat of fascism in Europe and the associated shift to the left. In constructing this analysis, the chapter first outlines the general political economic evolution of Europe after 1850, before turning to the emergence of modern forms of management, work and welfare.

3.1 INDUSTRIAL CAPITALISM AND NATIONALISM AFTER 1850

The pace of social change in the second half of the nineteenth century was dramatic. The economy boomed for two decades after 1850, carrying forward an unprecedented extension of capitalist industrialization and urbanization from the 'inner Europe' of Britain and North-western Europe, northwards to Germany and Scandinavia, and south-east as far as northern Italy (Hobsbawm 1962; Pollard 1982). Although still economically divided north-south and east-west, Western Europe had became a single, integrated economy by the 1870s, which made it the hub of the world economy by the end of that 'European century'. It was the most dramatic and rapid transition in the history of the world, then or perhaps since. However many of the most important developments were political as well as economic. The 1848 revolutions across European capitals had not in themselves been successful, but they posed two questions. First, how to find ways of granting political power to the industrial middle classes commensurate with their economic importance, and second how to address the conditions and aspirations of the urban masses, in order to exorcize the threat of the 'dangerous classes' or what Marx's *Communist Manifesto* called 'the spectre of communism'. By 1914 it had not proved possible to find an entirely workable solution to either question, though they had been more or less successfully integrated, within the competitive and increasingly mutually hostile nation states that were breaking free from aristocratic and church-dominated regimes.

The single most significant development was the emergence of a German military-industrial state, which under Prussian aristocratic leadership fought wars against Austria and France in order to establish a powerful fledgling 'empire' under the Kaiser in 1871. In contrast to Britain, the middle classes were a weak force in relation to the dominant military clique. In Italy a group of romantic bourgeois revolutionaries led a successful military campaign that established a new state, but did not have enough economic muscle to completely displace aristocratic and church influence. Elsewhere many thorny national issues still remained, particularly in the Balkans and areas dominated by the Austro-Hungarian empire. The period from 1848 until the early twentieth century has been seen as the age of the 'conquering bourgeoisie' (Bergier 1973). Nevertheless they had to make compromises and reach accommodations with traditional political classes, and they themselves also became differentiated into industrial, professional and increasingly important commercial/service sectors. States did increasingly extend votes to male workers, in efforts to cement mass loyalty to countries that were in economic, and increasingly, military competition.

The dominant forms of capitalism that emerged in Europe in the last quarter of the nineteenth century were thus aggressively nationalistic. Germany set the pace for other European countries, the prime aim being to build up roads and railways not just to establish distribution networks for markets, but also as military routes for challenging the ascendency of Russia to the north-east and France to the south. Prussian state traditions played an active part in the German industrialization process, unifying states into a single customs union (*Zollverein*) in 1833 and, with the aid of the banks organizing industry into cartels and holding companies which dominated rather than responded to market pressures. In both Germany and Italy, the state which had brought nations into existence was then able to play an active role in the industrialization process (Supple 1973). Although nation states sought to imitate or improve on British technology, they typically chose a very different social path. This happened to a certain extent in France from the 1850s, with Napoleon III pioneering statist forms of capitalist development based first on the urban reconstruction in Paris initiated by Baron Hassmann, and subsequently by underwriting the creation of a national railway system. However it was the German alliance between the Junkers and big business that enabled it as a late industrializer to take most advantage of the 'privilege of backwardness' to transform the early leads of Britain, Belgium and northern France increasingly into handicaps (Gershenkron 1962).

These nationalistic and militaristic tendencies were exacerbated by the economic downturn that lasted from the 1870s to the mid-1890s, the so-called 'Great Depression' associated with the deflationary effects of growing international economic integration and the import of massive supplies of North American grain. The chief European beneficiary of the latter was Britain as the 'free trade' conduit through which these imports occurred, and the general effect was to heighten both internal and external tensions. Germany in particular pursued a protectionist path in order to advance its interests within a European and world economy dominated by Britain. By the end of the nineteenth century Germany emerged as an industrial state (*industriestaat*) well placed to take advantage of renewed economic growth from the 1890s (Tilly 1996). Science-based industry was the key to Germany's emergence. Thus Frederick Bayer and Elberfeld, founded in the 1860s, pioneered the development of synthetic dyes from coal products before using them in heavy chemicals, fertilizers, medicines, ointments and photographic accessories. Electrical engineering also took off after Werner Siemens developed the dynamo and harnessed it first to steam engines and then to lighting, transport and electrical power generators. Innovative German manufacturers like Daimler and Benz vied with the French in developing the first cars with internal combustion engines in the 1890s (Henderson 1969).

Although Germany was the most spectacular European example of a 'late' industrializer, Sweden's development was almost as rapid, carried forward by finance capital with the acquiescence of the aristocracy. Reinvesting the profits of pulp, wood and iron ore exported to Britain and Germany, it rapidly built up an industrial structure with the help of foreign capital and escaped from being one of the poorest fringe economies of Europe (Gustaffson 1996; Pollard 1996). Italy after unification in 1870 was a more mixed story. Despite attempts by the state to underwrite the railway building companies, it was only with state public works and military spending from the 1890s that industrialization took off, and then only in the north. By the time of the first industrial census of 1911 there were two million industrial workers in cycles and motor cycles, cars, textiles, glass making and food production (Poni and Mori 1996). Other countries sought a niche within the European industrialization process; for example Denmark achieved efficiencies in agriculture to supply dairy and meat products to the expanding European population.

The economic downturn also helped to propel European powers into an imperialist scramble. The reasons behind the European military takeover of much of the globe at the end of the nineteenth century are complex and much debated by historians (see Porter 1994). However, it would be hard to deny the significance of political economic motives for safeguarding access to raw materials and export markets in what was regarded as an increasingly finite world. The outcome undoubtedly pushed Germany further down the militaristic road, as the chief land-locked loser of the 'scramble for empire' from the mid-1880s, without easy access to trade routes. As a result Europe up to 1914 was in a state of 'armed peace' (den Boer 1993: 76). Britain gained most from the imperialist carve-up, although in the long run this had economic costs, as it discouraged organizational and technological innovation to improve industrial efficiency at home.

Table 3.1 European mortality rates per 1,000 live population, 1851-1910 (ranked by mortality rates 1851-60 or 1886-90)

	1851-60	1886-90	1906-10
Denmark	21	19	14
Sweden	22	16	14
England	22	22	15
Belgium	23	20	16
France	24	22	19
Germany	26	24	18
Netherlands	26	21	14
Portugal	-	22	20
Italy	-	27	21
Austria	-	30	23
Spain	-	31	24

Source: Glass and Grebenik (1941-78: 6: 68-9), cited in Hamerow (1983: 75).

As it became the centre of a world production system dominated by demands for food, clothes, raw materials and land, so Europe's population boomed, more than doubling in the nineteenth century to reach 401 million by 1900 (Hamerow 1983: 59). Throughout Western Europe standards of living started generally to rise after 1860 and particularly towards the turn of the twentieth century, with the effects of falling food prices, due largely to cheap American imports (Hunt 1981). Rising wages and better less adulterated food, rather than access to medical care, was the major reason for a significant improvement in crude death rates, although improved popular knowledge about hygiene and public health measures also played a part (Anderson 1996; Sretzer 1988). The accelerated fall in mortality rates, which was most pronounced in Northern Europe, is shown in Table 3.1.

Although its course was uneven and variable in effect, in a short space of time an urban industrial life had emerged for an increasing number of European people, as indicated in Table 3.2 below.

Table 3.2   Population growth (000s) of urban Europe, 1850-1900 (ranked by size of largest city in 1850)

		1850	1900
Britain:			
	London	2,685	6,586
	Glasgow	345	776
	Manchester	303	645
	Birmingham	233	523
France:			
	Paris	1,053	2,714
	Marseilles	195	491
	Lyons	177	459
Italy:			
	Naples	449	564
	Milan	242	493
	Rome	175	463
	Turin	135	336
Austria:			
	Vienna	444	1,675
Germany:			
	Berlin	419	1,889
	Hamburg	132	706
	Munich	110	500
	Cologne	97	373
Belgium:			
	Brussels	251	599
Spain:			
	Barcelona	175	533
Sweden:			
	Stockholm	93	301

Source: Cook and Stevenson (1998: 241-2).

Urbanization was associated with pronounced cultural shifts to modern patterns of life during the last quarter of the century. One of the most significant of these, in the wake of mass education, was the rise of national newspapers which increasingly sought to shape European political opinions and national consciousness, and to influence consumer tastes through advertising. At the same time new forms of distribution, such as the cooperative movement and the department store, facilitated access to mass consumption. Shops like the *Bon Marché* in Paris that originally targeted prosperous bourgeois shoppers, started to stock a wider variety of less expensive items and to apply economies of 'scale' and 'scope' to the retail sector (Merriman 1996). Particularly in Britain, specialist national chains like Sainsbury's and W. H. Smith emerged. Revolutions in national transport enabled larger European markets to emerge, and facilitated the imperialist integration of the world economy through troop transport and innovations such as refrigerated shipping. Mass entertainments such as sport, music hall and subsequently the cinema also developed. Rising real incomes enabled more disposable income to be spent on consumer items, rather than just housing and staple food items. By the early twentieth century, when European capitalism ruled supreme across the world, it had resumed economic expansion and its products were increasingly enhancing the lives of urban people.

The First World War, the final rupture of growing tensions between imperialist nations, was a dreadful human disaster but also a critical catalyst of change. Mobilization of troops and production for the war effort vastly increased the role of the state in society. In turn it stimulated technical and organizational change in industry, and hastened craft dilution and mechanization. The war killed off the Austro-Hungarian empire, and disturbed patriarchal relations between the sexes and hastened female suffrage. It precipitated the Bolshevik revolution of 1917, and started to bring Western Europe into greater dependency on the USA. However it also left many pressing issues dangerously unresolved, which led to a 'repeat performance' on an even more horrendous scale involving millions of civilians little more than 20 years later. By 1917 Europe had fought itself into a bloody stalemate, and with Bolshevik Russia suing for peace, the balance of advantage had shifted to Germany. America's belated military intervention was decisive in Germany's defeat, and the shape of the peace negotiated in Versailles bore the imprint of its influence through President Wilson's 'Fourteen Points'. The USA, now the world's largest industrial power, participated in a conference which dismantled the Hapsburg empire, promoted the realization of nationalist aspirations in Eastern Europe, and established liberal democracies across much of Europe. The severe revenge punishments inflicted on Germany for its 'war guilt', including the loss of Poland and of its empires, and the imposition of heavy reparation payments, were particularly insisted upon by France and Britain. Having achieved some of its ends, the USA then withdrew into 'isolationism', with Congress voting not to join the new League of Nations set up to ensure world peace in the future. American capitalism boomed in the 1920s, and confidence abounded that it could be sustained by internal expansion alone. In the world economy as a whole the writ of British imperialism was shaken but not dislodged, as represented by the concerted efforts to restore the 'gold standard' pegging international currencies to the prewar sterling price of gold.

The story of the interwar period is not entirely one of unremitting gloom. The expansion of the middle classes in the interwar years and the emergence of social housing for many workers in regular employment led to a significant shift towards a European consumer economy based around household items like carpets, vacuum cleaners and even radios and gramophones, although cars remained luxury items. Yet this increasing general prosperity of course left behind the millions of unemployed. The growing influence of the state was not only felt in the authoritarian societies of Italy and Germany. Everywhere there were hesitant moves towards economic planning, and a growing acceptability of various forms of taxation which helped to finance growing welfare provision (Deaton 1976). This trend was reinforced by rearmament from the mid-1930s that finally started to lift the world economy out of the depression of the 1930s. A mass way of life was also signalled culturally by and 'disciplined' forms of entertainment like ballroom dancing. Therefore to an extent some of these trends validate the evolutionary account of a political economy responding to the pressures of a mass scale and urbanization.

However, only some. While, there were many problems in the 1920s, as represented by the growth of unemployment, the hyperinflation of Germany and Austria, and the fascist takeover in Italy. It was however the Wall Street Crash of 1929, and subsequent Great Depression which undermined the credibility of both political and economic liberalism, kindling anti-democratic forms of nationalism and protectionism of which fascism was the most virulent. The Crash in fact proved that the economies of Europe and the USA were closely intermeshed, for it was the calling-in of overseas loans by panicking American speculators that caused economic collapse in Europe, hitting Germany worst and enabling the Nazis to bid for power. With the collapse of the gold standard in 1933 no viable system of international regulation of currency or trade existed and each country sought to protect their own by imposing tariffs, leading to a decline in world trade. Various national paths out of depression were attempted. Britain hesitatingly developed forms of 'imperial preference' for the goods of the empire and dominions, while the USA and Sweden experimented in different ways with the new-fangled forms of state interventionism to revive the economy, advocated by John Maynard Keynes. In Sweden, the Social Democratic Party which was elected in 1932, and which has ruled for the most part ever since, launched a programme involving corporatist cooperation between capital and labour, involving a strong emphasis on both industrial investment and provision also for domestic consumption and social security provision. The American New Deal under Roosevelt sought to develop a more half-hearted national recovery programme, combined with state social security, and legal recognition of trade unions. Though this regime has sometimes been called 'Fordist', Henry himself bitterly opposed the efforts to extend union organizing rights to his workers (Navarro 1991; Clarke 1992). In France a short-lived 'Popular Front' government under Léon Blum from 1936-7 united socialists and communists against the right, and initiated reforms such as reductions in the working week, paid holidays, trade union recognition, and greater state regulation of the economy. The Nazis sought their own distinct route out of depression by state direction of private industry, and military conquest to expand markets and mobilize sources of forced labour. In all these various instances briefly described above, economic crisis and the political pressures arising from them, were the main stimulants rather any inherent logic associated with technologies of mass production.

3.2 AMERICAN MANAGERIAL CAPITALISM AND THE EUROPEAN RESPONSE

The growth of large-scale production for mass markets was most pronounced in the USA, where alongside it new managerial philosophies and approaches started to emerge. In what follows we dispute a purely 'functionalist' account which sees American managerialism as simply the most naturally efficient form of industrial organization, although that was of course part of its ideological or discursive power. We therefore seek to show how it was culturally and politically influenced, before turning to look at the extent to which Europe had, by the end of the interwar period, developed its own management styles, or copied American methods.

America was initially an offshoot of European capitalism that developed its own bourgeois path free from the constraints of a feudal aristocracy, a central state, and with access to vast natural resources. Despite massive European immigration before 1920, labour shortages persisted, leading both to more innovative labour-saving investments and wages on average 25% higher than in Europe, fuelling the development of the largest and most buoyant consumer market in the world. Mass production methods had first demonstrated their effectiveness for the North during the civil war of 1861-

65 and were subsequently applied to civilian consumer goods. American manufacturers were able to take advantage of the economies of scale offered by modern technologies to focus on consumer goods industries to a greater extent than in Europe (North 1965; McCraw 1988). By 1913 the USA had become the world's largest manufacturing nation, overtaking Britain (Parker 1996).

Until late in the nineteenth century it was still most common to describe factory relationships in terms of 'masters and men' (Williams 1976). References to 'mine managers' in the USA date from 1862, while the collective verb 'managed' appeared there from 1880. Yet it was only in twentieth-century American English, following the popularization of the term by Frederick Taylor in his *Scientific Management* that the paid agents (now of 'employers' rather than 'masters') generally became known as 'managers'. This shift in discourse reflected accelerated rates of change in the social organization of production. By the beginning of the twentieth century a professionalized managerial elite began to appear that had its own discrete philosophy based on a combination of Enlightenment positivism and pragmatic Puritanism. Taylor believed his system required 'a complete mental revolution' on both sides of industry (George 1972). The worker would trade control over the job for the high wages that would result from the application of Scientific Management, while management would take the trouble to redefine their relationship with workers, and invest in the necessary systems of research, planning, coordination and control to improve workers' performance. Whereas Braverman (1974) depicts Taylorism as the naked exercise of managerial power through technological design, Jacques (1996) draws attention to its important ideological dimensions. He suggests that high wages were rationalized as compensation for loss of individual workers' independence, 'reshaping' the 'American Dream' to fit the circumstances of the factory rather than the farm. Employees would thus accept subordination, and still perform their prescribed role in a 'perfect', Puritan way, while receiving earthly rewards as 'elected' consumers of material abundance. Taylorism also helped to mobilize immigrants with little industrial work experience or knowledge of English, by simplifying tasks and incentives.

In America an individualist 'liberal' suspicion of their competitors made entrepreneurs reluctant to establish the 'gentlemen's agreements' and cartels that emerged in late nineteenth-century Europe, which were declared illegal in the USA in 1890 and 1914. The only route to controlling their business environment and lessen the risks involved in heavy investment in plant was therefore through mergers and takeovers. Thus the increasing shift to multidivisional organizations integrating primary production, manufacture, distribution and even retailing was culturally and politically influenced rather than dictated by considerations of 'pure' efficiency (Fligstein 1985). This was the context in which capitalist transactions increasingly shifted from 'markets to hierarchies' (Williamson 1975), or as Chandler (1977, 1988) put it, from the 'invisible hand' of the market, to the 'visible hand' of managerial direction, which was first demonstrated in the establishment of the transcontinental railway system as the motor of American industrialization. A new social elite of managers were then trained in the required 'management knowledge', who would it was hoped become suitably motivated by the development of career structures focused on the long-term profit and expansion of the corporation. This was also consistent with a 'democratic' and meritocratic society where white male suffrage had been conceded as early as 1860. It formed a fertile environment for management education to take root as a form of 'expert' professional knowledge, in the expanding American universities (George 1972).

By the early twentieth century American managerial philosophy and practice were largely confined to large-scale firms in the USA, and had not spread far in Europe's generally smaller-scale capitalist enterprises. Culture and politics as well as the smaller scale of national markets were major impediments to the transfer of 'modern management' to Europe. Although a degree of business concentration did take place, especially in Germany, even there in 1913 only 24 German firms had capital assets of $20 million or more, compared to 280 American firms in 1917 (Cassis 1997: 4). Chandler (1990) contrasts the emergence of the 'Managerial Capitalism' that had taken root by 1914 in the USA, with the 'Personal Capitalism' associated with British family firms, and the more corporate and cartel-based 'Cooperative Managerial Capitalism' that had taken root in Germany.

These distinctions are admittedly rudimentary ones, which would be elaborated if there was more space. The main point to make is that Taylorism was part of the broader shift to American managerial capitalism in the USA which came to be known as 'Fordism' after Henry Ford's changes to production and work relations pioneered in Detroit in the first decades of the twentieth century. Part of the Fordist case, however, is that these shifts also necessitated a turn to an interventionist and welfare-oriented state. The role of the state will be considered in more detail towards the end of the chapter. However we have already seen that, with the exception of Britain and Belgium, statism was an inherent trend within European capitalism rather than something which responded to productive changes, and the American New Deal in the 1930s can therefore be seen as an accommodation in response to crisis, to dominant European traditions. Thus work measurement and Taylorism barely got a toehold in Europe before World War I. Most of Western Europe's nation states had long traditions of negotiated relationships between the state and business, well before the emergence of big business. There was greater legal tolerance of cartels and other 'gentlemen's agreements', and in an imperialist Europe based on national rivalries, these were consolidated through a closer alliance between big business and the state. This state-big business alliance may in some ways have held back the development of modern business methods in Europe, since it reinforced acceptance of bureaucratic government or military command hierarchical models, such as that of the influential Henri Fayol (McCraw 1988). Additionally it stemmed from the narrower geographical scope of most European markets and the enduring family, local and social obligations experienced by many capitalists. It was also inhibited by the widespread craft resistance to deskilling, the political legacy of the incomplete bourgeois-aristocratic settlements, and the emergence of strong socialist and trade union movements.

After the First World War experience of craft dilution and mass production, however, there was a gradual shift in Europe towards reorganizing industry in larger and more integrated units, professionalizing management and adopting Taylorist methods. The immediate postwar strength of labour, often involving demands for workers' participation or control, led employers increasingly to resort to 'neutral' intermediate groups to help them deal with this challenge to their legitimacy. Taylor's missionary emphasis upon the work engineer appeared to provide this required neutrality. Ironically, Soviet Russia under Lenin more wholeheartedly accepted the neutrality of Taylorist methods as the technological and organization 'base' for building a socialist industrial utopia (Littler 1982). As far as the broader attempt to professionalize management was concerned, the first International Management Congress was held in Prague in 1924, and journals were established to spread the message (Pellicelli 1976). 'Americanism' was criticized by the Italian communist Gramsci as the system associated with Henry Ford's annihilation of craft controls through extension of Taylorism to the whole process of automobile production, and the associated attempt to rule workers' lives within and beyond the workplace. Taylorism was more talked about than acted on in Europe in the 1920s, not least because attempts to apply it often gave rise to bitter struggles by workers and resistance or lack of interest by employers. The shift to protectionism and national autarchy in the 1930s further undermined managerial cosmopolitanism (Pellicelli 1976). Even in the USA Taylorism came under attack from the Human Relations school for failing to give insufficient attention to the 'human factor' in worker and management relations. Taylor himself had admitted that his ideal worker was an ox rather than a man. Before the Second World War European employers thus largely practised traditional paternalist or command management, based on the 'right to manage' and assumptions of total employee subordination, even though these assumptions had begun to be challenged by a rising labour movement.

3.3 WORK FROM THE 1880s TO THE INTERWAR YEARS

Urbanization and industrial capitalism went hand in hand, and from the end of the nineteenth century workers were increasingly massed into larger productive units under hierarchical systems of authority. Some of this involved applying more advanced technological methods to established industries but new, more process-based activities required larger-scale organization, such as steel production, chemicals, and a range of engineering-based consumer products such as sewing machines, bicycles and cars. The extent of the shift to process-driven industrial work in urban centres should not, however, be exaggerated, even in the core of industrial Europe now stretching from Scandinavia to northern Italy. Before the First World War unemployment and underemployment, both cyclical and seasonal, too, remained endemic, touching up to half the urban workforce and obliging them to live in constant insecurity. Large numbers of those with regular jobs still worked in physically arduous, non-mechanized occupations, such as the 1.5 million men in Britain, and 800,000 in Germany who dug out the coal on which industrialized economies depended. Except for Britain, where under 10% laboured on the land, agriculture was still Europe's biggest single pursuit, involving a third of all German workers and more than half of all Italian and Austrian (Crouch 1993: 121). Many with industrial jobs still lived in rural areas and had 'rural' attitudes. French miners, for example, fought furiously to defend working hours compatible with continuing agricultural activities (Trempe 1995). Manual work involved huge efforts, and was frequently carried out in hazardous and unhealthy conditions, although its rhythm varied considerably from one industry to another. Even in the new industries many processes still depended on hand or craft skills, and took place in workshops rather than factories.

The arrival of electric lighting permitted a standardization of the working day throughout the year. In most manual occupations work, when it was available and regular, consumed around ten and a half of workers' available waking hours for six days a week. Many of the new migrants to the cities immediately joined the substantial numbers of urban poor, living off their wits on the margins of increasingly wealthy societies. The decline of the putting-out system led to the increasing separation of residence from paid work, and 'productive' from 'domestic' life, and the boundaries of the sexual division of labour were redrawn. The abysmally low wages established for domestic work or garment sewing led significant numbers of women into prostitution, a major growth industry in European cities (Walkowitz 1980). The growth of urban centres, a consumption-oriented middle class, and expanding financial and commercial activities all served to germinate the expansion of heterogeneous service classes, as a prominent feature of industrial capitalism rather than a 'post-industrial' trend away from it as is sometimes claimed (Hartwell 1973; Kumar 1978).

Within the larger enterprises a 'new middle class' was emerging of company administrative officials, accountants and lawyers and university-educated engineers and designers, opening up avenues of mobility mainly for sons of aristocratic and middle class fathers. Below the 'professionals' in the employment hierarchy there were huge numbers of clerks and junior administrators which increasingly gave rise to low-paid openings for the educated daughters of middle class families. In 1871 the director of the British telegraph service reported that 'the wages which will draw male operators from an inferior class of the community will draw female operators from a superior class' (cited in Scott 1988: 415). Thus by the end of the nineteenth century there was a significant expansion of gender-segregated 'white blouse' jobs for women in offices, telegraph and telephone companies, as well as in the growing numbers of public service jobs like teaching and nursing. By the eve of the First World War, one-third of French women, nearly one-quarter of Belgian and British women, and nearly one-fifth of German women were already in paid employment (Hamerow 1983: 144). In general, however, such paid employment was reserved for single women, who were expected to leave employment once they married, a tradition which, despite the growth of feminism, often fitted in with their own plans and expectations (Bourke 1994).

For those relatively few who had, or were supported on, a skilled worker's wage or white collar salary, the trend from the early 1890s was towards improving living standards, greater security in 'better' jobs, and improved status. However even for these often highly literate workers, the work regime remained largely authoritarian and arbitrary, creating an increasing sense of disenchantment and dashed expectations. The growth of 'foremen' and supervisory staff also exacerbated tensions. Skilled, unskilled and some white collar workers and public servants started to join the emerging trade unions. Collective organization around mutual insurance and pay had secured permanent, although limited, bargaining rights for skilled male workers in most Western European countries. In Germany and Austria these were already structured by the industrial union branch, the form of organization also being promoted successfully by syndicalists in

France and Belgium. Where unskilled male workers had relatively permanent, non-seasonal jobs in workplaces such as the gas works, the railways or on municipal tramways, they too were beginning to join unions which were more often general or industrial.

Table 3.3   Western European trade union membership as % of the total labour force, 1910-14 and c. 1938

	1910-14	1938
UK	22.6	28.7
Denmark	13.0	27.3
Netherlands	12.2	24.5
Germany	11.4	-
Norway	8.5	34.3
Belgium	7.5	25.3
Sweden	7.1	36.0
Switzerland	5.7	20.0
Austria	4.8	-
Italy	4.0	-
Finland	3.4	5.0
France	1.9	18.8

Source: Reproduced by permission of Oxford University Press from Crouch, C. (1993: 117, 170), *Industrial Relations and European State Traditions*, Oxford: Clarendon Press.

Table 3.3 shows that trade union membership had taken off nearly everywhere in Western Europe by 1914, with Britain and Denmark leading the way. By the late 1930s, except in fascist countries, union membership had become customary for between a quarter and a third of all Western European workers, even higher among those working in industry. In the USA, however, union density among the non-agricultural workforce was 10% in 1914 and was still at that level (although rising rapidly) in 1936 (Mann 1995; Jefferys 1986).

Almost everywhere that craft unions existed they established or maintained substantial differentials between their wages and those of unskilled men. By the eve of the First World War localized bargaining for the more privileged unionized workers was widespread, and comparatively strongly centralized sectoral or branch multiple-employer collective bargaining was already present in Denmark, Switzerland and Britain. Only in Denmark and Britain, however, did workers have any form of regular representation within the workplace (Crouch 1993). European employers on the whole resolutely defended their absolute control of the workplace: most workers had no rights while employed on their employers' property. Many employers also felt paternalist obligations, the French foundry employers reminding association members in 1902 to look after workers 'like a father does his family'(quoted in Castel 1995: 262). Employment was considered a privilege, not a right. It was therefore not protected by legislation and was accessed through the goodwill of the foreman or employer, although in the handful of very large firms personnel officers were starting to introduce bureaucratic recruitment procedures. What tasks workers did, and how they were rewarded, was usually determined unilaterally by superiors than being subject to standardized rules. Only rarely before the First World War did Western European governments intervene in shaping substantive employment relations.

In the interwar years the trade union and labour movements were mostly on the defensive. A huge postwar membership peak in 1920 was followed by a considerable decline through most of the 1920s, and then steady renewal from the early 1930s as the European economy picked up and those workers in jobs regained the confidence to adhere to the collective organizations that had been largely absent from the devastating period of peak unemployment between 1929 and 1933. The political left, meanwhile, was seriously weakened by the split between communism and socialism after the Russian Revolution. Mostly, therefore, where reformist socialist parties made gains, as in Germany, Austria, Spain and France, these were largely cancelled out between 1933 and 1940 by the Nazis. The major exception was Sweden where in 1932 the Social Democratic Government pioneered a 'social' form of Keynesianism whose centrepiece was the 1938 *Saltsjobaden* corporatist agreement in which the trade unions consented to management prerogatives, capital investment and profitability, in return for union recognition, higher wages and state welfare. This alliance between capital and labour survived because Sweden was able to maintain neutrality during the 1939-45 war (Weir and Skocpol 1985).

The trade union movement itself took on a variety of organizational forms as part of wider labour movements during this period, and the extent to which these patterns could be derived from changing productive relationships was initially theorized by Touraine (1966). He argued that while craft workers were on the whole defensive in outlook and not politically radical, factory workers from the late nineteenth century tended to take an oppositional stance based on perceptions of a cleavage in class interest between themselves and their employers. His further argument that the technical and professional new middle class of the post-1945 period increasingly developed an alternative vision of a self-managed society, will be taken up in the next chapter. Hyman (1996), however, points out that this is far too sweeping and takes no account of the fact that unions are institutional creations which can also structure as well as reflect workers' consciousness. He points to the importance of dominant national traditions which articulate to the political in various ways. In Britain a labourist or 'economist' form of organization developed which pursued voluntarism in collective bargaining while channelling its political efforts separately into reformist socialism. This to some extent bears comparison with the 'business unionism' which had become dominant in the USA by the 1930s, and which was underpinned by the New Deal itself. Continental European trade unionism by contrast articulated in more direct ways with political movements of both left and right. The unions were themselves often creations of the parties of the Socialist International established in 1889. Their future course was then affected by the split between communists and socialists after 1917. Company unions did not gain a strong foothold in labourist Britain, except among the emerged employed middle class. They did in paternalist Germany, for example, at Krupps armaments factory. Nor did the Catholic trade unions which established themselves on the continent outside the Protestant countries of Scandinavia.

In their different ways, however, the aim of most unions was to reduce the exercise of arbitrary power in   workplace regimes, and this largely depended on the supply of labour in increasingly differentiated occupations. Where local transport, railways, manufacturing, and coal and steel provided a constant and strong demand for permanent labour forces and demand for craft skills were high, workers' organizations found spaces within which to exercise limited collective power. Yet even in these sectors the return of mass unemployment in the 1930s had devastating effects. In France, for example, while 'only' 12.6% of workers were entirely unemployed at its 1935 peak (compared to one in four male workers in Britain), more than half of those left at work had their weekly hours cut (Noiriel 1986). Where - and this was the experience of the overwhelming majority of Europe's workers - there were many small firms and largely unregulated markets, labour market bargaining opportunities and trade unionism remained extremely weak. It was this encompassing job insecurity that stimulated political action to secure a variety of forms of state protection from the consequences of industrial capitalism.

3.4 POLITICAL STRUGGLES AND EUROPEAN WELFARE: A LOGIC OF CITIZENSHIP?

If the political course of Western European capitalism was shaped initially after 1848 by varying deals between aristocratic and bourgeois classes, the rise of labour became the most pressing domestic political issue of the late nineteenth century. This manifested itself in 1871 just as the economic boom ended, with the short-lived Paris Commune, hailed by Marx as the first practical prototype of the 'worker's state' of the future. While labour had been relatively quiescent in the years of economic boom, the reappearance of economic instability in the 'depression' years from the 1870s to the 1890s, as well as the massing of industrial workers in urban industrial centres, fuelled social discontent and class consciousness. This was manifested in the growth of unions referred to above and the establishment of significant socialist parties across Europe which (Britain excepted) were formally Marxist or anti-capitalist in character.

Marx's predictions appeared to be becoming true as concentrations of workers in larger productive units in urban centres developed industrial and political class consciousness (Geary 1981; Mann 1995). Faced with this mobilization, European dominant groups had little option but to extend the franchise in order to contain the challenge of labour and to seek to address some of its problems. Table 3.4 shows that large minorities of workers from across Western Europe began before the First World War to vote in large numbers for the socialist parties that promised to control employment insecurity, to recognize the value of their work, and to deliver a 'new world'. Contrary to Touraine's (1966) claims, this was not a simple mechanical response to urbanization and proletarianization. Often it was the craft workers and workers in small towns as well as numbers of clerks and school teachers who were the most militant and politicized. Rural traditions of autonomy fostered anarchism and syndicalism as old and new came into conflict. By contrast, in many large enterprises in urban centres, especially in Germany, paternalistic employment relations and tied housing often discouraged militancy. Thus Krupps developed family housing for workers, shops, schools, medical and insurance facilities in order to secure the loyalty of workers at a time of rapid industrialization. Nor was the unionization of new industries like the car industry a foregone conclusion, which remained non-union throughout Europe for most of the period before 1940. The responses of workers were also shaped by the political context. In Britain the power of the middle class in civil society and a loosening of restrictions on union organizing was one factor leading initially to a reformist political consciousness and voluntaristic collective bargaining traditions. At the other extreme, Prussian autocracy pushed more workers into a revolutionary stance, whereas the statist but more democratic regimes of Italy and France led to greater political ambivalence among workers (Geary 1981; Crouch 1986). The extension of the male franchise undoubtedly pushed the socialist movement towards the pursuit of parliamentary reform or revolutionary overthrow of the state, which soon became reflected in the parties of the Second International, which defined anti-statist (and hence anti-parliamentary) movements such as anarchism and syndicalism as beyond the pale. Even so the viability of class society remained on open question, with an unprecedented growth of militancy and radicalism up to 1914 as prices increased faster than wages, and employers and states often mounted counter-offensives against spreading unionization. We prefer this interpretation by Geary (1981), to that of Hobsbawm (1987) who in our judgement one-sidedly views the late nineteenth century as the period during which working class people were smoothly integrated into parliamentary reformism.

Table 3.4 European socialism: founding dates and political structure (ranked by year of founding of socialist or labour party)

	Year party founded	Universal male suffrage	Universal female suffrage	Labour vote c. 1914 (%)	Industrial workforce, 1906-11 (%)
Germany	1875	1871	1919	35	39
Denmark	1876-8	1901	1920	30	24
Belgium	1885	1895	1948	9	45
Norway	1887	1898	1913	26	26
Austria	1889	1907	1918	16	24
Sweden	1889	1907	1921	30	25
Italy	1892	1919	1945	18	27
Netherlands	1894	1917	1919	19	33
Finland	1899	1906	1906	43	11
France	1905	1848	1944	15-20	30
UK	1900-6	1918	1928	6	45

Sources: Sassoon (1996: 10); Siaroff (1994: 98); Droz (1977: 341); Bernstein and Milza (1990: 60-1). Siaroff reference from 'Work, welfare and gender equality: a new typology', in Sainsbury, D. (ed), *Gendering Welfare States*, London: Thousand Oaks, New Delhi: Sage. Reprinted by permission of Sage Publications Ltd.

In the new era of nation states and growth of the left, the right did not stand idly by. Its political centre shifted from the liberal nationalism of 1789 and 1848 to conservative and then to more aggressive forms of reactionary nationalism (Mann 1995; Merriman 1996). In a parliamentary era, the right also increasingly sought a mass base that ranged from British pragmatic conservatism to the Catholic and confessional politics that was influential in Germany and continental Europe. The latter was reinforced by the 1891 Papal Bull *Rerum Novarum* 1891 which launched a contradictory project of preventing socialism and control of the masses, but also greater social justice (Mann 1995). At the same time more openly authoritarian and anti-democratic movements started to emerge around the notion of the nation as a primordial and ethnically constituted community, often rooted in Darwinian conceptions of the struggle of the fittest and racist ideas derived from imperialism.

The growth of parliamentarism was closely associated with the beginnings of European welfare states, the foundations of which had been laid by 1914 (Thane 1996). In this era however welfare provision was almost everywhere a defensive reform enacted from above and intended to stem the advancing power of labour and socialist parties rather than a direct product of class struggle around state intervention. In any case socialist movements at this time had not fully accommodated themselves to capitalism and often rejected 'reformist' measures (Sassoon 1996). As we saw in Chapter 2, the first modern capitalist social policy was the British 1834 Poor Law, enacted in the wake of middle class enfranchisement in 1832. Its disciplinary and centralizing ambitions were not always successful. Riots sometimes prevented workhouses being built and, in any case, cyclical unemployment periodically threw more out of work than could be contained within their walls (Fraser 1973). By the last quarter of the nineteenth century Europe's ruling groups were becoming increasingly aware that something more than a repressive and residual social policy was required. To secure a stable class-stratified society many understood they would have to integrate the urban masses into the nation state, while others prioritized investment in the economic and physical 'fitness' of the population. The area of social provision where this was recognized earliest was mass education. Many middle class conservative and aristocratic politicians saw the need to build national loyalty through national education systems, while many employers acknowledged the value of instilling time discipline and developing a basic proficiency in literacy and numeracy among the population (Hamerow 1983). It took some time, however, for the same logic to be applied to social security and health care.

Chancellor Bismarck in Germany grasped the nettle by employing a determined 'stick and carrot' method to lay the basis for the development of a contributory social insurance. Having banned the socialist Social Democratic Party in 1878, he initiated a series of reform measures in the 1880s to cement the loyalty of the German masses to the new German state. Thus he initiated a series of health and welfare reforms that broke from earlier poor law provisions, and sought to extend the paternalistic company welfare schemes pioneered by employers such as Krupps, and the more mutal schemes organized between miners and their employers, to the German state as a whole. Compulsory insurance covering occupational injuries and health were introduced in 1883 as were maternity payments, and old age pensions in 1889. The statist and paternalistic traditions of the Junker elite, and the weakness of the middle class, also facilitated state intervention in social security benefits which were initially low and limited to an elite of male industrial breadwinners, with particular classes of women, mainly widows and pregnant women, also being included. The major missing elements in Bismarck's system were any social assistance to the unwaged, to establish a citizenship right to a minimum income, or any unemployment insurance. These did not come until 1927 under the postwar left coalition German government (Zöllner 1982), as shown in Table 3.5.

Table 3.5 Years of introduction of social welfare schemes in Western Europe (countries ranked by year of introduction of measures on occupational injuries)

	Occupational injuries	Health	Pensions	Unemployment
Germany	*1884*	*1883*	*1889*	1927
Austria	*1887*	*1888*	1927	*1920*
Norway	*1894*	*1909*	1936	*1938*
Finland	*1895*	1963	1937	
Italy	*1898*	1928	*1919*	*1919*
Holland	*1901*	1929	*1913*	*1949*
Sweden	*1916*	*1953*	*1913*	
Denmark	*1916*	1933	*1922*	*1944*
France	*1946*	1930	*1910*	1967
UK	*1946*	*1911*	1925	*1911*
Belgium	1971	*1944*	1924	*1944*

Source: Flora *et al* (1983: 454). Reproduced by permission of Macmillan Press Ltd.

The moments and specific influences upon social welfare measures varied considerably within each nation state, but in the four social policy areas listed in Table 3.5 every country except Belgium has at least one institutional marker in the30 years between 1889 and 1916. What is also striking is the bunching of initial welfare developments into two main periods: the first between the 1880s and the First World War (shown in *bold italic*), and the second following the Second World War (shown in *italic*).

In the years that followed ruling groups throughout Europe followed the German example of using welfare as a nation building instrument. The first welfare benefits in other Western European nations were usually meagre and restricted to particular key groups of male workers who represented 'human capital' worth investing in (Rimlinger 1971). Paternalistic and patriarchal 'maternalism', seeking to enhance women's mothering capacities for the nation, was embodied in provision of maternity benefits and 'protective legislation' restricting women's entry into designated occupations (Bock and Thane 1991; Koven and Michel 1993). France, where the low birth rate and high infant mortality rate particularly exercised the minds of national leaders in the wake of the German defeat of France in 1870, pioneered free medical care, child welfare clinics, supplies of free milk, and family policy generally (Quine 1996). However the weakness and divisions of the French trade unions and socialists diminished the incentive to introduce social insurance (Thane 1996). In Britain medical reports indicating the poor physical condition of working class volunteers for the Boer War (1899-1902) helped to create a climate of agitation for 'national efficiency', but pensions in 1908 and national insurance in 1911 were Liberal Party measures intended to stem the growth of the Labour Party (Fraser 1973; Ritter 1983).

Housing also became an increasingly important area of intervention, often as a development on from public health intervention. In France rehousing of displaced workers was one of the features of Haussmann's rebuilding of Paris and establishment of a sewerage system. In the early stages of industrialization employers had often provided housing or hostel accommodation for workers for the reason that the first factories were in remote rural locations. Only later did 'model' employers seek to provide decent housing, often as part of a wider paternalistic concern to supervise the lives of workers and families. In Britain, Quaker employers were the main initiators of such moves at Bournville and Port Sunlight, alongside paternalistic voluntary organizations like the Peabody Trust. By the 1870s the Liberal Mayor of Birmingham, Joseph Chamberlain, was pioneering the 'gas and water' socialism praised by the Webbs which included slum clearance and municipal housing. On the continent company housing was more common, the case of Krupps already having been mentioned. There was also a more planned approach generally to urban development which sought to avoid the worst problems of urban squalor associated with the British industrial revolution. Distinct cultural preferences emerged, with small housing favoured in Britain and Northern Europe and apartment living elsewhere (Power 1993).

Between the wars social policy became an established and significant activity of the state. Expenditure rose as the forms of social insurance established before and after the First World War matured, and as social costs rose with the increase in numbers of older and unemployed people. Pierson (1998) argues that welfare was 'depauperized' and increasingly became a benefit of national citizenship. Socialist parties, now embracing reformism and starting to appear as partners in coalition governments, stimulated pressure for the extension of welfare measures. At the same time governments of the authoritarian right in Italy and Germany as well as in republican France and social democratic Sweden, implemented eugenicist pro-natalist policies to encourage the growth of large families, to counter the effects of mass emigration (Quine 1996). Housing ceased to be seen purely as a public health issue, and in the wake of wartime rent controls what has been termed a 'European paradigm' of non-profit or social housing by municipal authorities and voluntary organizations began to emerge (Doling 1997).

The 'doubled-edged' nature of modern welfare regimes was thus established. On the one hand there were some genuine benefits on which more extensive rights could later be built. On the other the regimes fostered social control, not just because they 'diverted' workers and other subordinated people from more radical change, but also because they extended the disciplinary reach of the state and professions into people's lives, and 'normalized' approved attitudes to health, work and family (Donzelot 1979; Foucault 1977).

3.5 CONCLUSION

This chapter has shown how industrial capitalism in Europe was profoundly shaped by political contingencies, particularly by state traditions, the nature of bourgeois-aristocratic settlement, and the evolving economic and inter-imperialist competition between nations that led to two horrifying wars. Alongside these dominant considerations the mobilization of labour from below also began to shape the political responses of governments to labour and social questions. Initially state interventions were largely conservative measures aimed at forestalling demands for radical change. However, in the interwar period, as trade unions grew in strength and socialist parties gathered in more voters, these interventions started to go further. But these tentative movements towards restraining neo-liberal capitalism were virtually crushed across continental Europe by 1940. The growing triumphs of dictatorial governments cannot just be dismissed as fascist 'interludes' along an inevitable road to 'organized' capitalism, as it was only eventually defeated by massive military force. The next chapter shows how following that defeat, a renewed mobilization from below, and a closer integration of Western European and American capitalism, were decisive in shaping the postwar patterns of management, work and welfare in the so-called 'Golden Age'.

4. The Political Economy of Europe in Capitalism's 'Golden Age', 1945-75

This is the first of two chapters reviewing West European capitalism's most successful period, the so-called *Trente Glorieuses* or 'Golden Age'. It analyses the *political* economic landscape within which the patterns of management, employment relations and social policy, analysed in Chapter 5, emerged and developed. It seeks to show that the construction of stable forms of social and political regulation were the preconditions for, rather than the consequences of the economic and technological developments that took place during this extraordinary period. Thus rather than seeing full employment, workers' rights, welfare states and the neo-corporatist institutions underpinning them as the 'natural' consequence of organized capitalism's evolution towards large-scale industry, it follows Lane (1995: 25) in arguing that there is little evidence that postwar employment security was an economically determined consequence of a system 'stable mass markets' under 'mass production' somehow 'logically connected to the regime of accumulation'. The chapter also seeks to demonstrate that political as well as economic influences were central to the strains that these arrangements came under from the late 1960s onwards.

A fundamental argument underpinning this chapter is that these domestic European formations have been crucially affected by external global political economic pressures throughout the post-1945 period. This contrasts with forms of analysis that suggest that European states in this period enjoyed national autonomy, which has only latterly been undermined. European arrangements, and their national variants, were crucially affected by the global political framework and a world market primarily constructed through the military and economic power of the USA, confronting its former Soviet ally as a Cold War adversary. Both the military defeat of Germany and the reconstruction of Western Europe itself were projects with uncertain outcomes, and deeply influenced by outside forces. Germany never surrendered but was defeated by a temporary but remarkable cooperative effort between the USA and Russia who, emerging as superpowers from the contest, redrew the European map at Yalta in 1945. 'Western Europe' was the subsequent Cold War project, framed after 1945 by Stalin's domination and closure of Eastern Europe, and the construction of the rest of the continent as an American sphere of influence. However, Western Europe was also politically shaped from below, particularly through rising aspirations and a shift to the left in popular consciousness at a time when most forms of conservatism were discredited. If Western Europe was to become economically and politically viable, ways had to be found of reconciling two sets of potentially contrary influences, American liberal universalism and European state collectivism. The resulting compromise was a limited, partial and uneven Americanization of Europe, where most state traditions, including taxation, welfare provision and the regulation of economic and employment relations, remained markedly different from those in the USA. For a generation, this compromise was remarkably successful: Western Europe's capitalist states were largely set down the road of stable parliamentary democracy with an unparalleled economic prosperity, democratization of work relations and expanding social protection.

The chapter starts by charting the West European leftwards shift, showing how the hidden and not so hidden hand of the USA played a central stabilizing role in limiting its impact. Having traced the course of this compromise, it turns to consider the turbulence which emerged from the late 1960s, when renewed challenges from below and changing political economic conditions destabilized the postwar settlement between America and Europe. It shows how in the short run this produced new domestic social compromises in the 1970s that substantially extended the scope of those achieved in the straightened circumstances of 1945.

4.1   EUROPE TURNS LEFT AND THEN STABILIZES

There were a variety of reasons why, as Hobsbawm (1994: 165) puts it, Western European politics were generally 'skewed to the left' by the end of the Second World War. Traditional economic approaches had patently failed in the interwar period, and Europe's right-wing parties and most employers had generally displayed sympathy for authoritarian and fascist regimes. Nazi Germany had now been defeated by the international alliance between liberal capitalism and communism, with extensive involvement at national levels of socialists, communists and trade union representatives. During the war national alliances were already working on plans for postwar reconstruction involving extensive state planning, extensions of workers' rights and enhanced health and welfare provision. The war itself had led to a massive increase in the role of the state, and had been responsible for a growing integration of science and industrial investment (Cardwell 1994), and fostered a collectivist mentality. There could be no simple return to uninhibited free market economics for, as the economist Joseph Schumpeter put it in 1943: 'The all but general opinion seems to be that capitalist methods will be unequal to the task of reconstruction' (cited in Armstrong *et al.* 1991: 5). This new opinion produced tangible results even before the war ended. For example, in 1944 the British Government acted on one of the key elements of the 1942 Beveridge Report by issuing a White Paper on Full Employment, the first instalment towards the creation of a comprehensive welfare state (Timmins 1995). In the Netherlands clandestine negotiations took place during the Nazi occupation between employers and unions, paving the way for the Special Decree on Industrial Relations of the centre-left government coalition established in 1945. The government received powers to veto all collective agreements in return for promises to maintain full employment and provide an expanded welfare state (Ruysseveldt and Visser 1996). In 1943 the French National Resistance Council adapted a strongly radical programme for postwar modernization involving national economic planning, widespread nationalization and comprehensive social welfare that was substantially implemented after Liberation in 1944 (Jefferys 1997).

A centre-left consensus and associated political settlements were not, however, easily achieved. To many at the time 'capitalism in Europe appeared to be in mortal danger' (Sassoon 1996: 189). Millions of lives had been lost, 50 million more had become refugees, and ordinary people everywhere were experiencing exceptional material difficulties. In continental Europe normal and social and economic life was close to collapse (Laqueur 1992). Europe's capacity to feed people had been devastated by the war and around 100 million people were on the edge of starvation (Briggs and Clavin 1997). Armstrong *et al.* (1991) argue, however, that the greatest threat to the system at the time was not so much physical destruction as the undermining of capitalist relations of production between worker and employer. Labour had emerged strengthened and confident from the war. In Britain by 1945 the upsurge in unionization that had been sustained by wartime full employment was followed by the election of a Labour Government. In Germany the collapse of Nazism left many workers in effective control of factories, out of which local anti-fascist committees were formed, often demanding the nationalization of key industries. All major political parties, communist, social democratic and Christian democratic, initially called for radical anti-capitalist economic policies. The greatest shifts to the left, however, came in France, Italy and Greece. In France the Communist Party's role in the resistance placed it at the head of the popular unrest that erupted with the retreat of German forces. In the October 1945 elections the communists became the largest political party and with the socialists won more than half the vote (Jefferys

1997). In Italy, where waves of strikes in the industrial north hastened the end of Mussolini's government in 1943 and industrial workers played a key role in driving out the German army, the Committee of National Liberation set up 'councils of management' in factories severely curtailing employers' powers (Armstrong *et al.* 1991). In Greece the departure of German troops led to civil war and the real possibility of a communist takeover (Wegs and Ladrech 1996).

At the same time as Europe was veering leftwards, the USA set about the task of reconstructing the postwar world. Previously American universalism, as a product of the American Revolution of 1775 and the Enlightenment philosophy of progress, had beckoned to the world to come to the land of opportunity and freedom and seek a new life and American identity. Up to 1914 millions of Europeans had answered the call. Now this philosophy was to become a prescription *for* the world, in direct competition with Soviet communist universalism. America took on the mantle of saving the world for freedom, and restoring capitalism to health by underwriting the restoration of an expansionist world based on the pre-1914 liberal principles of 'free trade', facilitating American foreign investment, and providing access to raw materials and export markets. Hence the world monetary system of fixed exchange rates based on the dollar standard established at the international Bretton Woods conference in 1944, where the USA dominated financial institutions, the World Bank and the International Monetary Fund (IMF) were also set up, initially with the prime aim of reconstructing Europe. Hence also, the 1947 General Agreement on Tariffs and Trade (GATT) codifying the ground rules for international trade to achieve the mutual tariff reductions required for American hegemony through reciprocal 'most favoured nation' provisions (Armstrong *et al.* 1991).

The reconstruction of Western Europe was the essential piece in this global jigsaw. The USA wanted both to prevent the resurgence of protectionist prewar Europe, and to prevent a slippage into communism, especially at the weak points of Italy, France and Greece. It had some leverage as an occupying power, but it chose to adopt a more active approach through the 1948 $13 billion Marshall Aid programme to assist the economic recovery in Western Europe. The largest programme of foreign aid in history, it had a variety of explicit and implicit objectives, including: locking European and American economies into mutual interdependence; creating stable democracies in which parties of the right were strengthened and parties of the left became wedded to reformism; restoring European economies and dampening unrest; and encouraging European federalism and combating nationalism and protectionism. Above all Marshall Aid provided the economic platform from which to launch the

North Atlantic Treaty Organization (NATO) in 1949 that set the seal on Western Europe's Cold War alliance with the USA (Urwin 1997). It also benefited America directly because most of it took the form of grants for commodities produced in the USA (Foreman-Peck 1995), the equivalent of a 3% yearly boost to the American GDP over a four-year period (Maddison 1987: 66). In 1951 Marshall Aid ended and was transformed into the Mutual Defense Assistance programme with a narrower focus on military aid.

Marshall Aid thus helped stabilize Europe politically and to kick-start stagnant economies. It was accompanied by a huge propaganda campaign. For example, with slogans such as 'You Too Can Be Like Us', Italian people were shown films of American workers actually driving to work in their own cars (Ellwood 1998)! It encouraged people to aspire to American consumerism and to support a 'politics of productivity' which, building on earlier state traditions, underpinned postwar neo-corporatism. The campaign also underlined the need to accept changes to the labour process, on the assumption that these would later bear fruit in higher wages and welfare benefits (Maier 1981). This deepening of the social base of the postwar capitalist state contributed to establishing the necessary confidence for renewed private investment and higher growth. It led also, as Millward (1997) has pointed out, to renewed popular support for the nation state in Europe as one which provided 'security' both internally through full employment and welfare states, and externally against the 'communist threat'. Compliance in Germany, Austria and Italy was also influenced by the fascist disciplinary inheritance, and in the first two was imposed by occupying powers (Maier 1981). France was exceptional, in that political stability was not achieved until de Gaulle took power in 1958, as the result of the ongoing contest between socialists and communists.

A key condition of Marshall Aid was that European countries should start dismantling trade barriers and set up a pan-European organization to administer aid and oversee economic recovery, the 1948 Organization for European Economic Cooperation (OEEC). From 1960 this became the broader Organization for Economic Cooperation and Development (OECD) embracing the world's major capitalist economies. The other key development was the creation of the European Coal and Steel Community (ECSC) in 1950, the forerunner of the European Community. Although European federalists, especially Jean Monnet (the 'father of Europe') initiated it and influenced its technocratic centralism, primarily imitative of France planning, the sponsorship of the USA was not far away. Once it had been decided to restore the German economy it was strategically necessary to lock it into a permanent embrace with its old rival France. At this stage, and even when the Treaty of Rome in 1957 took the process a stage further, partial economic integration did not take away power from European nation states, but boosted national forms of welfare capitalism (Millward 1997).

Emergent European federalism was thus heavily influenced by the USA (Anderson 1997; Wallace 1997). It accorded with its strategic economic and military interests but cannot wholly be reduced to them. It was made possible by the prior existence within the USA of a political project to model the world political economy on its own developing domestic structures. By 1945 these had shifted from classic liberalism to a more corporatist 'associative state' involving collaboration between big business and the state, a process accelerated by the New Deal's recovery programmes and planning during the Second World War (Hogan 1987). However Marshall Aid was predicated on a degree of state planning, neo-corporatism and welfare in Europe that was never acceptable to the dominant groups in the USA where union rights were curtailed by the 1947 Taft-Hartley Act, and where there were no significant postwar welfare reforms (Garson and Bailey 1990). What emerged out of this American global project was what Ruggie (1982, 1994) calls a world economy governed according to principles of 'embedded liberalism' that flourished in Europe in the 1950s and 1960s, involving a liberal international order supportive to varieties of stable nation-based systems of welfare capitalism, based on compromises between key social groupings.

Thus rather than seeing the 'golden years' as determined by some inherent 'Fordist' tendency for mass production technology to 'require' a nation-based form of welfare state and regulated capitalism (e.g. Jessop 1990), the evidence presented above indicates that 'embedded liberalism' emerged from a politically constructed American-European compromise. We now turn to how European nation states exercised their 'relative' degrees of autonomy within this global compromise, according to the terms of national-domestic settlements between labour and capital.

4.2   VARIETIES OF NATIONAL SETTLEMENT UNDER WELFARE CAPITALISM

Across the countries of Northern Europe some variant of democratic neo-corporatism, encompassing political democracy, social protection and centralized Keynesian economic management, and the involvement of labour and capital as 'social partners', became the norm. Postwar social democratic ideology built upon familiarity with and support for wartime statism, and sought to turn it to the socially progressive ends of postwar reconstruction. It drew its strength from a predominantly working class social base, but also from its 'programmatic' appeal to other classes, involving plans to socialize industry, to instigate substantial state planning and to deliver comprehensive citizenship rights to social welfare, at a moment when 'capital had lost the right to dominate' (Padgett and Paterson 1991: 12). Social democracy appealed primarily to 'rational' and self-interested working class collectivism, but also to 'ethical' elements in the middle classes who wanted to see the state promoting greater social equality rather than simply mopping up social casualties (Keating 1993). Although the basic shape of European political institutions, social conflicts and party systems had been established in the early twentieth century, when social cleavages around religious, urban-rural, centre-periphery, and class relations had been moulded into varying but durable institutional forms (Rokkan 1972), the nature of the post-Second World War European settlements themselves thus varied according to the relative strength of social democratic and Christian democratic forces.

The social democratic left took parliamentary power in 1945 more emphatically in Britain than elsewhere where it initiated a programme of widespread nationalization and universal systems of health and welfare. However, the weak condition of the British economy restrained its left reformist ambitions. The major industries nationalized such as rail and coal were essential but unprofitable, and Labour's welfare reforms were largely extensions of early twentieth-century social liberalism (Miliband 1972). France was a rather different case. In appearance the Fourth Republic established in 1947 by the coalition of forces involved in the Resistance was a weak parliamentary democracy, prone to instability because the single largest political party, the communists, were excluded from governing coalitions (Keating 1993). However, the executive took charge of reconstruction. France's 'statist' political culture, rooted in Bonarpartism, had already laid the basis for a strong form of postwar national planning. Not only was the resulting French 'indicative' planning more interventionist than Britain's, but its state enterprises, including the country's major banks, the Renault car firm, and many public utilities were also efficient and profitable (Tipton and Aldrich 1987). In theory tripartite and politically accountable, *Le Plan* was in reality monopolized by cordial relations between civil servants and business leaders who had been fellow students at *les grandes écoles,* France's elite postgraduate universities.

Statist traditions were also strong in Italy where a new republican constitution was presided over by the vehemently anti-communist Christian democrats. This party, founded in 1943 emerged in 1948 as the dominant political force, helped by the north-south split and confessional-influenced women voters. Marshall Aid was channelled through two huge public corporations or holding companies headed by entrepreneurs. Italy's planning system, though not as effective as France, was facilitated by the 'corporatist' traditions originally established by Mussolini. The right's hegemony was aided by a weak and politically divided trade union movement and a left whose influence was confined largely to the north. The position of the Catholic Church was officially recognized within the constitution through a concordat, as it had been under fascism. Since the socialists were divided, the communists were Italy's second most important political force, making the country a potentially weak link in the European chain of capitalist nation states. It thus became a prime beneficiary of American aid that was targeted towards the Christian democrats from 1947 once they had agreed to expel the communists from the coalition government (Keating 1993).

The onset of the Cold War resolved the USA's indecision about whether to rebuild West Germany economically, which was then seen as a necessity overriding France's desire for a weak neighbour. As the dominant occupying power the USA exercised great influence over West Germany's political and economic structures. It decided that its interests required only limited 'de-nazification' of prominent posts, but that the anti-fascist committees should be disbanded. Equally, while IG Farben, whose wartime Auschwitz industrial plant had been the largest in the world, was split into three it was allowed to continue operating. The Allies also insisted on a more decentralized state, on stronger constitutional limits to politics (the Basic Law) and a more liberal economy (the Social Market Economy) than became typical of the rest of Western Europe. These conservative tendencies were reinforced domestically by the emergence of the Christian Democratic Union (CDU) as the dominant parliamentary force in the first elections in 1949 (Urwin 1997).

In Italy too Christian democracy curtailed the shift to social democracy. The existence of Christian parties in the Benelux countries, Belgium, Luxembourg and the Netherlands, played a similar role but not to the same degree because they were not as hegemonic, and governments were typically formed through coalitions (Keman 1996). These countries also experienced attempts through neo-corporatist structures to secure the representation of various interests in policy making through direct involvement in educational and welfare provision ('pillarization'). Belgium was the best placed to revive economically after the war as its industry had experienced less destruction. It also benefited by selling Congolese uranium to the USA and received payments from the Allies for using the port of Antwerp. From 1944 the Benelux countries started to coordinate economic planning, presenting a joint front for Marshall Aid that prefigured wider moves to European integration (Tipton and Aldrich 1987). In Portugal, Spain and Greece, however, authoritarian governments overlaid by a thin veneer of constitutionalism continued to rule. They were backed by the Church and propped up by massive American aid to ensure that they remained part of the 'democratic' West. Thus postwar social democracy made scarcely any impact on state policy in Southern Europe (Urwin 1997).

With Labour voted out of office in Britain in 1951, only in Scandinavia did social democracy remain the dominant political force into the 1950s, where it built on its economic success. Sweden emerged from the war in a strong economic position because it had remained neutral during it, selling iron ore and ball bearings to both sides. Denmark, Norway and Finland had suffered more war damage, and the latter was forced to pay reparations to the USSR (Tipton and Aldrich 1987). Though Scandinavian political systems varied, all combined adversarial electoral politics with neo-corporatist consensual policy-making structures. Left-right polarization by class, weak religious divisions and low levels of right political mobilization, have been a pronounced feature of Scandinavian politics and party formation since the early twentieth century, with social democracy strongest of all in Sweden (Esping-Anderson 1990).

With these varying movements towards social and Christian democracy, the legitimacy of Europe's nation states within an international political economy and power politics shaped by American dominance was confirmed, thereby facilitating the economic recovery and sustained growth that permitted the delivery of rising living standards and improved social welfare, and ensured political stability until the end of the 1960s.

4.3   GROWTH AND PROSPERITY IN THE 1950s AND 1960s

Achieving social cohesion was crucial to the revival of European capitalism, but in the context of raising the rate of investment, and in the cause of pursuing the Cold and Korean Wars. This meant that working class aspirations and bargaining strength had to be increasingly constrained by deflationary policies and currency devaluations. In this setting Marshall Aid was an important economic fillip to European economic recovery, and was 'spectacularly successful in removing trade barriers, and promoting recovery of output' (Maddison 1987: 66). It also politically contrasted with the way Stalin imposed communist regimes and asset-stripped Eastern Europe to rebuild the USSR and secure its borders, helping to cement Western Europe's alliance with the USA. Gradually employers and their political representatives regained legitimacy, and won support for postponing present consumption, as both reformist socialism and Christian democracy shifted to the right and a firm ideological to 'the West'. This was materially underpinned by the rapid and to some extent unexpected economic recovery. The pieces in this jigsaw fitted together so well that by the early 1960s Europe was experiencing full (male) employment and sustained economic growth, as shown in Table 4.1.

Table 4.1 European economic growth, 1948-63, and unemployment, 1960 (ranked by rate of growth in GDP)

	Annual average % rise in GDP 1948-63	Unemployment % of total labour force 1960
UK	2.5	1.3
Belgium	3.2	3.3
Sweden	3.4	1.7
Switzerland	3.4	-
Norway	3.5	1.2
Denmark	3.6	1.9
France	4.6	1.4
Netherlands	4.7	0.7
Austria	5.8	2.4
Italy	6.0	5.5
West Germany	7.6	1.0

Sources: Laqueur (1992: 170); OECD (1996: 45). Laqueur reference is from *Europe in our Time: A History 1945-1992* by Walter Laqueur, copyright (c) 1992 by Walter Laqueur. Map copyright (c) 1992 by Viking Penguin. Used by permission of Viking Penguin, a division of Penguin Putnam Inc.

The powerhouse of European economic recovery was the Western German 'economic miracle' (*Wirtschaftswunder*). Industrial production there increased sixfold from 1948 to 1964 and unemployment fell from nearly 9% in 1948 to an all-time low of 0.4% in 1965 (Laqueur 1992: 205). The renewal of industrial plant destroyed by war, combined with the weakness of a labour movement extinguished by Nazism led to large productivity gains. The Allies also imposed a juridical and consensual system of industrial relations. Currency reform in 1948 heavily squeezed living standards and shifted resources to investment. A massive influx of refugees from Eastern Europe provided ready supplies of cheap labour and further checked workers' bargaining power. As these workers were absorbed by the end of the 1950s, a second wave of immigration was then encouraged from Southern Europe and particularly Turkey. The Italian and Austrian postwar performances were almost as impressive, and again the relative weakness of a labour force used to fascism, alongside state planning, facilitated a significant shift to capital formation. In Italy the power of labour was undercut by internal migration from the south. Maier (1981) argues that it is no coincidence that, the USA excepted, the world's three most successful postwar economies, Germany, Italy and Japan, all experienced fascism and then military occupation (Maier 1981).

Britain's postwar economic growth was the least impressive, although unemployment fell to among Europe's lowest. This was partly because it did not immediately need to renew its industrial plant after the war, and partly because of entrenched conservatism by both sides of industry, reinforced traditions of foreign investment established in the imperialist era. However it did start from a higher level of prosperity with a much smaller proportion of its workforce engaged in agriculture. Spain, Portugal and Greece also lagged significantly behind the rest of Western Europe but started to develop in the late 1950s with the help of American economic aid designed to prop up their authoritarian governments. Growth occurred mainly in their relatively small industrial sectors and in tourism, but their agriculture often remained inefficient. Sweden and the Nordic countries were a rather different case. While the post-1945 political settlements brokered by the USA had largely passed them by, their export economies were closely integrated into, and able to take advantage of, the postwar expansionist world economy. Although its growth rates were relatively modest, by the mid-1960s Sweden had the highest national wealth of any country in Europe, the highest living standards, and the highest level of social expenditure (Tipton and Aldrich 1987).

Under American patronage the European Economic Community was formed in 1957 by Germany, France, Belgium, the Netherlands, Luxembourg and Italy, as the EC6. It led to some standardization of external trade barriers and facilitated a wider global liberalization through GATT. Its formation, and that of the rival European Free Trade Association (EFTA) clustered around Britain and the Scandinavian countries, also helped to sustain the boom into the 1960s. The upsurge was primarily sustained by trading in manufactured goods *among* European countries just as it had been in the years before 1914. From the late 1950s, the recovery of Europe was underlined by the fact that the trading deficit with America was turned into a surplus, the technological gap was closing, and the 1960s represented a decade of considerable economic achievement (Williams 1994).

The rapid increase in investment in the context of an increasingly open international economy led to a rapid rise in the importance of multinational enterprises. In the first two postwar decades the most rapid expansion occurred in American Multinational Corporations (MNCs), particularly those operating in Europe. By 1966 there were 9,000 subsidiaries of American firms rooted in Europe. British MNCs, mainly exploiting

Commonwealth links outside Europe, were the next most significant group, followed by West German MNCs (Pollard 1997). These varying degrees of industrial concentration were also mirrored by variations in research and development. According to OECD data, of one hundred major innovations between 1945 and the late 1960s about 60 were introduced by American, 14 by British and 11 by West German companies (Foreman-Peck 1995: 258).

According to the nature of their political settlements, Europe thus adopted 'modified' forms of the American consumer economy whose character for many 'was the real political issue of the 1950s' (Sassoon 1996: 207). Europe continued to experience greater state involvement in the economy, a polity based on neo-corporatist institutions, integrative industrial relations systems and a more rapid increase in social expenditure. Significant divergence overlaid a slow underlying tendency towards convergence. From 1950 to 1973 there was a substantial growth in Western European government spending from an average of 27% to 37% of GDP, but there were no major extensions of the postwar nationalizations to disturb their basic capitalist character (Maddison 1987). A great deal of this was on social expenditure, with provision of education, health care, housing and social security joining defence as the principal activities of modern governments. The biggest change from prewar Europe came with the establishment of full employment and widespread job security. Unemployment fell to average 2.9% in the 1950s, and it dropped again to average 1.5% in the following decade. Between 1960 and 1968 unemployment ranged from 0.1% (in Switzerland) and 0.7% in Germany to 5.0% in Ireland (Aldcroft 1993: 137, 234). This was both an impressive achievement compared to the prewar unemployment, and it provided access for Europeans to sample the emerging 'consumer society'.

Linked to related improvements in nutrition and developments in health technologies was postwar population growth. This arose out of the combination of lower mortality rates and the 'baby boom' that occurred throughout North-west Europe. Widely attributed to couples reuniting after the war, it was sustained by rising living standards into the 1960s, and was accompanied by the further decline of the rural population engaged in agriculture, an accelerated urbanization that included slum clearances and the construction of mass social housing, and by mass migration and immigration. Between 1950 to 1970 the overall proportion of the urban population of the EC12 countries rose from 65 to 74%. The growth of urbanization was slower in countries which were already highly urbanized, such as Britain, the Netherlands and Belgium, but it was particularly pronounced in France (up from 56 to 71%) and in Southern Europe, notably Spain (Champion 1993). Between 1959 and 1965 as many as five million workers migrated from the Mediterranean regions to the industrial cities of

Northern Europe (Aldcroft 1993: 136) while significant levels of immigration occurred from Europe's former and present colonies. Between 1945 and 1975, but particularly after 1960 an unprecedented 30 million people entered Western Europe as workers or workers' dependants, 'one of the greatest migratory movements in human history' (Castles *et al.*1987:1), as shown in Figure 4.1.

Whereas before the Second World War only a handful of Europe's large cities could genuinely be described as cosmopolitan, by the 1970s most large urban centres had become ethnically diverse. These internal and external population movements were associated with dramatic changes in the economic and social restructuring of urban spaces, involving shifts within and between manufacturing industries, and between industry and public and private services. These in turn gave rise to new patterns of residence and forms of inequality. As some intergenerational upward social mobility occurred among 'native' Northern Europeans, there was an increasing correspondence between unskilled and migrant labour (Castles *et al.* 1987).

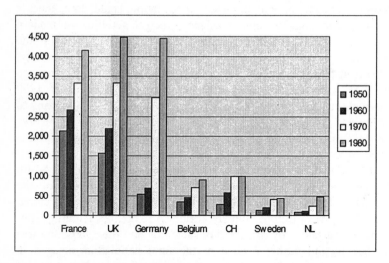

Notes: i. For France and the Netherlands data excludes 'nationals' emigrating from colonies
ii. CH = Switzerland

Source: Castles *et al.* (1987: 87).

Figure 4.1   Growth of 'foreign residents' ' in selected European countries (000s), 1950-80

If the return of political conditions for investment was the initial stage of the European economic recovery, the consumer boom of the 1950s and 1960s that fed, clothed and housed the growing numbers of Europeans represented its completion. More than one commentator has seen growing consumerism as indicative of a growing 'Americanization' of Europe (Therborn 1995; Sassoon 1996). This can be seen as associated with the increasing adoption of American products like Coca Cola, increased inward investment, and a broader cultural transformation involving the adoption of American 'ways' in work, feeling, and behaving. It is difficult and sometimes unhelpful to separate these elements as, for example, the mass media, particularly television and cinema, are both American products and a means of transmitting American values. However, the significance of 'Americanization' in this period should not be exaggerated. The 1929 level of American car density was only, for example, attained in Europe after 1960 (Therborn 1995: 145). What did occur was that the consumer durables such as cars, TVs, telephones, and washing machines identified with American consumerism spread unevenly across Europe in the wake of rises in real wages and shifting patterns of household expenditure. Average European hourly wages had also risen significantly by the mid-1970s and were rapidly closing the differential with the USA, as shown in Figure 4.2.

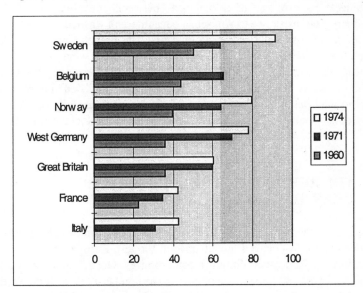

Source: Wegs and Ladrech (1996: 163).

Figure 4.2   Average hourly wages in manufacturing as a % of American hourly earnings

This catching-up even extended to Southern Europe. Thus on average 60% of Spanish household expenditure went on food and housing in 1958, while by 1973-4 this proportion had fallen to 42% (Therborn 1995: 140). There remained a gap in living standards between Europe and the USA, but it was fast closing and between 1953 and 1970 real wages in Italy, Holland and Germany rose by roughly 150% (Sassoon 1996: 194). The highest European living standards, in Sweden, then measured around three-quarters of the GNP per head achieved in the USA. Despite this rise in European living standards there remained a substantial wealth gap between the most prosperous countries and those on the economic periphery such as Greece, Portugal, Spain, and Ireland. Significant regional inequalities persisted even though all societies were on an upward trajectory. And there were also important cultural differences between Europe and America, many of which stemmed from Europe's more collectivist traditions in which labour movement organizations and parties of the left played a vital part. Most European societies were generally less unequal than the USA, even before the redistributive effects of taxation and social security transfers (Maddison 1989).

While there were important contrasts between Western European nations, the general pattern was of a 'balance' between consumer and welfare capitalism. The resistance to American consumerism was led by the left and drew in nationalistic and economic interests. The French Communist Party wanted to ensure that 'Coca Cola does not triumph over wine' and a number of European countries sought either to ban or tax it (Sassoon 1996). On the whole, however, European societies adapted and modified the American model to national cultural purposes, perhaps most successfully in Sweden's fusion of technologically advanced urban living with social democracy, a kind of 'social' consumerism.

4.4   THE REVIVAL OF THE LEFT AND THE REAPPEARANCE OF CRISIS

While the initial impact of the Cold War from 1947 and of the economic boom of the 1950s checked the advance of the left, Europe's right was still constrained by its postwar domestic compromises. Outside Scandinavia and Southern Europe, although democratic governments of the right were in power, they largely operated within the parameters of postwar social democracy. France and Britain were 'deviant' cases. In France the exclusion of both Gaullists and communists led to unstable and divided centre-left governments, which were plagued by colonial difficulties in Indochina and Algeria. The French generals' rebellion over Algerian independence brought de Gaulle back to power in 1958, forcefully ending the Fourth Republic and creating a new constitution in which the legislature was subordinated to the presidency and executive, and restored a form of authoritarian politics institutionally closer to Southern than Northern Europe (Keating 1993). Britain was also exceptional as the only country outside the southern perimeter where the traditional Conservative Party had survived as a significant political force, although during this period it was ideologically similar to continental Christian democracy. Scandinavia was the one place in Western Europe where the left enjoyed unchallenged parliamentary power in the 1950s. Its distinct form was influenced by the cultural inheritance of a 'family of nations' with strong central states and radical political traditions, which were then fused with a modern class politics (Castles 1993). While elsewhere in Europe conservative parties were the chief beneficiaries of the economic recovery, in Scandinavia it strengthened the hegemony and reputation for economic management of left parties, whose popularity in the 1950s was extended by the rapid expansion of social welfare measures (Wegs and Ladrech 1996).

The 1960s, however, saw the revival of more overt class conflict, and the emergence of cleavages around other social issues. After nearly two decades of full employment in Western Europe during which labour market power had been slowly exercised more effectively by the trade unions, there was a European-wide explosion of conflict in 1968-9, pushing employers and governments onto the defensive again. Nearly everywhere workers had higher expectations and greater confidence and, drawing inspiration from the postwar anti-colonial 'liberation' struggles and the Vietnam war, women, and ethnic and national minorities also started to press their demands. The rise in levels of conflict after 1967 was thus linked to a world-wide challenge to American hegemony. Economic prosperity also meant that West European politics could, for the first time, focus on exercising choices under conditions of plenty, releasing irresistible pressures to extend postwar settlements and the boundaries of social and economic democracy.

A Weaker America and the End of the Boom

The 1960s saw Europe becoming less economically dependent on the USA, as reflected in the growing strength of the European Economic Community, which Hobsbawm (1994: 241) has described as a 'growing gap between the overwhelming military, and therefore political, domination of the alliance by Washington, and the USA's gradually weakening economic predominance'. America's weaker economic grip primarily resulted from a complacency born of its overwhelming technological lead, and a postwar preference for foreign investment rather than modernization of domestic plant (Armstrong *et al.* 1991). This was compounded by the costs of both military involvement in Vietnam and a domestic 'War on Poverty' designed to dampen black social unrest. The result was a crisis of confidence in the ability of the US dollar to maintain the Bretton Woods system of fixed international exchange rates. Precipitated by speculative French government purchases of gold, America abandoned its attempt to regulate the world's currencies in the early 1970s, leading to floating exchange rates. At the same time the economic expansion of both Europe and Japan led to over-production and market saturation, bringing the long boom to an end (Williams 1994). The emerging recession was magnified by the rise in oil prices that resulted from the greater independence displayed by America's Middle Eastern client states after the 1973 Arab-Israeli war. The outcome was increases in both inflation *and* unemployment, an unheard of combination in Keynesian orthodoxy.

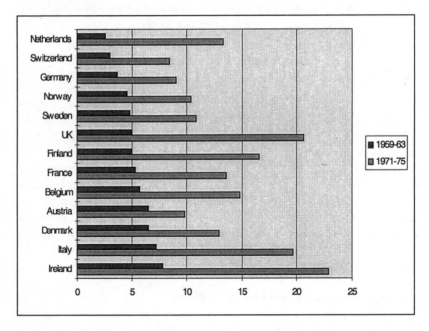

Source: Reproduced by permission of Oxford University Press from Crouch, C. (1993: 229, 256), *Industrial Relations and European State Traditions*, Oxford: Calerndon Press.

Figure 4.3   Western European 'discomfort' index: inflation and unemployment rates for 1959-63 compared to 1971-75 (ranked by degree of discomfort in 1959-63)

In the 1970s the postwar economic boom faltered. Crouch (1993), following the American economist Arthur Okun, provides a 'discomfort' index, combining the unemployment and inflation rates, enabling us to see its rise and national distribution across Europe in the 1970s, as shown in Figure 4.3.

From 1959 to 1963 Western European inflation averaged 3.2% and unemployment 2% a year. By 1971 to 1975, inflation averaged 10.9% and unemployment 3.1%. The Western European 'discomfort' average had risen by 171%. There were extremely high 'discomfort' counts, at around or above three times the 1959-63 level, in Ireland, Britain, Italy, Finland and France and also above-average increases in the 'discomfort' indices for Belgium, the Netherlands and Switzerland. This experience coincided with, and fuelled further discontent in, the governing centre-right parties and coalitions that appeared to have ushered in the growing uncertainty. Initially it generally gave a boost to the left-leaning political parties and coalitions identified with the founding of postwar prosperity and welfare security. Inflation also promoted union activism to recover lost ground, as it had around the turn of the twentieth century.

Table 4.2   Left votes in selected Western European elections, 1931-85[i]

	Number of countries	Electorate (millions)	Left vote (%)
1931-5	11	105.3	27.2
1936-40	9	31.7	29.1
1945-50	13	147.0	33.5
1951-5	13	154.6	33.4
1956-60	13	163.0	32.9
1961-5	13	169.7	33.6
1966-70	13	176.3	35.9
1971-5	13	188.8	35.4
1976-80	13	202.7	36.8
1981-5	13	211.4	34.2

Notes: The 13 countries used since 1945 are: Austria, Belgium, Denmark, Finland, France, West Germany, Ireland, Italy, the Netherlands, Norway, Sweden, Switzerland and Britain.

Source: Bartolini and Mair (1990: 122).

The first responses to the reappearance of 'crisis' were therefore increasing militancy and an electoral shift to the left. The renewed electoral support for left parties and the growth of union membership came not just from manual workers but also from the expanding 'middle ranks' in industry, and public and private services. The growth of welfare had generated new battalions of workers, the majority of them women, with a stake in sustaining and expanding state welfare. Table 4.2 outlines the fortunes of the European left over the 50 years from 1931, the shaded periods signalling the important swings towards the left in the postwar period, and at the end of the 1960s and of the 1970s, before the pendulum swung away in the 1980s.

While the left remained electorally weak in Southern Europe and in France until 1981, overall in the 1970s more Europeans voted 'socialist' than ever before, and by 1975 left parties were in power in Sweden, Austria and Britain, were the main party dominating coalition governments in Norway, Germany, the Netherlands and Switzerland, and junior coalition partners in Finland and Ireland. Even in Belgium and Italy 'Christian or other quasi-labour parties' participated in government (Crouch 1993: 252-3).

The Radical Challenge

The most significant consequence of this renewed left influence was a significant extension of the ways in which European welfare capitalism sought to advance employment and social rights, and promote greater social equality. For the first time, as Hobsbawm points out (1994: 284), 'welfare expenditures - income maintenance, care, education, etc - became the *greater part* of total public expenditure, and people engaged in welfare activities formed the largest body of all public employment'. This second wave of welfare and industrial relations settlements arose mainly from demands to rewrite the national-domestic postwar political compromises that had now become somewhat tarnished during the intervening years, and no longer satisfied a rising generation. The precise terms exacted depended upon the different ways in which national labour movements had acquired strength and influence over the previous two decades, and the extent of challenge of the emerging 'new left', student and feminist movements. While the shocks of May 1968 in France, and of the 'hot' Italian autumn of 1969 failed to realize the hopes of its most radicalized participants, they pushed social democracy to the left and put governments in a mood of compromise aimed at containing pressure from below. New issues were put on the political agenda such as ecology, and real advances were made in implementing women's demands around divorce, discrimination, abortion and contraception. In Southern Europe by the end of the 1970s the challenge from below had toppled all the authoritarian regimes.

This period was the heyday of electoral *and* ideological success of social democracy. When problems started to appear, they were initially attributed to 'too little' Keynesianism rather than too much, giving rise to still more interventionist 'indicative planning' (Padgett and Paterson 1991). French planning was often seen as the model, which was emulated by the British Labour Government after 1964 through Wilson's 'white heat of the technological revolution', spreading also to West Germany. This was accompanied by an extension of neo-corporatist attempts to integrate big business and organized labour into these processes, often through incomes policies. Growing political centralization and 'scientization' evoked further, if diffuse, demands for decentralized democracy and more genuine forms of equality. These demands became the basis for a rise of a 'new left', the driving force behind which were often middle class intellectuals who also tapped growing grassroots discontent among younger industrial workers and growing numbers of university students. Bobbio (1987) has argued that these new movements represented a democratic challenge from below to the hierarchical bureaucracies of 'organized capitalism'. One possible explanation for their emergence is a new cleavage within the middle class: a conflict over control over work *within* the growing ranks of the 'new' middle class, between those who direct, the managers and technocrats, and those who exercise skills in private and public organizations, the latter forming most of the recruits for the new movements. As we saw in the previous chapter Touraine (1966) argued that the new corps of scientific and technical workers were prone to develop a utopian consciousness.

However, though suggestive, this argument has tendencies to reductionism, and Kriesi *et al.* (1995) argue that the threats to personal autonomy and other undesirable effects of the 'managed society' themselves gave sufficient cause for radical discontent. Third World 'liberation' movements and the anti-Vietnam war movement in challenging American postwar international domination also stimulated diverse forms of activism, each seeking their own form of 'liberation', whether for women, gays, or disabled people. Such movements were typically anti-technocratic, emphasizing self-help and self-management. They occurred across the industrialized world, but with a crucial difference between Europe and the USA. In Western Europe the rise of 'new social movements' coincided with the revival of worker militancy, whereas in the USA the white working class 'silent majority' was mobilized against the peace, black and feminist movements by the American right, initially by Nixon and later by Reagan.

The 'rebirth' of the West European feminist movement was certainly one of the most notable developments of this time. However, the notion of a 'second wave', building on the 'first wave' of nineteenth-century feminism, does not fit Southern Europe where feminism only emerged as a 'first wave' in the 1970s. Both the shortage of labour that compelled employers to recruit women, the growth of women's education, dramatic improvements in health, and potential access to technologies of reproductive control, were strong influences on the movement's emergence (Kaplan 1992; Anderson and Zinsser 1988).

To summarize, Western European politics from the end of the 1960s to the mid-1970s were characterized by both heightened distributional conflicts *and* demands emerging from new identified social movements. There were significant variations in the extent of, and institutional forms taken by the rise of new movements and worker militancy across Western Europe, but the waves from the left and from below were felt in all European countries. In part a challenge to social democracy, the new politics also embodied attempts to extend traditional egalitarian concerns for 'citizenship' into areas such as 'race', disability and sexuality. While its most radicalized manifestations were a challenge to existing parliamentary politics and the way that keeping to the 'rules of the game' maintained the status quo, it also led to the radicalization of formal left politics through what Kriesi *et al.* (1995: 112) call the 'programmatic renewal' of social democracy. With the benefit of hindsight, it is now apparent that a neo-liberal right critique of managed capitalism was also crystallizing which, though largely marginalized at the time, would subsequently make a concerted bid for popular legitimacy as a way out of the deepening problems of economic and social malaise associated with the 1970s. However, before these issues are considered, the next chapter first shows how the developments analysed in this chapter impacted on West European patterns of management, work and welfare.

5. Management, Work and Welfare in the 'Golden Age'

This chapter fleshes out the patterns of management, work and welfare associated with the postwar political economic contexts analysed in Chapter 4. It expands on the theme of a restrained 'Americanization' of European societies in the areas of management and work, with a much smaller influence still over welfare. In essence, this period saw largely American-originated technology and management practices gradually introduced alongside European interventionist and regulatory state traditions. We start with management as this was one of the main cultural and political economic mechanisms through which the processes of 'Americanization' occurred. We next consider work as being profoundly shaped by these processes, but restrained by working class mobilizations. Finally we consider state welfare as a primarily European creation building on prewar traditions, although nonetheless subtly affected by America's influence over the postwar settlements. The developments of this period are evaluated in a broadly positive light as they were associated with fairly evenly distributed rising prosperity, workplace democracy and extensive social provision. However we are not blind to the negative features of the so-called 'Golden Age' which formed the background to the amplification of social discontent during the 1960s and 1970s.

5.1 THE GROWTH OF WESTERN EUROPEAN MANAGEMENT

Management occupies a central place because the emergence of the postwar Western European social stratum of modern managers has both been a significant organizational phenomenon that influenced the way Europeans work, and a political catalyst encouraging changes in European welfare and society at large. Its contemporary history really begins after the war. An historian of European management education wrote in 1965 that 'over the last two decades there has been, in Europe, a shift from patrimonial management to professional management' (Mosson 1965: 147). The shift, which had only largely been completed by the 1990s, referred not just to declining family ownership of medium and large-sized firms, which occurred more slowly in continental Europe than in Britain because of easier access to external sources of capital but also crucially to management 'style'. 'Patrimonial' management operated, in essence, on the assumption of the (nearly) 'divine rights' of ownership and command, vested in the force and charisma of the individual entrepreneur. It was effective within a stable socio-economic environment where relatively high levels of trust occurred between networks of gently competing firms and interests, or where state interventions and institutions restrained over-aggressive competition. As the dominance of national ruling class networks came under challenge, both from below or from international competition, and as firms grew in size due to successful competition on price and quality, managers were obliged to become more 'professional'. They needed to rely more on procedures and bureaucratic rules than ownership or force of personality, a development enhancing the claims of an emerging managerial 'profession', and potentially amenable to 'American' academic approaches that were more analytical, adaptive to environments and 'participative' in style (Harbison and Myers 1959). Thus 'managerial rights' became increasingly conditional. Rather than deriving merely from property rights or charisma, they increasingly sought legitimation from expertise in achieving business coordination through the application of standardized rules, and in exercising authority through 'professional' codes. Since before the 1980s there were very few ways of directly verifying managerial performance, professional 'self-responsibility' received particular emphasis.

While the growing influence of this 'managerialism' was socially linked with the rise of the new middle classes, it in part was also a product of the welfare state. While Chapter 7 argues that in the 1980s and 1990s managerialism has become particularly influential in the renewal of the right and the shift to a neo-liberal state, here we note that between 1945 and the 1980s while Europe's welfare states helped expand management numbers, their 'modernizing' social democratic governments were closely associated with the technocratic and managerial concepts of planning and efficiency. We first trace the postwar growth in management functions, and the increasing influence of American management thought and practices upon them. We then show how Western European cultural and political traditions generally restrained the influence of American managerialism up to the end of the 1970s, with discernible differences in management culture between European countries.

Management as an Emerging Force

The growth in managerial numbers to the mid-1970s was largely due to two related processes. Europe's postwar nationalizations and creations of vast national health and welfare systems directly created hundreds of thousands of managerial posts, many of which were organized along national civil service administration lines, while simultaneously they stimulated strong demand for consumer goods and services, enabling many European firms to increase sales and output and to grow substantially in size. Fifty British, 29 German and 24 French firms all employed over 20,000 workers by 1973, a total of 93 firms compared to the then American total of 211 such firms and Japan's 28 (McCraw 1988: 477). As they grew, firms expanded the layers of management dedicated to administering increased numbers of workers and coordinating complex labour processes. Explaining the different ratios of managers used in different subsidiaries, Unilever's chairman reported to its AGM in 1958 that:

> The pattern that emerges is that the higher the degree of mechanisation and the more sophisticated the environment, the higher will be the ratio of managers required (quoted in McGivering *et al.* 1960: 58).

Thus increasing technological complexity, expansion of companies' product ranges, and the growing importance of marketing, all led to rising numbers of managers within large manufacturing firms up to the end of the 1970s and beyond. The expansion of the scale and scope of public welfare had comparable effects.

This unprecedented growth of managers occurred across Western Europe, although definitional differences make precise comparisons difficult. In France the proportion of *cadres*, classified as those holding management positions in public and private sector companies, rose from just 8% of the total working population in 1954 to 18.6% in 1975 (Marchand and Thélot 1991). In Britain about 10% of the working population were managers and professionals in the public and private sectors in 1911. This rose rapidly after 1945 to reach 23% by 1979 and 30% by 1988 (HMSO 1991; HMSO 1981). In Sweden the proportion of managers, professionals and white collar salary earners (*övriga arbetstagare*) employed by affiliates of the Swedish Employers' Federation had risen by 1994 to 44 % (SAF 1996a).

This growing occupational group of 'professional, administrative and managerial employees' has been depicted by John Goldthorpe (1995) as one 'service' class or 'salariat' whose relationship with their employers are primarily determined by 'trust' rather than by contract. This analysis oversimplifies a considerable diversity in functions and positions (Butler and Savage 1995). At the top end of the extensive management spectrum the managerial class blends with the old bourgeoisie, while at the other it embraces those with very limited supervisory responsibilities and no independent means or networks.

Marshall Aid and the Partial Progress of American Managerialism

As the numbers of European managers began to rise after the Second World War their employers began to seek training for them, but by the 1960s as they started to carry their coordinating skills between firms, many managers themselves increasingly sought 'professional' qualifications to enhance their mobility, especially if they lacked access to traditional 'networks'. The meritocratic features of American managerialism therefore often appealed to this group. However, expanding European management training was also a product of the political dependency associated with postwar Marshall Aid.

The notion of management as a meritocratic 'profession' operating on universalistic principles was primarily an American construct. It was particularly associated with the assertion that a 'managerial revolution' had effectively shifted control from the owners and shareholders to the managers of enterprises. Burnham (1945), a former American Trotskyist, now believed that this had made the overthrow of capitalism irrelevant, as the needs of complex and large-scale production required managers to be in charge, whoever technically 'owned' the means of production. One implication of this was to 'depoliticize' productive relationships, which now became seen as solely contoured by technical requirements. Within this discourse, managerial 'missionaries' saw themselves as a key mediating force that would obviate the need for class conflict, establishing a 'scientific' foundation for hierarchy through the realization of the productive potential of 'industrial society' in the interests of all. This universalist doctrine was summarized in 1951 by one of the earliest American management gurus, Peter Drucker:

> Profitability is the only yardstick of economic performance... Regardless where the profits go, regardless who owns the legal title, regardless how the management is selected and to whom it is responsible, the management-worker relationship is bound to be the same (quoted in McGivering *et al.* 1960: 83).

In 1952 the American Management Association defined the political objectives of management as 'the preservation of a free society' through 'putting the real meaning of a free society to work within the organisation for which each individual executive is responsible' (quoted in Carew 1987: 196).

While America promoted its organizational methods as an ideological means for holding communism at bay, it was also seen as a mechanism to secure the opening of European markets to American business. For both these reasons, the expansion of 'management education' became a significant element of Marshall Aid between 1947 and 1951, and a major conduit through which Taylorism and American free market ideology were introduced to European managers throughout the 1950s. This occurred partly through American-influenced training, campaigns and consultancies, and partly through direct funding of universities.

Between 1947 and 1951 Marshall Aid was administered by the American Economic Cooperation Agency (ECA), and in Washington the Republican Chair of the Senate Foreign Relations Committee had insisted that in exchange for bipartisan support the ECA 'shall be under the effective control of adequate business brains' (cited in Carew 1987: 92). A former car salesman and President of Studebaker was therefore made its chief administrator, its senior policy-makers included the presidents of *Time* magazine and Chase National Bank, and its national heads of mission were top businessmen. In 1948, in response to a series of adverse reports on British industrial practices by American businessmen returning from visits to Britain, the Labour Government's Chancellor of the Exchequer, Sir Stafford Cripps, and the ECA, established the Anglo-American Council on Productivity (AACP). Between 1948 and 1952 this paid for nearly 1000 British managers, workers and specialists to spend between four and six weeks each in the USA on 138 separate trips. Their reports sold over 600,000 copies, and on their return team members often 'spread the word' to thousands of industry opinion-formers at dozens of meetings (Carew 1987).

The ECA also exerted pressure on other European countries to create national productivity centres, funding the French *Association française pour l'accroisement de la productivité*, and the German *Rationalisierungs Kuratorium der Deutchen Wirtschaft*, with an Italian centre that was soon criticized for organizing seminars in marketing, accounting and industrial engineering that were one-sidedly for the benefit of managers. Similar study-visits to the British ones followed, for example involving nearly 4,000 French employers, *ingénieurs* and *cadres* between 1950 and 1953 (Carew 1987; Mosson 1965; Boltanski 1987). According to Carew (1987: 139-40) 'the teams formed a highly favourable view of American management with its great professionalism'. From this base the ECA engaged in wider 'information work'. For example, in Germany the ECA Labour Division came under the influence of a former United Steelworkers of America union official who argued in 1951 that the controversial co-determination proposals of the Christian Democratic Government would result in more rapid dissemination of American production methods. The ECA then used its influence with the American government to ensure that the occupying powers remained neutral, and to end the hostile campaigning by the

American National Association of Manufacturers. While co-determination departed from the desired American managerial model, it was seen as strategically necessary to stabilize German labour relations (Carew 1987).

An additional influence helping to redesign European management came from the rapid growth of management consultancies strongly influenced by the latest American thinking. Thus CEGOS (*Commission d'études générales des organisations*), the largest French industrial training consulting firm until the arrival of subsidiaries of American parent firms in the late 1960s, ran training programmes based on combining rationalization with the 'human relations' approach. This had been developed in the USA by Elton Mayo in the 1930s, and provided a more sophisticated understanding of group and individual influences on work behaviour than that offered by Taylorism (Rose 1986). CEGOS grew from 40 employees in the 1950s to 600 by the mid-1960s, when consultants operated in Spain, Holland, Italy and Belgium. Its board of directors included directors of the main banks and the head of British Petroleum in France. Its principal rival and parent of the French polling company SOFRES, SEMA (*Société d'économie de mathématique*), grew from 120 staff in 1960 to 2,000 in 1969 (Boltanski 1987).

Managerialism in Europe's Universities

In 1951 Marshall Aid to Europe became 'Conditional Aid'. Henceforth, American bilateral agreements with its European 'partners' providing loan funds to industry and the promotion of productivity projects were to be conditional upon changes in cultural values and industrial practices. The expansion of university-based management education was crucial to this process, since as well as reinforcing its 'professional' and meritocratic basis, it permanently institutionalized new management practices which thereafter appeared more 'home grown'.

Thus the American National Management Council encouraged Fiat and Olivetti and the local Turin Manufacturers' Association in 1952 to establish the independent postgraduate management institute IPSOA (*Instiuto post-universitario per lo studio dell' organizzazione aziendale*) to promote professional management. In its first eight years, the bulk of IPSOA's teaching was undertaken by 34 professors from 19 American business schools funded under Conditional Aid. By 1953 it funded between 60 and 100 Americans at any one time working in European agencies like the Belgian *Office Belge pour l'accroissement de la productivité* (Carew 1987; Mosson 1965). By 1956, 40 British universities or research institutes were in receipt of grants under Conditional Aid. Some universities also received money through agencies like the American 'Inter-University Committee' that also distributed some of the Ford Foundation funding for the Dunlop, Harbison and Myers research programme into 'The Labour Problem in Economic Development' (McGivering *et al.* 1960). This was a huge fillip to British academic research in production engineering and personnel management. Building upon this momentum, seven universities started traditionally taught postgraduate diploma courses in management, administration or production engineering, while from 1953 Oxford and Cambridge each organized month-long summer schools or extramural classes for about 40 experienced managers (Mosson 1965).

In 1953 the European Productivity Association (EPA) was established as part of the Paris-based Organization for European Economic Cooperation (OEEC), that remained dependent on Conditional Aid until it became the OECD in 1961. In the 1950s the OEEC started to hold regular international conferences on Business Management Education, while the work of the EPA focused on popularizing techniques such as quality control, cost accounting, production planning, work organization, marketing and personnel management (Mosson 1965). In its first four years the EPA ran 340 courses in management techniques for 15,000 managers, just as the highly influential Ford Foundation-funded research programme referred to above into how the world's labour force could best be structured and managed harmoniously started to come on stream. Based at the universities of Chicago and Princeton, and led by John Dunlop, Clark Kerr, Frederick Harbison and Charles Myers it involved 90 academic researchers in the USA and overseas and gave birth to 36 books and 42 articles and papers, including Dunlop's *Industrial Relations Systems* (1958) and *Industrialism and Industrial Man* (Kerr *et al.* 1973), whose analysis suggested that the rest of the world would gradually converge towards the 'pluralistic industrialism' of managerial America. Both the OEEC and the EPA were strongly in favour of introducing American-style business schools into Europe and targeted the large-scale training of European businessmen and management teachers. From 1956 onwards the EPA also mounted a European seminar programme led by American consultants on the theme of training for management, and paid for significant numbers of university lecturers to attend training courses in the USA along with several other American-based or funded organizations (Mosson 1965).

Although different aspects of this ideological re-engineering of European management training were often resented and resisted by European employers' associations, the long-term impact was considerable, having what Carew (1987: 223) calls a 'cumulative' and 'pervasive' impact. Belgium provides an example of how this operated. In 1953 a committee of the employers' Federation of Belgian Industries proposed establishing a new centralized 'staff college' for management, with courses based on exchanges of experience and teaching by practicing managers. This conclusion ran counter to American concerns to create business schools through which to introduce free enterprise ideology from the 'outside'. So the EPA-funded Belgian Productivity Centre campaigned against this decision, successfully overturned it and in 1956 founded the *Fondation industrie-université pour le perfectionnement des dirigeants d'enterprises* (Industrial Foundation for Training Leaders of Industry) to link the network of decentralized training centres attached to the five universities it had been funding since 1953 (Mosson 1965).

By the 1960s the process of the Americanization of European 'professional' management education had begun. Of the 20 management schools listed by the European Association of Management Training Centres in 1961, only one had been founded before the Second World War. All too often from the American perspective, however, the dominant national characteristics of the Europeans' educational and class systems had subverted the new institutions away from the establishment of 'pure' management education, and were still giving it a limited priority. Between 1930 and 1959 American-based business schools conferred a total of about 40,000 masters degrees; in the 1960s expanded provision conferred 89,400; and in the 1970s some 385 American institutions awarded 344,800 new masters' degrees in business. In Britain, by contrast, the National Scheme of Management Studies that was launched in 1947 had by the mid-1950s merely succeeded in embedding low-level non-graduate part-time evening management education into approximately 250 technical-level colleges (Carew 1987). By 1962, when just under 2,500 students had enrolled on the new replacement Diploma in Management Studies (DMS), it was only available full-time at two colleges, with 11 offering block-release courses (Mosson 1965). Therefore, the pace of European adaptation should not be exaggerated. It was only in the 1960s that 'management' started to emerge as a university subject in its own right, rather than a series of discrete specialisms, and management was still a long way from becoming a 'graduate profession' (Carew 1987).

The 1960s' Management 'Movement'

From 1960 there continued North American criticism of the inadequacy and amateurism of Western European management, combined with the rising demand from the growing numbers of new managers for fully professional qualifications, prompting more rapid change. Pellicelli (1976) points out that after 1960, just as Europe sought to close the technological gap with the USA, a similar 'management' gap was perceived, in the contexts of the shift to large-scale production, European economic integration, and an ideological climate of student unrest. He sees this as part of a growing emphasis on technocracy in the 1960s which devalued the 'classical' European education and sought to widen recruitment to the European elite, in the context of extended state planning, the rise of large European firms and growing labour unrest.

In 1957 Nestlé founded IMEDE (*L'institut pour l'étude des méthodes de direction de l'enterprise*) as a part of the University of Lausanne in Switzerland, with Hoftstede's (1980) research (discussed below) as one of its notable products. In 1962, INSEAD (*L'institut européen d'administration des affaires*) was founded at Fontainbleau by the EPA and the International Chamber of Commerce. In both instances the Harvard Business School played a central role in designing syllabi and staffing the new colleges (Mosson 1965). In Britain in 1964 the British Institute of Management (BIM) was founded and the endorsement of management education in the government's Robbins Report into Higher Education of 1963, resulted in the establishment of the London and Manchester Business Schools in 1967.

Once new institutional providers had been established or old ones had begun to teach management, the structure, content and pedagogical methods of European management courses were reshaped in line with the new American orthodoxy. From the 1960s the top European business schools and universities began, hesitantly at first, but by the 1980s with enthusiasm, to teach management largely according to the precepts of the Harvard Business School model. This was considerably facilitated by the intensive marketing of American management textbooks by American publishers, and the populist revelatory texts of 'gurus'. In the 1970s there was a widespread adoption of the typical American MBA curriculum:

1. *Core knowledge courses* in such subjects as statistics, accountancy, marketing, production, economics, psychology, law and management theory.

2. *Elective courses* which permit specialization in chosen areas such as finance, etc.

3. *Integrative courses* which variously synthesize existing knowledge and seek to develop strategic and problem-solving skills through projects, case studies and business games.

Management issues were placed at the centre of the educational process, relegating the significance of 'background' subjects, and breaching Europe's traditional authoritarian teaching style by adopting more participative, critically reflective and active teaching methods. This reinforced the 'democratic', meritocratic, professionally disinterested and universalistic image of American management while at the same time underlining the twin core messages of 'self-responsibility' and of a standardized, rule-based approach to business. By the 1980s a European version of an American MBA had become a key requirement for aspirant managers, even when as in Germany and Sweden this remained 'packaged' within a national degree. The MBA model in fact reshaped European management education at all levels, from the school classroom upwards. A study of the emergence of *cadres* within French society between the 1930s and the 1980s confirms that their rise owed much to:

> the importation of value systems, social technologies, and standards of excellence from the United States, in conjunction with (or even in some cases prior to) the Marshall Plan... As these technologies spread to other areas of collective life (such as social work and even the parochial school system), they helped to establish new forms of social control (Boltanski 1987: 97-8).

Yet it is important not to exaggerate the extent to which American managerialism penetrated Europe in this period via the Marshall Plan and business education. Even in Britain, which is often seen as closer to the American model of liberal capitalism than the rest of Europe, there was substantial resistance to it. Zeitlin (1999) points out that while British union leaders were enthusiastic supporters of a politics of productivity and associated American methods, engineering industry leaders were not fully convinced. They saw it first as a vehicle of intrusion into their affairs by the state and the labour movment, and also not necessarily adapted to British market conditions which required smaller production runs and more flexible production methods. American production methods and forms of organization like the multidivisional firm were adopted in the spate of mergers of the late 1960s onwards, by which time they were arguably becoming outmoded. This is just one example of a broader pattern of continued diversity between European and American managerialism, and among European capitalist nations themselves.

European Managerial Diversity

> In Germany, in Sweden, in Denmark, and even in France, there are a lot of checks and balances against management freedom of actions, there are supervisors' reports, there are workers representatives on the board and there is much more government intervention... On the other hand, British management is much more beholden to its shareholders than European management is. We have to pay far more attention to the attitude of our shareholders (British manager, cited in Calori 1994: 23).

Readers who have followed the analysis presented in previous chapters will be aware that the differences which the perceptive British manager is describing have deep historical roots. Britain was always closer to the American model of liberal capitalism, even if it could not emulate its scale and dynamism by the third quarter of the twentieth century. This was particularly the case with the basic elements of business structure in which joint stock companies that raised capital on the stock market and as a result had to pursue short-term profit for shareholders above everything else, and the requirements of finance capital exercised a dominating influence. In continental Europe this was much less the universal pattern and this was associated with a different approach to business organization within wider political economic structures in which the state exercised a guiding hand, and the banks were directly involved with companies in developing enterprises. This facilitated the development of cultures of regulation and paternalism, and led to more of an emphasis on investment, long-term growth, and a stronger desire to secure market domination rather an absolute obsession with short-term profit. These traditions therefore led to even greater tendencies, despite the Marshall Plan, to resist many of the aspects of American managerial capitalism, even though there was a recognition of the need to close the technological gap between Europe and the USA. This was starting to change by the 1960s. Even so, reviewing the situation at the end of the 1960s, Sampson (1968) was careful not to exaggerate the extent of a European 'managerial revolution' which was remodelling itself along American lines. In many countries even the largest firms often remained firmly under family control: the Wallenbergs in Sweden, the Bercots in France, the Agnellis in Italy, the Pilkingtons in Britain, and so on. In addition rather than expressing American values of meritocracy, Europe's new managers remained wedded to socially exclusive traditions

> because they are grafted on to the old bourgeois traditions: the old classes in which Europe took such pride, its armies, priests, imperial administrators, have transferred themselves into this new élite (Sampson 1968: 112).

This judgement is supported by Wegs and Ladrech (1996) who show that a 'plutocracy' of Europe's very rich remained powerful, that the political managerial elite continued to largely exclude women, and that the grafting-on process varied in different countries: via the Oxbridge 'establishment' in Britain, through the *grandes écoles* system in France, and by acquisition of a university law degree in Germany. This occurred in the context of higher education systems which, despite significant postwar expansion, remained firmly elitist with severely restricted access for children of manual workers.

Cultural analysis does reveal something about the socially embedded nature of management practices. Evidence of continuing distinct national differences in European management cultural styles was uncovered by Hofstede (1980). Analysing attitudinal data collected by IBM between 1967 and 1973 on its 116,000 white collar employees in 48 different countries, he found that despite its strong American corporate culture there were distinct European cultural 'clusters' around four dimensions: 'power distance' (the degree of hierarchy between boss and subordinates); 'uncertainty avoidance' (the extent of formalized rules and fixed life patterns enhancing security, and emphasizing avoidance of risks); 'individualism or collectivism' (looser or stronger ties between people in terms of loyalty and expectations of organizations, friends and families); and 'masculinity' or 'femininity' (the extent of emphasis on material achievements as opposed to concern with interpersonal relationships and the quality of life). There was an 'Anglo-Scandinavian' cluster including Britain, the Netherlands, Norway and Sweden, where attitudes exhibited relatively low 'power distance' and low 'uncertainty avoidance' scores, although Scandinavian countries were distinctive by their low 'masculinity' scores and Britain was strongly 'individualist'. The 'Germanic' cluster of Germany, Austria and Switzerland was characterized by relatively low 'power distance' and high 'uncertainty avoidance'. Finally, countries like France and Belgium, as well as Italy, Spain and Portugal exhibited both high 'power distance' and high 'uncertainty avoidance'.

Hofstede's study inspired many attempts to replicate his results. One review of these revealed that for management and work roles Europe clustered into 'Anglo', 'Nordic', 'Germanic' and 'Latin' countries. Greece was treated as a European outlier, with characteristics closer to 'Near Eastern' societies (Ronan and Shenkar 1985). More recently significant attitudinal differences on a range of factors, including risk tasking, were found among managers in several European societies (Daniels and Radebaugh 1995). However, such evidence on 'culture' must be treated with caution. While it does link management cultures to wider social processes and institutions such as collectivism, religion, authoritarianism and democracy, it is often divorced from a concrete and dynamic analysis of relationships in the labour process (Thompson and McHugh 1995). Nor does the notion of distinct national managerial cultures take sufficient cognizance of cultural diversity within societies (for example between northern and southern Italy, and even different parts of the USA), and different economic sectors such as manufacturing and services, public and private, and so on.

Evidence about culturally shaped management attitudes needs to be connected to an institutional analysis of firms and the wider political economic contexts in which they operate. A number of models have been developed in this direction. Garrison's (1994) framework uses the dimensions of economic management and political governance. Thus Britain, even before Thatcher, was characterized by a relatively liberal economy and a parliamentary system of governance which largely saw 'pressure groups' as an external influence on government decisions. Both 'Nordic' and 'Continental' systems of political economy have, in different ways, emphasized 'partnership' within the process of economic management, and have fostered a more fully 'corporatist' system of political governance closely enmeshing organizations of workers and employers into the state's activities. The southern regimes in the period under review in this chapter displayed an authoritarian character, with limited political democracy but some role for corporatism in the economic sphere.

Different European management styles thus broadly appear to reflect the complex mix of historically embedded values that we saw emerge in the pre-modern era, that were reconfigured by the shift to industrial capitalism at the end of the nineteenth century, and crucially by the post-1945 political settlements with labour. As one moves from the East towards Europe's Western seafront so external trading and related competitiveness attributes become more important, while as one moves from South to North (and away from Rome), so assumptions of 'divine' managerial authority require greater legitimation and which the patriarchal family plays less of a central role as an organizing principle of social life. Within these general trends, different clusters rather than distinct 'types' of managerial and business systems can be identified. Thus Calori (1994) points out that while Britain can be seen as part of an Anglo-American cluster there were distinct differences from the USA. These included a more pragmatic approach to business problems, and a reluctance of family firms to delegate to managerial professionals. In the wider context, other important distinctions were the stronger role of the state in the wake of two twentieth-century war economies and strength of reformist labour movements, and in the establishment postwar of a welfare state based on citizenship entitlements. These more regulatory and socially oriented dimensions are a more central feature of continental business systems and political economies which cluster around the German or 'Rhenish' model (Albert 1991). The essential features of this system have already been described and their link to the formation of an industrial military state at the end of the nineteenth century. We have also touched in the previous chapter on the way that these traditions were reshaped rather than dismantled by the USA after the Second World War. Calori (1994) also groups Japan with this cluster and there are certainly significant similarities: an anti-liberal industrialization programme led by a feudal elite with military considerations in mind. Its authoritarian and paternalist traditions turned under American occupation labour movement pressure towards partnership, and production shifted from military to consumer-oriented production. Their emphasis on paternalism, cooperative working, corporation growth and domination of markets, and production of high-quality goods that consumers appreciate, were a highly successful combination as a viable and increasingly effective managerial tradition and system of political economy, that increasingly gave traditional American managerial and individualist capitalism a run for its money (Albert 1991). Although there is no space to embark on a full comparative discussion here, there were important differences in that group loyalty to the group and the company as the foundation for a way of life became particularly pronounced features of postwar Japanese capitalism (Dore 1972). In Germany, however, there was more worker individualism, pluralist industrial relations, a more liberal political economy and, as we shall see, more extensive welfare as features associated with the postwar 'social market economy'.

Within this framework the Scandinavian systems (which also vary significantly among themselves) can be more appropriately seen, as Calori (1994) argues, as variants of the Rhenish model than distinct types in their own right. Sweden's distinctive traditions of statism led to a more centralized system of industrial relations corporatism and welfare provision from 1938 that was undisturbed by the Second World War and proved itself highly competitive in the postwar international economy. Calori also puts considerable emphasis upon 'the Latin way of doing business', locating France as something of an exception and distinctive model within this group. This tradition is seen as having strong tendencies towards statism, protectionism, hierarchy rather pluralism in the firm, and intuitive management. In Italy there are strong traditions of both family and state-owned firms, whereas in France there is as we have seen a particular emphasis on planning conducted by elite managers and civil servants. Southern countries are claimed to put more emphasis on 'credentialism' as a route to high managerial position, and 'management by chaos' in response to pressure rather than by following procedural rules.

Despite these important differences among European countries, there was much that was similar in Western European management traditions as they developed during the third quarter of the century, and they were becoming more like each other than those that dominant in the USA. Even Britain is only a partial exception in this respect. By the 1990s this had changed dramatically in ways that will be discussed in Chapter 7. However by the 1970s the three key approaches that distinguished Western European management from American approaches (the authoritarian south apart) were: (1) a broader set of goals than short-term profits, (2) a greater reliance on non-competitive networking with other firms and the state, and (3) a greater acceptance of state and employee involvement in structuring workplace rules. In the confrontation between Western Europe's long history of ruling class networking and the democratic and leftward turn after 1945, its management processes had been forced to become significantly pluralist. Nevertheless, the institutional and ideological legacy of Marshall Aid and American business education in Europe should not be underestimated as the foundations were laid in this period for a future more radical shift to American methods of business organization, production and a liberal political economy, whose emergence it was already possible to detect in the late 1960s (Sampson 1968). The extent to which this happened varied, as well as the timing, and will be explored in the latter half of the book. However, the turn happened first in Britain whose culture was most historically receptive to the message in the first place, while continental European societies were, as we shall see, dragged along later and rather more unwillingly.

However defined, the three or four broad country clusters on managerial business systems and state traditions identified above also broadly map onto different approaches to work and industrial relations, and social policy and welfare provision, to which the chapter now turns.

5.2   WORK AFTER 1945

Working lives in Western Europe changed dramatically during the 25 years after 1950. Besides the impact of the gradual professionalization of management just discussed, and the associated extension of mass production methods, the two key and interlinked elements of this transformation were full employment, the growth of welfare states as sources of employment and protection against risk, and the enhanced political influence enjoyed by northern European labour movements. Work in Western Europe not only became plentiful, it also became more urban, more feminine, less physically arduous and less private. There was rapid movement away from working on the land although, as shown in Table 5.1 below, this process took longer in Portugal, Spain, Finland and Ireland and is still by no means complete in Greece. By the early 1960s only one in five employees in Austria, Denmark, France, Holland and Norway worked in agriculture, and by 1994 just one employee in 20 throughout the EU15. In Hobsbawm's (1994: 291) words, 'the peasants of agrarian Europe stopped tilling the land'. After 1945 Europe's workers entered a post-agricultural age. Even those left on the land experienced dramatic changes in their work: horses were replaced by tractors, and the constant availability of electrical and petrol-based power, and modern farming techniques, ensured that most agricultural tasks were less back-breaking but also more intensive and less communal than previously.

Table 5.1   The decline of agricultural work in Europe 1950-94 (ranked by the size of the agricultural workforce in 1950)

	Agricultural workforce as % of total workforce	Agricultural employment as % of persons in employment	
	1950	1974	1994
UK	5.1	2.8	2.3
Belgium	12.1	3.8	2.9
Switzerland	16.5	7.5	4.0
Netherlands	18.8	5.7	4.0
Sweden	20.3	6.7	3.4
Germany	23.2	7.0	3.3
Denmark	25.6	9.6	5.1
Norway	25.9	10.6	5.3
Austria	32.3	11.4	7.2
France	33.0	10.6	4.8
EU15	-	*11.7*	*5.5*
Ireland	39.6	22.8	12.0
Italy	40.0	17.5	7.9
Finland	46.0	16.3	8.3
Spain	-	23.2	9.8
Portugal	-	34.9	11.5
Greece	-	36.0	20.8

Sources: Crouch (1993: 201); OECD (1996: 42). Crouch reference from Crouch, C. (1993), *Industrial Relations and European State Traditions*, Oxford: Clarendon Press. Reproduced by permission of Oxford University Press.

Although the absolute numbers of Western Europeans at work increased as a result of postwar population growth, the participation rates of those aged 15 to 64 remained stable at around two-thirds: younger people delayed entering the labour force to go into further and higher education, and the provision of near universal pensions enabled or required older workers to retire earlier. As families decreased in size, and housing improvements and electrical technologies made household work easier, and as the economy boomed, women spent more of their lives in paid work. While there were wide variations within Europe the EU15 male average participation rate fell from 96% in 1960 to 81% by 1984, while women's participation rose from

42 to 50%. Economic growth and tight labour markets drew many more women into manufacturing, clerical and private service sector jobs, while health and welfare services became heavily reliant on cheap female labour. More women remained in paid work after marriage or returned to it after their children had started school. Women's participation varied nationally according to culture, levels of economic development and welfare policies. In the poorer and more agriculturally based societies it tended to be lower than the European average, though the data may not adequately recognize women's informal contribution on farms. Belgium (42%) and the Netherlands (30%) were two richer northern countries where there was less cultural acceptance of women's participation which remained far below average in 1974. Only in Sweden, Britain and Denmark were there large increases in the proportion of women working, and only in these countries along with Austria, Norway, Finland, Switzerland and (just) France and Germany did more than half of all women have paid work by the mid-1970s (OECD 1996).

The 1960s and 1970s saw growing numbers of non-manual or non-industrial jobs created in servicing, administering and managing the rapidly expanding welfare state, and in design, sales and marketing for the new mass consumers' insatiable appetites for new and enhanced products. By 1975 a small majority of workers in the EC9 worked in the services sector and 8.3% of employment was in public administration and 5.6% in finance and insurance (Eurostat 1977). Between 1960 and 1974 the share of total employment provided by EU15 governments as a whole rose from 11.2 to 15.2%. Since the war private employers had seen their span of command fall from covering nearly 95 in every 100 workers to less than 85, and to only three out of every four workers in Sweden (OECD 1996) The increased administrative complexity of both business and welfare administration also generated new layers of supervisory personnel.

The shift from agriculture, the modernization of much of European manufacturing, the growth of services and the rising levels of participation by women, all contributed by the 1970s to the significant reduction in the volume of physically exhausting and overtly hazardous work that had dominated employment since the industrial revolution. The growth of lighter assembly line work and spread of reasonably effective health and safety legislation saw industrial accident rates tumbling from the 1960s. With the continuing exceptions of seafaring, construction and mining, accidental death at work became a rarity (OECD 1989). However, alongside the reduction of these health risks, new ones arose associated with first the growth of mass production technology and the stresses of intensive and subordinated work implicated in cardiovascular disease, second, the petrochemical and process industries were responsible for increases in occupationally related cancer, and third public service work itself involved dealing with people's needs at times when they were often in distress. Women workers also had the added burden of balancing home and work demands (Cooper *et al.* 1988; Doyal and Epstein 1983). With such evidence in mind, it is important not to paint too rosy a picture of working conditions in capitalism's so-called 'Golden Age'. The impact of these advancing forms of working helped to fuel the discontent of the 1960s and campaigns against technocracy, more humanistic working conditions, and a genuine workers' democracy, as significant factors in the upheavals of the late 1960s.

State Regulation of Employment Relations

Nevertheless, social relations at work underwent a profound transformation during this period. Gradually the discretion of employers was narrowed as work became increasingly regulated from above by the state, and negotiated from below through the actions of strengthened labour movements. In a full employment situation, workers could also take the 'exit' option and move jobs, as well as exercising 'voice'. Both in the late 1940s and again in the 1970s under left-influenced governments, national legislatures imposed many curbs on employers' freedom to dispose of 'their' assets without considering their employees' or the 'national' interests. This was done partly by nationalizing individual firms or economically strategic industries, and partly by imposing employee consultation requirements or collective bargaining obligations on individual or associations of employers.

Nationalization went furthest in France, Britain and Italy, where most of the public utilities, mining, transport, parts of the finance sector and some manufacturing firms were taken into public ownership. The newly (1949) founded Federal Republic of (West) Germany, where the employers successfully resisted union demands for the large-scale nationalizations that were anathema to the American occupying force, nevertheless had to tolerate significant restraints upon employer autonomy through the system of co-determination introduced by Christian Democratic Government. The 1952 Works Constitution Act gave employees in firms with more than 500 employees one-third representation on their supervisory boards. This measure built upon the cooperative works councils that had kept production going in the chaotic days after defeat in 1945. Later, the 1976 Co-determination Act extended parity representation rights for workers on supervisory boards in all companies with more than 2,000 employees (although that representation did not include a veto over the personnel director).

Several other countries also extended industrial democracy in the aftermath of the Second World War. In France, De Gaulle acted quickly to institutionalize and limit the powers of the workers' committees that in many large firms risked usurping the 'natural' chain of command. In February 1945 *comités d'enterprise* were made mandatory in all industrial companies with 50 or more employees, but unlike the German *Betriebrat* they were not permitted independence or any real powers. They were to be chaired by their employer (or his representative) and had little direct influence over company policy. Their formal rights were limited to being informed and consulted about the general state of the company, in particular when redundancies (*plans sociaux*) were involved. In Britain the wartime Joint Production Committees had strengthened trade union influence, so while the unions wished to maintain them, the employers did not. Support for the British tradition of 'voluntarism' by both unions and employers meant there was no positive intervention on union rights, but the anti-union legislation passed in the wake of the 1926 General Strike was repealed by the 1945 Labour Government. Only in the 1970s did legislation significantly extend workers' legal rights with the 1974 Health and Safety at Work and the 1976 Employment Protection Acts. In Italy in the 1950s, the weak and divided labour movement combined with Christian Democratic political power led to weak labour legislation and minimal worker influence on the enterprise or the state. The flow of cheap labour from the south to the dynamic northern regions also undercut the power of labour. This only changed with the growth of workplace militancy in the late 1960s, when governments sought to channel this into institutional forms of labour protection and national collective bargaining agreements (Butera 1985).

Sweden departs from this pattern in that postwar developments were built more directly on prewar foundations of the 1938 Saltsjöbaden Agreement between the Swedish employers (SAF) and the central manual union confederation (LO). Since the LO had secured recognition rights and centralized collective bargaining, it successfully resisted government plans to introduce works councils to regulate pay, hours and conditions, for fear of being sidelined under 'dual representation' (Leion 1985). Another unique feature of the Swedish system was the agreement that private industry would not be nationalized, in return for high taxation to fund a strong public sector in health and welfare. This compromise was strained by increasing worker militancy in the 1970s and by the trade union campaign for 'wage earner funds' to place a share of profits under the investment control of the unions.

An emphasis on collaboration between employers and workers at national level also underpinned the Dutch system of industrial relations, where perhaps the most conservative labour movement in Europe gave central priority to rebuilding the nation after the war. In return for this they won rights to participate in national wage agreements and in corporatist arrangements for social security and social welfare. However they voluntarily surrendered influence in the workplace, and statutory works councils actually stymied the development of plant-level union organization. As elsewhere in Europe this system came under pressure in the 1970s from workplace militancy leading in 1980 to a revised framework where unions could use works councils as a tool for workplace organization and collective betterment of working conditions (van Zweeden 1985).

Minimum European Labour Conditions

Following the Second World War several Western European countries not only intervened to establish procedural conditions for the conduct of industrial relations, but also laid down minimum substantive conditions. Governments often introduced or extended minimum rates of pay or, as with British Wages Councils, laid down statutory forms of pay resolution in specific low-paid sectors. By the early 1980s France, Luxembourg, the Netherlands, Portugal and Spain had statutory minimum wages set by government while in Belgium, Denmark, Germany, Greece, and Italy, they were negotiated through collective bargaining (Bridgford and Stirling 1994). European states also established minimum health and safety levels. Before the Second World War what limited legislation existed was generally ignored by employers, poorly policed by the state, and inadequately punished in law. However after 1945 and especially as a feature of 1970s' political settlements, the notion of workers' rights to a safe working environment became embedded within welfare capitalism. By the early 1980s most states had health and safety provisions and pressures mounted to harmonize them across Europe. There was still very considerable national diversity in approach and inspection, enforcement arrangements and sanctions varied considerably. In Greece, Italy and Portugal basic provisions are part of written constitutions, while in Germany, Holland and Spain they are laid down in national legal codes, and in Denmark, Ireland and Britain they are defined by common law (Health and Safety Executive 1991; Bridgford and Stirling 1994).

It should not be assumed that all in the European 'garden' was rosy by the 1970s. Poverty remained widespread; wealth remained highly concentrated; gender and race discrimination were endemic; production line jobs were often pressured and alienating; trade unions often acted sectionally, increasing wage differentials (although not in Sweden) and excluding outsiders (often women and minorities). However the differences between the prewar context of widespread job insecurity and the postwar job security were profound.

Trade Union Growth and 'Advance'

Workers' own independent organizations, the trade unions, were playing a key role in the generation of confidence in employment security by the 1970s. Standing (1997) sees workers' sense of job security being underwritten by the fact that in Western Europe by the late 1960s and early 1970s the employers widely recognized and bargained with trade unions. In this way an independent and collective voice was provided for most manual workers as well as for many of the growing numbers of white collar ones. Trade union structure and ideology varied widely across Europe. In postwar Germany and Austria the 'fresh start' led to an industrial unionism focused on sectoral collective bargaining outside the workplace. Sweden, too, experienced a growth in manual industrial unionism in a national framework of collective bargaining, but accompanied by a stronger and more independent workplace unionism. Elsewhere religious and political divisions often cut across craft, industrial and regional divides, in often bewilderingly complex ways: in France no less than five discrete national confederations had emerged by the mid-1960s within a labour movement that emerged with late industrialization. In Britain early industrialization had led to the survival of craft unionism on which industrial and general unionism was grafted, and a fairly weak single central confederation (Bridgford and Stirling 1994).

These institutional differences contributed to significant national and sectoral variations in trade union ideology, objectives and effectiveness. The overall story, however, is one of advance in numbers and growing influence up to the mid-1970s. By 1975 half or more of the whole labour force were members of unions in Sweden, Finland, Norway, Austria, Denmark, Belgium and Britain. Everywhere else (except Southern Europe) at least one in three, and virtually the entire skilled workforce, were union members. Even in France, where less than one in five workers held a paid-up union card, well over half the eligible workforce voted for trade union representatives in works council elections when given the chance (Labbé 1994). In Italy nearly half the non-agricultural labour force was unionized, and in West Germany and the Netherlands about one-third, with almost everyone unionized in manufacturing (Crouch 1993). These high levels of union membership signalled the unions' emergence as a significant political force and pressure group on the local and national state, with many leading trade unionists taking jobs in the labour movement-led governments of the mid-1970s. It also reflected the recognition by many employers that they had no choice other than to recognize the unions because of the tightness of the labour market.

In the 1970s the appearance of economic crisis and more general industrial conflict was dealt with by labour compacts that resulted in extensions of the postwar settlements. It was only in Britain that weakly established corporatism collapsed entirely after the 1978-9 'winter of discontent' and election of the Thatcher government. Table 5.2 details the expansion of Western European trade unionism to its highest level in the twentieth century.

Table 5.2   Western European trade union membership density, c. 1950 compared to c. 1975 (ranked by density levels in 1950)

	Trade union membership as % of total labour force	
	1950	1975
France	18.8	17.8
Finland	20.2	67.6
Italy	23.2	32.9
Germany	24.5	29.3
Switzerland	28.1	29.2
Netherlands	30.0	32.3
Denmark	38.5	61.2
Norway	40.3	60.0
UK	41.1	48.1
Austria	41.8	51.2
Belgium	42.2	61.3
Sweden	50.3	77.7

Source: Reproduced by permission of Oxford University Press from Crouch, C. (1993: 197-8, 252-3), *Industrial Relations and European State Traditions*, Oxford: Clarendon Press.

There was nothing 'automatic' about this trade union growth. In country after country, and in sector after sector, employers vigorously contested it, only fully embracing pluralist strategies of incorporation and cooperation where they were either legally constrained to do so or where, as in Britain and Scandinavia, periods of left government effectively legitimized a significant trade union presence. It was also in Britian and Scandinavia, both with strong traditions of solidarity and welfare universalism, that trade unionism spread effectively in the 1960s and 1970s to white collar and professional workers in public and private employment. In Scandinavia and Belgium, where trade union densities rose to over 60%, the state gave the unions a direct role in distributing unemployment insurance. The most notable outlier in terms of low levels of union membership was France where postwar laws formally required employers to jointly run the social security system with the unions at national level, to collectively bargain at sectoral level and to hold minimal consultations with elected *comités d'enterprise* inside plants with more than 50 employees (Jefferys 1996). However the absence of an effective 'compromise' between labour and capital was reflected in the major political postwar strike waves, and most notably in 1968 (Shorter and Tilly 1974). The political exclusion of communist-voting workers, the aggressive resistance of the employers, and political divisions among unions led to lower unionization, little or no workplace collective bargaining, and volatile strike explosions among non-unionized workers (Jefferys 1996).

Countries with similar proportions of workers participating in 'mass production' industries thus had hugely different levels of membership and organizing traditions. To understand the influence of Europe's national trade union movements by the 1970s requires examining nationally embedded approaches to authority (Black 1999) as well as the balance of class forces and the unions' mobilizing capacities over both of which political and religious cleavages play a major role. Governments everywhere had the capacity to legitimize unionization and collective bargaining and to reinforce the ideological concept of the 'responsible' employer. Whether they used this capability or not to 'insulate' the labour movement from market forces, and if so how extensively, was shaped by the relative pressures governments experienced from employers and unions (Western 1998).

Among the different forms of pressures exerted by the trade unions were strikes, although the extent to which these reflected strength or weakness varied. Figure 5.1 compares the recorded days lost per 1,000 workers during three selected five-year periods between 1946 and 1975.

In all three periods the Netherlands, Austria, Norway, Switzerland, Germany and Sweden (those on the right of Figure 5.1) registered consistently low levels of industrial disruption, with generally less than 100 days lost per 1000 workers. Meanwhile another six, Finland, Italy, Belgium, France, Ireland and Denmark (on the left of Figure 5.1) registered not less than 150 days lost per 1000 workers and generally well over 200. As with union membership, no simple distinction can be drawn between the dominant production system of one group of six compared to the other. The 'lower conflict' countries tended to exhibit either higher economic growth rates, or stronger state regulation of conflict resolution, or both, than did the 'higher conflict' countries. But the only general (and still not universal) trend was for the numbers of working days lost to rise between the early 1960s and the first half of the 1970s (the exceptions being the smaller countries Finland, Norway, Austria and Switzerland). This trend reflected two opposed developments: on the one hand the growing challenge of workplace unionism from below, partly triggered by the higher inflation levels of the 1970s that encouraged activism to maintain earnings levels; and on the other a rougher economic climate that began to pressure employers to offer greater resistance to union demands.

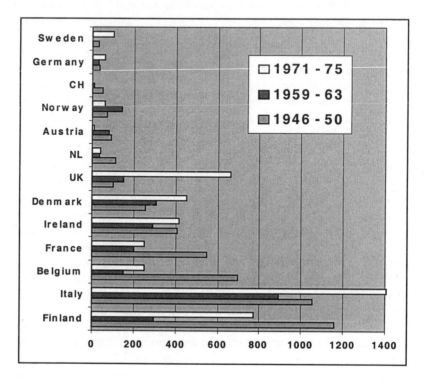

Note: CH = Switezerland

Source: Reproduced by permission of Oxford University Press from Crouch, C. (1993: 203, 228, 255), *Industrial Relations and European State Traditions*, Oxford: Clarendon Press.

Figure 5.1   Conflict in Western Europe during three periods from 1946-75: days lost per 1,000 workers

Authority Relations at Work

The decade after 1965 was associated with the rising political, economic and democratic expectations of a generation of younger workers, as the first postwar generation of trade union leaders formed by the defensive experience of the 1930s, was replaced by leaders whose formative experiences were of growing trade union strength and influence. On the shop floor many workers began to acquire considerable powers of restraint over managerial authority. Throughout Western Europe in the 1970s, therefore, the workplace regimes of most manual and white collar workers became more 'democratic' than ever before. Workers still carried out orders, but they frequently had a 'right to reply' and exercised their 'voice' through trade union or works council representatives of whom their immediate managers and supervisors had to take notice. This 'voice' did not resemble workers' control, although some consultation on decisions at levels remote from the workplace was introduced in Germany in 1976, in France in 1982 and proposed but never implemented in Britain by the 1977 Bullock Report.

The bottom-up pressures were reinforced by other influences. Earlier in this chapter we traced an acceleration in the professionalization of European management in the 1960s. Yet while American accounting, marketing and sales methods were readily diffused, European managers did not find it feasible to implement American personnel methods, rooted either in non-unionism and union avoidance or in legally enforceable workplace contracts in the main with strongly business unions. However, the American argument about the need to standardize, rationalize and regulate labour markets did correspond with certain trade union interests. Under tight labour market conditions trade unionists at both national and local levels saw the creation of more elaborate systems of rules and 'rights' as a way of diminishing the arbitrary exercise of managerial power. As we shall see in the next section of the chapter, these rights were reinforced by rapidly expanding 'social security' against a range of risks associated with wage labour such as unemployment, ill health, and poverty in old age, which diminished their traditional disciplinary effects.

Employment security and access to many of the fruits of postwar economic growth allowed workers many more choices about the work they did, where they lived, and the way they lived their lives, than previous generations had experienced. Leisure opportunities multiplied as shorter working hours and access to telephones, televisions and cars gave many workers the means to construct broader identities than those dictated by the need to earn a living. Low-cost air travel and the expanding European motorway network enabled greater numbers of Northern Europeans to take their longer holidays in other (mainly Southern) European countries.

During the third quarter of the twentieth-century the dominant work trajectory shifted from the prewar experience of more physical and less secure jobs under a harsh, insecure and undemocratic work regime, towards physically lighter work with secure employment and slightly more democratic work regimes. However, with the spread of largely American-originated mass production techniques in both manual and white collar work, there was another counter-dynamic towards increasing work measurement and supervision (Braverman 1974), involving an uneven shift for many skilled workers from 'responsible autonomy' to the managerial assertion of more 'direct control' over work processes (Freidmann 1977). This was a factor in the growing worker discontent since, despite greater job security and higher living standards, the 'affluent' worker was not only denied real participation, but also remained aware of continuing societal inequalities. There remained, too, another work trajectory: a minority 'secondary labour' market, the underemployed, casual trajectory that had been typical of Europe at the end of the nineteenth century and which remained more common in large parts of the non-union labour market of the USA. It had now become thoroughly feminized and racialized in Western Europe, with few employment rights to job security, workplace democracy, access to training or decent wages. The welfare state offered less effective protection to such workers and their families, and its dualistic labour markets often exploited their labour (Doyal *et al.* 1981).

5.3   WELFARE UNDER 'WELFARE CAPITALISM'

The expansion of Western Europe's welfare states after 1945, from institutional foundations already laid by the end of the interwar period, is without doubt one of the defining features of 'welfare capitalism'. It was an essential element in the implicit postwar arrangements that the ruling elites made with Europe's working classes: the rebuilding of industrial capitalism would not be achieved by fear and compulsion but by consent, without resorting to the risks of unemployment, and poverty in sickness and old age that had always underpinned earlier imbalances in employment relations. Demographic issues also loomed, in that the loss of life during the war encouraged countries to provide social security incentives to raise the birth rate. It also preserved the 'liberal' framework of society. The welfare state would not be fascist, but neither would it be communist, and it was therefore a form of 'security' that did not fundamentally remove responsibility from the individual. However, it did embody a form of paternalistic commitment that society's rulers would 'look after' people, in return for support for the Western side of the Cold War. The welfare state was thus the essential ingredient in the political, social and ideological stabilization and subsequent economic rebuilding of Western Europe.

Once re-established, the expansion of European welfare states themselves became a significant influence upon, and not just simply a reflection of political economic forces. We have already seen that the welfare state became a significant sector of employment and trade unionism, accelerating the shift to services and the expansion of managerial layers. As Esping-Anderson (1990: 221) put it:

> The contemporary welfare state is not merely a passive by-product of industrial development. With its institutionalization, it becomes a powerful societal mechanism which decisively shapes the future.

Welfare states were therefore an *embedded* element of European political economies, rather than a 'superstructure' outside the productive system. They were therefore an integral feature of a 'demand-side' society, in which the responsibility of the state was to provide employment, protect social casualties, and provide 'public goods' like health and education, partly out of paternalism, and partly because it was deemed to be indirectly productive. There was an assumed 'virtuous circle' in which there was a broad consensus that welfare expenditure enhanced skills and 'human capital', expanded employment, improved morale, and maintained consumption among non-working sections of the population (Gough 1979). And for 30 years after 1945, the 'virtuous circle' seemed to work very well. However, while this 'functionalist' case has some merits, while welfare states were part of the glue which led to the undoubted economic success of postwar European capitalism, they were also a cost to capitalism that grew as expectations expanded in the 1960s and as Western economies were hit by the oil recessions. As in the field of employment relations, employers and conservative parties often went along with welfare capitalism for pragmatic reasons rather than always being convinced in their souls of its merits. Thus pressure from below in a democratic era had ensured that welfare states were now accepted to be 'social rights of citizenship' (Marshall 1950). However the extent to which this occurred was shaped by political mobilizations, which underlined the differences between Europe and the USA, and also between European nations themselves.

Constructing Europe's Postwar Welfare States

Thus precise configurations of postwar welfare states varied, and were often shaped by past inheritances and the strength of political mobilizations. Nevertheless, the key influences were first, the fact that Sweden had shown since the 1930s that welfare capitalism could work, and second the publication in Britain of the 1942 Beveridge Report, which provided a blueprint of how a Keynesian strategy of full employment could be combined with centralized state social policy. Beveridge sought to defeat the 'five Giants of Want, Disease, Squalor, Idleness and Ignorance', through comprehensive social security, a National Health Service, housebuilding and town planning, full employment, and universal secondary education. In contrast with the Bismarckian corporatist system of decentralized compulsory insurance, Beveridge's plan envisaged the state taking full command of social security and health by establishing uniform nationwide systems. It was not only rational in the context of the wartime experience of national planning, but it also dovetailed with the political spirit of universalism and common citizenship. Only through a single, state-run system could health and welfare provide the same benefits to everyone without distinction of rank or social position. Neither Beveridge nor Keynes were socialists; indeed they may properly be dubbed 'reluctant collectivists', social liberals, who sought to preserve rather than transform capitalism by preventing a return to the mass unemployment of the 1930s (George and Wilding 1985). Nevertheless the restraints upon 'free market' capitalism implicit in their approach to economic and social planning led it to be taken up by left-reformist politicians, and it subsequently became seen as the lynchpin of social democracy.

Beveridge's plan was largely enacted by the postwar Labour Government, elected largely because British voters believed that it would be more likely to deliver on it than would Churchill (Addison 1977). The circumstances of postwar Britain were economically daunting and the American-British international compromise constraining, but Labour did implement its major planks through National Insurance and National Health Service Acts in 1946 and a National Assistance Act in 1948. Two other significant measures, universal compulsory secondary education and the crucial 1944 White Paper setting full employment as the first goal of government economic policy had been introduced under the wartime coalition government. In continental Europe the outcome of the postwar social reforms was more often an extension of the Bismarckian system. This was not predestined, but was the direct result of the shift to the right that occurred after 1947 with the onset of the Cold War. Wartime Dutch, French and German leaders exiled in London had been strongly attracted to the Beveridge model. Resistance coalitions in Italy and the Netherlands seriously discussed the possibility of establishing a centralized, state-run system of social security towards the end of the war. A major factor deflecting European states away from this path was the political rise of Christian democracy whose neo-corporatist and 'social market' bias became an important force within European societies (van Kersbergen 1995). In Germany, too, as an occupying power the USA was able to steer political choices away from Beveridge-style welfare or a strong form of Keynesian economic intervention, whereas they had to accept that Britain was going down that road. In Europe, too, the Bismarckian approach had a popular base, in that trade unions wished to remain significant 'stakeholders' in welfare, whereas the interwar depression had convinced many British trade union leaders that this was not desirable (Whiteside 1997; Crouch 1999).

If the extension of Bismarckian variants of welfare became the norm in Germany, Austria, the Benelux countries, France and Italy, in the 'core' of continental Europe, two contrasting departures from it were found to the north and south. Towards the north the Scandinavian 'family of nations' (Castles and Mitchell 1993) exhibited strong tendencies towards the Beveridge model. While Sweden had already started developing its system in the 1930s, the postwar expansion of Scandinavian welfare states was nevertheless strongly influenced by principles of universalism. Nevertheless the unions were accorded the role of administrators of the system (which was also a feature of social security in some Benelux countries, the so-called 'Ghent system' of state delegation. The resulting Swedish 'model' uniquely combined big business success in export markets, peaceful industrial relations and neo-corporatist economic planning with high rates of domestic taxation to finance health and welfare provision. Its economic strength enabled it to pay high wages and deliver higher living standards than elsewhere in Europe while also pursuing solidaristic income policies, low levels of unemployment, and generous welfare benefits. Sweden's path was emulated with national variations by Denmark and Norway and with greater difficulties by Finland.

The postwar authoritarian regimes of Spain, Greece and Portugal cannot however be considered seriously as 'welfare states' until the 1980s. They differed from the prewar fascist governments of Germany and Italy, in that although they were also undemocratic, they did not actively subordinate civil society to the state and did not see welfare as a way of extending their influence into the nooks and crannies of civil society (Rose 1996). After the war Southern Europe's still strongly agricultural authoritarian regimes were therefore reluctant to spend on welfare and were 'laggards' both economically and politically. Instead, the extended family and the Church continued to play the central role in social provision, alongside some patchy occupational social security particularly aimed at securing the loyalty of state employees. The fact that these tendencies were also reinforced by the fact that regimes were propped up by military and economic assistance from the USA should not be overlooked. The picture was therefore very different from that in North-western Europe, where welfare capitalism represented an alternative to both prewar fascism and postwar communism, and the 'welfare state' was associated with a liberal polity based on representative democracy, a regulated economy with varying degrees of state intervention, and a state which worked in cooperation with flourishing civil societies.

In this brief review we have seen how welfare capitalism took a distinctly 'European' path after 1945, but that this was influenced generally and often also specifically by countries' positions in the European-

American alliance and how that intersected with domestic politics and the relative strength of social and Christian democracy. One of the most interesting aspects of this is that the USA did not accept the need to follow the same path. Its welfare provisions under the 'New Deal' in the 1930s had been a belated copy of Bismarck's system, and were not universalized after 1945. In contrast to Europe there were no universal child allowances or social assistance scheme. Dominant groups in the USA agreed that welfare capitalism was a pragmatic necessity for Western Europe, but it was not going to be extended to American workers. The demographic pressures were also not as intense in the USA, and in the absence of either social democratic or Christian democratic political traditions, workers were not in a position to make them think differently.

The Rise of Welfare Expenditures

Table 5.3   Social security expenditure in Western Europe as a % of GDP 1950-77 (ranked by spending in 1950)

	1950	1965	1977
Norway	5.7	10.9	19.6
Switzerland	6.4[a]	8.5	16.1
Finland	6.7	10.6	19.3
Netherlands	7.1	15.7	27.6
Sweden	8.2	13.6	30.5
Denmark	8.4	12.2	24.0
Italy	8.5	14.8	22.8
Ireland	8.9[b]	10.3	18.3
13-country average	*9.3*	*13.4*	*22.4*
United Kingdom	10.0	11.7	17.3
Austria	12.4	17.8	21.1
Belgium	12.5	16.1	25.5
France	12.6[a]	15.8	25.6
Germany	14.8	16.6	23.4

Notes:
a.   1952.
b.   1953.

Source: Alber (1983: 157).

There was thus nothing inevitable about the dramatic rise in postwar levels of welfare expenditure. Under the influence of Western Europe's initial shift to the left welfare took on a breadth of meaning that included social provision in health, social security, housing and social services, within a broader social totality with strong normative connotations. 'Social security', meaning freedom from the fear of poverty, was popularized by the Beveridge Report and became enshrined in the UN's 1948 Universal Declaration of Human Rights. The 'welfare state', a term apparently first used in a positive sense by Archbishop Temple in Britain in 1941, was initially contrasted with the Nazi totalitarian and militaristic 'warfare state', but was later also contrasted with totalitarian communism. The Americans did not like the term, and so since Britain was initially heavily dependent on American aid, it was not commonly used in Britain until the early 1950s when it became generally accepted throughout Western Europe (Lowe 1999).

In the 1950s, despite governments of the centre-right becoming the norm in Europe outside Scandinavia, the 'welfare states' remained protected. They appeared to provide political stability as a bulwark against communism, they were highly popular, they contributed to, or at least did not undermine, the unprecedented expansion of the economy. They created jobs, and under full employment were relatively inexpensive. Throughout Europe in the 1950s and 1960s, governments of the right vied with left parties in promising improved welfare, and in slowly raising welfare expenditures. However, when these circumstances changed in the 1970s, the perspective of Europe's ruling groups started to alter. With the growth of social unrest and new demands on the welfare state by women and other groups, with the reappearance of recession and higher unemployment, and as welfare costs rose transferring substantial proportions of national wealth away from market to non-market areas, then the misgivings of Europe's ruling elites rose to the surface.

The massive expansion of welfare expenditures up to the 1970s is highlighted in Table 5.3, which shows how social security expenditure on items such as pensions, child benefit, unemployment insurance, health care and social assistance, grew continuously as a proportion of Gross Domestic Product (GDP). The countries that expanded their social security expenditure most as a proportion of their GDP were often those with the highest rates of economic growth, such as Germany, Austria, Italy and Sweden. By contrast comparatively poor economic performers like Britain and Ireland expanded their social security expenditure to lower levels. This observation seems to lend some support to the argument that welfare expenditure is conditional on economic growth (Wilensky and Lebeaux 1965). However the two do not always run in parallel. For example, Switzerland and Norway experienced similar rates of growth between 1948 and 1963 (see Table 4.1), yet Switzerland's social security expenditure rose by only 25% between 1950 and 1965 compared to Norway's 90%. Outside Europe, the USA and Japan were two other successful economies which did expand social protection in this period, but in a 'laggardly' fashion judged by the European average. By 1975 America's social expenditure was 18.7% of GDP, while Japan's was 13.7% (cited in Pierson 1998: 128). Political and ideological influences rather than economic performance must therefore account for most of these differences.

The major political influence on the expansion of European welfare states was the contest for manual and salaried workers' votes between social democracy and Christian democracy. It was in the Scandinavian countries where social democracy enjoyed unchallenged political power that welfare expenditure expanded most rapidly up to the mid-1970s. The countries with Bismarckian social security systems, such as Germany, Italy, the Netherlands and Belgium also experienced rapid growth in social security. These were countries where Christian democracy in one configuration or another sanctioned the expansion of corporatist welfare in the 1950s and into the 1960s (van Kersbergen 1995). France was slightly different, only acquiring a stable 'authoritarian' Conservative Government when de Gaulle came to power in a virtual coup in 1958, establishing the Fifth Republic based on Presidential power and a weakened parliamentary system. Thereafter there was a rapid expansion of social security, particularly after the shocks caused by the May 1968 uprising. In Britain where politics was organized around class divides, the smaller growth in welfare expenditure to 1965 reflected the strength of Conservative Party rule from 1951 to the 1964. Labour's return to power then saw a renewal of welfare expenditure similar to that occurring elsewhere in the more radicalized and crisis-facing Europe of the 1970s. The significance of political rather than largely economic factors in shaping national welfare patterns there appears indisputable.

Different 'Worlds' of Welfare

The political processes underpinning the expansion of social security provision under advanced capitalism have been shown by Esping-Anderson (1990) to lead not just to differences in levels of expenditure but also to different effects. He classified welfare regimes according to their ability to provide citizenship rights to a decent standard of living through social security entitlements independent of people's work experience ('decommodification'). Largely using data for 1980, reflecting the end of the period of left advance, Esping-Andersen grouped the effects of welfare provision into three main types or models: 'liberal' regimes that reinforced wage labour markets through providing minimal benefits and tight eligibility criteria and which therefore had low decommodifying effects; 'social democratic' or 'socialist' regimes that provided universal access to generous benefits, thereby partly insulating workers from the free labour market and which decommodified labour power very considerably; and 'conservative' or 'corporatist' regimes with only modest decommodifying effects because their benefits were closely allied to earnings and offered more to higher paid workers. The countries which most consistently clustered in these different 'worlds' are shown in Table 5.4.

Table 5.4   The 'three worlds of welfare capitalism' 1980

Type of regime	Decommodification score	Country
Liberal	Low	Australia
		Canada
		Japan
		Switzerland
		USA
Conservative	Moderate	Austria
		Belgium
		France
		Germany
		Italy
Social Democratic	High	Denmark
		Netherlands
		Norway
		Sweden

Source: Esping-Anderson (1990: 52, 74).

The differences in decommodifying effects, Esping-Andersen argued, were closely allied to patterns of political mobilization and alliance-building between social classes. He acknowledged that mobilization of the traditional manual working classes behind left parties is important, but he argued they were too numerically small to secure decommodified welfare by themselves and needed to forge alliances with other key social groups. After 1945 the expanding salaried classes became the key group and it was the failure by manual workers and/or the left to effectively woo them that shaped the strong emphasis on private and occupational insurance, and residualism, associated with liberal welfare regimes. By contrast within conservative regimes the strength of Christian democracy diluted working class political power, facilitating more privileged welfare for the salaried classes. Only in Scandinavia was the manual working class powerful and unified enough to forge alliances with the salaried middle class and secure equal access to social citizenship rights.

Esping-Anderson's approach links work and welfare by directly assessing how variations in social security rights and welfare benefits reinforce or mitigate work obligations under market capitalism. However there have been criticisms of this approach. Some have sought to qualify the emphasis on social classes in what is the 'social democratic thesis', by placing more emphasis on occupational groupings and 'risk groups' (Baldwin 1990). The notion of just three clusters of welfare regimes has also been criticized, and Esping-Anderson (1993) has acknowledged that there are exceptions within types, with Denmark as a more 'conservative' socialist regime, and the Netherlands combining elements of 'socialist' social security with conservativism. Neither does Britain's mix of universalism with low benefits and an underfunded NHS fit happily into the model (Jefferys 1995). For this reason, Ginsburg (1992) has dubbed the British regime 'liberal collectivist'. Furthermore Esping-Anderson's 'Nordic-centric' view tends to over-romanticize Scandinavian regimes. He implies that decommodified labour relaxes social discipline in the labour market, yet Sweden's 'active labour market' policy has always sought to rapidly reintegrate claimants back into the wage labour system, and the social assistance system can treat social 'deviants' such as drug takers rather harshly. Recent revelations of eugenicism in sterilizing thousands of young women with learning and mental disabilities, which continued until it was prohibited in 1976, have also tarnished the benign image of Swedish welfare (Armstrong 1997).

Esping-Anderson has been strongly criticized for focusing one-sidedly on class inequality to the exclusion of gender, 'race' and age inequalities (Ginsburg 1992). His model effectively ignores unpaid, 'pre-commodified' work performed by women that remains the majority of care provided in all types of regime. As Lewis (1993: 14) puts it, women 'only enter into Esping-Anderson's analysis when they enter the labour market'. Langan and Ostner (1991) stress that the Scandinavian model, although giving the appearance of achieving equality for women through integration into paid labour, often fell short of its ideals. If patriarchy is more hidden in the 'social democratic' welfare state, with work becoming highly sex-segregated in both private and public sectors, it is much more explicitly a feature of conservative systems where welfare benefits are biased towards white, male breadwinners, and the state only intervenes when there is a demonstrable lack of social capacity in civil society. Patriarchy is thus reinforced under the Bismarckian emphasis on family self-reliance and the Church's role in welfare. However liberal residual regimes are little better in providing women access to the social rights of citizenship. Through combining 'equality in the market' (exercised through exhortations or obligations on individual firms not to discriminate on gender or racial grounds) with minimal welfare protection benefits, the sick and the women who care for them, older people (a strongly feminized grouping), single mothers and many married women with child-rearing responsibilities often received mean treatment.

Welfare states of all varieties came under radical criticisms in the 1960s and 1970s for failing to attack the root causes of social problems. This generated new demands to tackle 'relative' as well as 'absolute' poverty and to address the social causes of ill health, and to stop operating in oppressive socially controlling ways. This criticism had a significant impact on the second wave settlements referred to in Chapter 4, encouraging higher levels of welfare expenditure, as represented, for example, by the 1969 'Equality Programme' of the Swedish Social Democrats, and by the election of a Labour Government in 1974 in Britain on its most radical manifesto since 1945. There was also qualitative change, with a new emphasis on tackling 'race' and gender disadvantage. It was in this context that the Swedish sterilization programme was finally prohibited in 1976.

5.4   ASSESSING POSTWAR WELFARE CAPITALISM IN EUROPE

In assessing Europe's welfare states up to the 1970s we must thus acknowledge that they did not transform the basic inegalitarian features of capitalist societies. Although there was some narrowing of income differentials in Scandinavia, Germany and Austria and a general growth in the share of national income taken by wages, these were not primarily the results of equalizing or redistributive welfare states (Padgett and Paterson 1991). This was because welfare states primarily involve horizontal rather than vertical distribution, between the employed and non-employed and the sick and the well.

While perhaps not quite 'golden', the era of full employment, state intervention and developed welfare states strengthened the position of labour in society and delivered real benefits to the broad majority. General improvements in living standards went hand in hand with the expansion of the 'social wage' of social security, health care, public housing, and access to education. It is true that the middle classes often received preferential health and welfare, formally through earnings-related benefits, informally through occupational 'fringe benefits' and their ability to assert themselves in technically egalitarian state educational and health care systems (Le Grand and Goodin 1987). As we have seen welfare systems varied in this regard, with Bismarckian systems having the greatest tendency to reproduce existing gender and class inequalities. However, because rights fundamentally derive from participation in paid work, they may have had less exclusionary effects on 'race' than citizenship or nationality-based systems of welfare (Crouch 1999). Paradoxically, however, middle class inclusion in state welfare was a major fact ensuring its political durability in Europe, and its marginality to it in the USA facilitated attacks on residual welfare for the poor. Welfare also became a major employer, offering many new routes for social mobility, creating a professional middle class grouping with a significant material stake in state provision as well as often exploiting the cheap labour of women and migrants. This dualism was a growing feature of European welfare states, which witnessed a growing minority of workers 'missing out' from the expanding prosperity within which there were high levels of 'relative' poverty.

Despite these problems our balance sheet would be a largely positive one, not least because by the 1970s real attempts were being made to tackle some of the underlying inegalitarian and oppressive features lurking beneath the benign surface of 'welfare' capitalism. In the face of the renewed challenge from below, European social democracy was starting to respond to radical critiques, reinvigorating the welfare settlements established in the straightened circumstances of 1945. It was at this very moment that these settlements came under concerted attack from the neo-liberal right, in a period of economic uncertainty. The remaining chapters of this book therefore focus attention on this challenge, and its impact upon the European political economy and associated forms of management, work and welfare.

6. The Growing 'Americanization' of Western European Political Economy

'Our days of weakness are over' – Ronald Reagan 1984 (cited in Urwin 1997: 286)

The American-European compromises in favour of promoting national 'welfare capitalisms' within a postwar liberal world economy underpinned by the US dollar and Cold War political loyalties came under increasing strain from the late 1960s. As was seen in Chapter 4, pressures bubbled up from below to extend the postwar settlements at the very time when Western capitalism was facing growing political economic problems associated with the collapse of the dollar standard, and the consequent oil recessions of the 1970s. The current chapter shows how Western Europe's ruling groups have sought increasingly to resolve these social tensions and economic difficulties by repositioning Europe on 'liberal' trajectories that involve greater accommodation to an 'American' model of individual contract capitalism, in the long run threatening to undermine European social models. It appears as if the scope for compromise between American and European models has narrowed, calling into question the postwar domestic compromises between Western Europe's ruling elites and peoples. Some of the major specific trends associated with this shift, analysed in greater depth in this and the three following chapters, are summarized in Table 6.1. They are intended to serve mainly as a checklist for analysis, as they do not of themselves indicate what causal mechanisms underlly such changes. As ever, the extent and timing by which European countries move down this road has been subject to significant national variation.

This chapter proceeds by first discussing the major changes in the rates of economic growth and unemployment that have made European governments particularly susceptible to internal self-doubt and external political economic pressures. It then shows how the latter have been manifested through the growing influence of international financial interests, riding on the back of new communications technology. These are then connected to two major political developments, the renewed impetus since the 1980s towards European and political integration, and the resurgence of the new right as an ideological influence on European conservatism and Christian and social democracy.

Table 6.1   Key features of Western Europe's political economy at the end of the 1990s

Issue	Contrast with the 1970s	Issue	Contrast with the 1970s
American power over international trade	Contested but now largely hegemonic	**Right-wing political ideology**	Highly influential
Social democracy	Abandoning equality goals	**Christian democracy**	Abandoning interventionism
Economic policy aim	Control of inflation rather than maintenance of full employment	**Welfare policy aim**	Stimulate labour markets; increasingly selective and conditional
Taxation	More regressive, preference for taxes on consumption than income and capital	**Keynes**	Nearly forgotten
Economic growth	Slower	**Technological change**	More rapid
Unemployment	Higher and of longer duration	**Establishment size**	Smaller
Industrial structure	Increasingly dominated by services rather than manufacturing	**Occupational structure**	Low demand for unskilled male labour; more managers and 'knowledge' workers

Stock markets	Increasingly important, free flow of capital across national boundaries	**Central banks**	Increasingly independent of national governments
Public services	Subjected to principles of 'new public management', contracted out or privatized	**Public producers and utilities**	Mainly privatized
MNCs	Increasingly important players, more European-wide and global in focus	**Production**	More international, exchange of 'best practices' between sites
National economy	More integrated into European and world markets	**Employment**	More feminized; less job security; relative decline of union influence; higher mobility across Europe but tough immigration policy
Collectivism	Less	**Social inequalities**	Widening

The impact of these changes on European 'lifestyles' is then briefly outlined, the chapter concluding with a theoretical discussion of how these pressures may be causally connected. Consistent with the general approach of this book, technologically determinist and economic reductionist explanations are criticized. Rather than viewing political economic changes as 'necessary' responses to autonomously generated pressures, the chapter suggests that neo-liberal 'globalization' is significantly affected by mobilization through international institutions supported by the American government and multinational companies. Encouraged particularly by the collapse of communism and the boom in American capitalism in the 1990s, they have increasingly sought to remodel the world in their own image - and have met with not inconsiderable success.

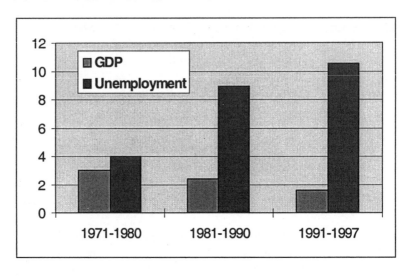

Sources: EC (1995: 13); Eurostat (1997: 2, 5).

Figure 6.1 Growth and unemployment among the 15 members of the European Union, annual average rise (%), 1971-97

6.1 SLOWER ECONOMIC GROWTH AND HIGHER UNEMPLOYMENT

One of the chief characteristics of European capitalism since the 1980s has been its inability to lift itself out of the doldrums. While the triad of major world capitalist trading regions, Europe, North America and Japan, were all affected by the onset of lower rates of growth after the mid-1970s, the Western European economy turned down more sharply in the 1980s than the USA or Japan. Between 1985 and 1995 the 2% annual average growth rate of real GDP across the 15 EU members was one-third less than that achieved from 1971 to 1980. Rising real compensation (i.e. real income) per employee, however, slowed even more, by two-thirds, while between 1985 and 1995 EU15 unemployment averaged 9.9%, nearly one and a half times higher than it had been between 1971 and 1980 (EC 1995; Eurostat 1996). Figure 6.1 graphs the contrasting trends in growth and unemployment from the 1970s to 1990s. Nevertheless, despite slower growth, by the late 1990s Western European per capita income was three times higher than it had been in 1950, and the income gap between richer and poorer European countries had narrowed significantly (Schulze 1999: 372). Slower growth should not therefore be seen as conclusive signs of a pathological 'Eurosclerosis', a diagnosis which, as we shall see, influenced the European turn to the right.

The major blot on the European economic landscape has been high unemployment: economic growth is no longer sustaining high levels of job growth. By 1996 there were 18.9 million citizens of the EU registered as unemployed (OECD 1998), not as high a proportion as in most countries in the 1930s, but huge in comparison to the experience of the post-1945 generations. Table 6.2 presents unemployment data since the 1973 oil price shock and collapse of the Bretton Woods exchange-rate system for 11 European countries where comparable standardized unemployment data exists, using work availability definitions.

Table 6.2   Standardized unemployment rates in Western Europe (% of total labour force), 1974-98 (ranked by unemployment in 1974-79)

	1974-79	1980-89	1990-98
Ireland	8.4	15.2	13.8
Italy	6.6	9.5	10.8
Belgium	6.3	10.8	8.6
Spain	5.2	17.5	20.3
UK	5.0	10.0	8.5
Netherlands	4.9	9.7	6.0
France	4.5	10.8	11.2
Finland	4.4	4.9	12.2
Germany	3.2	5.9	7.7
Sweden	1.9	2.5	7.3
Norway	1.8	2.7	5.1

Sources: OECD (1991: 40); OECD (1999b: 224).

Though unemployment was already rising sharply after 1973, the contrast between the 1970s and the two subsequent decades could not be more stark: only 3 of these 11 countries averaged unemployment over 6% in the last six years of the 1970s; but seven did so in the 1980s. Then, between 1990 and

1997, 10 exceeded 6% and only Norway, with the exogenous benefit of North Sea oil, faced unemployment at about the 5% level. Unemployment had not been 'cured' by the leftist governments of the 1970s and returned, seemingly permanently, to reconfigure labour markets and to haunt political and business decision-makers. It rose everywhere in the 1980s, and in seven countries it was even higher in the 1990s, with falls being recorded only where part-time work substituted for full-time jobs, in Ireland, Britain, the Netherlands and Belgium (see Chapter 8, Table 8.2). Comparing the patterns of European unemployment, however, brings out both continuities and discontinuities between the 1970s and the 1990s. Germany, Sweden and Norway have among the lowest levels of unemployment and Ireland has among the highest in each of the three periods shown in Table 6.2. Spain climbed from fourth highest to pole position between the 1970s and the 1990s, and the comparative rankings of Finland and France also worsened.

The combination of enduring unemployment patterns in some countries with the variability of some others points to the significance of national politics and institutional arrangements in mediating the impact of European wide and global pressures. However, a common feature of the European unemployment is that rates are higher, and duration tends to be longer, than in either Japan or the USA. Unemployment is also higher among young people, and among older workers due to increasing resort to 'early retirement'. Thus in 1996 unemployment in the 15-24 age group averaged 21.5% across EU15 countries, but it was above average in 'Southern' countries such as Ireland, Spain, Greece, Italy and Portugal, and the Northern countries of Belgium and Finland. Spain's youth unemployment rate was phenomenally high at 42.4% (Leat 1998). This links to the EU's difficulty in creating jobs to replace those lost in agriculture and manufacturing. Its average 60% participation rate for those of working age in 1996 is also well below those of Japan and the USA (EC 1997a).

It is claimed that the relative success of American job creation is due to greater labour market 'flexibility', lower rates of unionization, less statutory employment protection, higher immigration, greater occupational interchangeability and lower wages, all of which are said to encourage firms to take on more workers and thus create jobs. This informs the neo-liberal OECD (1996a, 1996b), which recommends 'supply-side' measures to create jobs, including provision of training to enhance skills and job take-up, reduction of restrictions on employers to hire and fire, and cuts in and restrictions on the availability of unemployment benefit. Increasingly European Commission policy documents such as its 1993 White Paper on *Growth, Competitiveness and Employment*, and EU national governments have endorsed and acted on this advice which have been strongly influenced by EU employers' lobbies. While technological change and some limited relocation of mass production industry to less-developed countries have lowered demand for Western European workers with limited skills, other factors have been more important in slow rates of job creation. Lower inflation in the 1980s in the context of reduced growth rates reduced the scope open to individual firms to adjust to more intense competition by passing price rises on to their customers. They became more likely to reduce labour costs and cut labour. In 1991 the Maastricht Treaty intensified the pressure on European employment by targeting lower rates of price inflation rather than job creation. The Treaty 'inscribed the monetarist project into the EU's agenda for the rest of the present century and beyond' (Grahl 1997: 129) by laying down five targets for monetary convergence: limits on government deficits, on accumulated public debt, inflation, long-term interest rates and requirements for exchange-rate stability. Not surprisingly, annual price inflation in the EU15 after Maastricht fell further and was just 1% by the end of the 1990s.

6.2   THE MARKETIZATION OF EUROPE'S FINANCES

The EU monetarist project was closely dovetailed with the extension of financial deregulation, and the increasing subjection of both public and private finances to the forces of global finance markets. As previous chapters have made clear, in Britain the role of the securities markets and investing institutions, with a significant bias to realizing short-term profit, were already critical for fund-raising well before the 1980s, whereas private companies and traditional banks were more important in the rest of Western Europe (Lane 1989). The 1980s and 1990s, however, witnessed a remarkable increase in the significance of finance capital, and it has been argued that a 'second financial revolution' at the international level has occurred of comparable significance to that which occurred at national levels in the initial shift to industrial capitalism (Cerny 1997). This was accelerated by the collapse of the Bretton Woods regulated international economy in 1973, and the political triumph of Reagan and the neo-liberal right in the world's largest economy, the USA, in 1980. The four main components of this pronounced shift were: (1) the internationalization of the American financial system; (2) a growth in savings in financial investments and the associated concentration of Europe's banking and finance sector; (3) the increased dependence on the financial markets by most European firms; and (4) the extensive privatization of nationalized industries and services.

The European deregulation of financial markets began in Britain with the election of a Conservative Government in 1979 which immediately dismantled its foreign exchange controls, and was largely completed by moves to the Single European Market by 1992. Since both Britain and West Germany had already opted for complete freedom of controls, all other EU countries too were obliged to abolish their restrictions on internal and external capital flows from 1990, with a two-year delay for Spain. This mirrored developments at the level of the world economy, leading to 'the emergence... of a globalized financial system' based on 'the internationalization and deregulation' priorities of 'the US financial system, which is characterized by very high degrees of competition among large numbers of financial agents' (Grahl 1997: 155). New computing and telecommunications technologies played a key role in enabling US financial agents to escape their remaining domestic controls and operate anywhere in the world, although they were not themselves the root cause of the shift. Thus financial capital has been significantly 'globalized'. Not only does it virtually escape regulation at the level of the nation state level, but the decisions of speculators and pension fund managers increasingly shape the policies of national governments. Governments which do not act according to the precepts of neo-liberal principles are likely to see a run on their currency, the prospect of which has served as an increasingly powerful disciplinary on left-leaning governments. The power of financial markets in relation to European governments was amply demonstrated in 1992 when sustained speculation forced Britain out of the European monetary system and a large devaluation of the Swedish krone.

Table 6.3   Institutional investment in selected European countries as a % of total household assets, 1980-90

	1980	1985	1990
Italy	-	2.9	6.1
France	10.6	23.6	36.3
Germany	22.6	23.6	36.3
UK	41.5	53.1	58.6

Source: Hirst and Thompson (1996: 43).

Governments have further lost power to financial institutions by the increasing latitude within the euro currency area given to the European Central Bank and in Britain to the Bank of England to regulate interest rates, along the lines of the German Bundesbank. Since high relative interest rates are the main monetarist measures that keep currency speculators happy, inflation low and unemployment high while simultaneously suppressing economic activity, this ensures that Keynes lies dead and buried, and the management of national economies is effectively 'depoliticized'.

States then have to shift their attention to achieving 'international competitiveness' within this framework, usually implying the deregulation of labour markets, the reining-in of welfare expenditure and the shift to more disciplinary forms of social policy.

Table 6.4   Europe's largest banking and insurance merger bids, 1989-97

Year	Target	Bidder	Bid value ($bn)
1989	CFV	Suez	5.88
1990	Nacionale-Nederlanden	NMB Postbank	6.86
1992	Midland Bank	HBSC Holdings	6.51
1995	TSB Group	Lloyds Bank	9.24
1996	UAP	Axa	8.48
1997	Bayerische Hypobank	Bayerische Vereinsbank	4.75
1997	Scottish Amicable	Prudential	4.67
1997	CRPL	Banco Ambrosiano	5.14
1997	Winterthur	Crédit Suisse	8.51
1997	AGF	Generali Assicurazioni	9.30
1997	BAT	Zurich Group	10.00

Source: *European,* 6 November 1997: 12.

The deregulation of finance markets also generated a boom in 'collective savings' in the 1980s, through their transformation into financial assets. This took off in Italy, grew in importance in France and Germany and became the dominant form of 'saving' in Britain where it had always been significant. Table 6.3 traces the rise in these countries of the proportion of assets held in financial investments compared to total household assets. The 'savings' generated from increased spending on individual pensions and financial debt and debt-servicing helped fuel a huge upsurge in international lending, with new forms of financial securities, and increasing size and concentration of financial conglomerates. The annual average level of borrowing on international capital markets doubled from $203 billion in the first half of the 1980s to $427 billion in the second half, and was $819billion in 1993. By the early 1990s sales of the new 'derivative' securities that move directly 'over the counter' between finance houses, bypassing the traditional stock markets, already exceeded sales conducted at the world's stock exchanges (Hirst and Thompson 1996). In the 1990s huge banking and insurance mergers surged ahead, as shown in the bids reported in the press shown in Table 6.4 above.

The 1997 merger of the Swiss-based Zurich Group with the British BAT created an asset management and insurance giant with a paper value of $34billion; that of the Italian Generali Assicuriazioni and France's second largest insurance company, Assurances Générales de France, formed a $22billion company. In the 1990s more Europeans than ever before personally owned shares or were dependent for at least a part of their pension on the performance of the securities markets and have their future financial well-being tied up in the hands of a small number of giant financial companies.

The liberalization of exchange controls, banking deregulation and the growth in European-wide financial companies, is eroding one of the distinctive features of European capitalism. British banks had traditionally invested overseas rather than domestically, and British industrialists had often resorted to stock markets to raise finance, leading to a focus on short-term profits for shareholders. By contrast in Germany one-third of the 259 largest firms in the late 1970s were still privately owned and controlled, and in France at the end of the 1980s, 28% of the top 180 industrial and commercial firms were under 'active' family control with a further 16% under 'passive' family control (Mayer 1992: 95-6). Yet in the 1990s, the slower levels of European growth coupled with the spread of marketization and the creation of the Single European Market have significantly increased the exposure of firms on the traditionally closed continental stock markets to foreign shareholders. By 1992 16.9% of all manufacturing employees in France worked in non-French-owned firms; in 1990 the Irish figure was 45.6%. This proportion rose from 13.7% in Britain in 1986 to 18.2% in 1992 and over a full 10 years from 1985 to 1995 it doubled from 6.6 to 13% in Germany and more than doubled in Sweden from 7.7 to 18%. With world-wide cross-border mergers and acquisitions growing at 21% a year between 1987 and 1990, at 30.2% between 1991 and 1995 and at 44.9% between 1996 and 1998, and with the EU countries alone responsible for 36% of all FDI inflows and 60% of all outflows, the interpenetration and interdependence of Europe's capitalisms increased enormously (UNCTAD 1999: 10, 18). The exposure of Europe's capital markets increased still more dramatically in 1999 as the new Euro currency devalued in comparison with the dollar, the yen and the pound. The result of a growing dependence upon inward investment is that, whether they like it or not, the recipient companies 'are forced to bend before the demands of the Anglo-Saxon investors' (*Le Monde*, 8 March 1997).

By the late 1990s more Europeans than ever before were exposed to the effects of economic decisions emanating from financial interests dwelling beyond their national borders. This exposure is, perhaps, most clearly seen in the full or partial privatization of many previously wholly publicly owned enterprises and utilities, a process often carried out through share offerings made on European stock markets. The sale of manufacturing firms like British Leyland and Renault and of many banking and insurance firms has 'rolled back the state' from much of Europe's market sector. Under pressure from the EU, Europe's governments proceeded with or have made plans for the full or partial privatization of their telecommunication companies and national airlines. In one week alone in October 1997 European investors were encouraged to buy into the national telecommunication companies of France, Italy and Spain. A year later three million French individuals bought shares in the second-round sell-off of France Télécom. Britain, governed continuously by new right governments from 1979 to 1997, went further down this road than other European countries. It also privatized the railways, most local public transport services, water and sewerage, sold off the best social housing to tenants, and moved (though more cautiously) towards the marketization of the state health service and parts of the civil service. As a result, many American and continental European firms are now delivering local services to British citizens. For example, France's Générale des Eaux owns the electricity generating power plant of Leeds General NHS Trust, Britain's biggest chain of private hospitals, BMI, the South-east's commuter railway network, Onyx, the cleaning contracting company and Three Valleys Water. Privatization and contracting out also have the effect of removing government responsibility for pay and working conditions, and research suggests that the main way privatized firms secure a return on capital has been by lowering labour costs and particular staffing levels (PSPRU 1996).

Table 6.5   Employment (% of working-age population) in European government services (ranked left to right in terms of most recent peak data)

	NL	Spain	Italy	Germany	Belgium	UK	France	Sweden
1979						15.0		
1982	7.3							
1985								26.2
1990					11.2			
1991				10.5				
1992		7.9						
1993			9.3			11.3		
1994			9.2		10.5			
1995	6.2	7.8		9.7			16.4	22.9

Source: Max-Planck-Institut (1998: Table 1.1.2.3).

Slowly but surely public services throughout Europe are being increasingly owned, managed or offered 'consultancy services' by private capital, whose priorities are substantially shaped by market considerations. As part of the cuts imposed by the Maastricht criteria, the growth in European public sector employment everywhere except in France was reversed by 1995, as illustrated in Table 6.5.

The variations in government services employment confirm the continued significance of national political influences. Whereas only about one in twenty work in Dutch government services, this figure is roughly one in five in Sweden and roughly one in ten everywhere else except France. Given that Europe's citizens generally have access to the same kinds of services, these reflect political choices about the best way to structure a society and deliver those services. New computer technologies have without doubt facilitated the development of financial instruments based on American methods of centralized discipline and decentralized responsibility, though they do not determine the political choices involved in adopting them.

6.3   THE ROLE OF NEW TECHNOLOGIES

By the early 1980s American business leaders were becoming increasingly concerned that they were being overtaken by more efficient and quality-oriented production methods developed by postwar Japanese capitalism. However, during the next 15 years of aggressive de-unionization and a panoply of 'flexible' production measures such as downsizing, outsourcing, relocating, subcontracting, lower real wages and rising income inequality, American capitalism re-established a still more pervasive global hegemony. Around 1990 it entered a decade of economic boom that enabled the New Democrats under Clinton to clear the huge burdens of debt accumulated in the Reagan-Bush eras. In part this recovery was due to the reinvigoration of American managerialism and its enhanced political muscle, discussed in the next chapter. In part, too, the revival reflected the hold the world's largest economy had over the new microchip technologies. American firms have traditionally been highly innovative, introducing new products with short lives to realize quick profits for shareholders, often in collaboration with university research departments (in pharmaceuticals and biomedicine) and supported by government grants (especially in defence). Thanks also to a huge new wage of immigration the American economy boomed while European firms experienced slower growth and increasing overseas share ownership. Their room for manoeuvre was slight. Whereas during the postwar upswing European firms could delay investing in new technology and still increase output and attain profitability by using old technologies more extensively, in the 1980s and 1990s delay often proved fatal. Sharp competitive pressures were exerted on them to invest in what were largely American microchip technologies. This was partly because of the economic downswing, but it was also because the new microchip technologies of the 1980s and 1990s have had a more rapid universal impact than most earlier technologies. They immediately affected not only how products were made and services delivered, but also what would be available.

Processes of production and consumption in advanced industrial societies became rapidly telescoped. In manufacturing the power, complexity and quality of many products were all considerably enhanced, while the production process was still further automated through computer-driven robots to ensure greater reliability and standardization of outputs. However the growing service sector was even more profoundly transformed by microchip technologies, which enabled Taylorist principles to be applied to white collar and service sector workers, often for the first time, implementing 'efficiency, calculability, predictability and control' the 'four alluring dimensions' that Ritzer (1996: 9-11) considers to be 'at the heart of... McDonaldization'. Economic advantage became as dependent upon knowledge-based as upon material-based resources, enhancing the position of those workers who possessed the knowledge while lowering demand for, and downgrading the position of unqualified operatives.

The widespread introduction of microchip technologies had at least three important consequences for the European political economy. First, Europeans found themselves increasingly dependent upon American-developed hardware and software. By the 1990s, Apple, Hewlett-Packard, IBM and IBM-compatible computers, Microsoft and a handful of other major American software manufacturers were supplying over 80% of Europe's computer and software markets. Competition from European and Japanese computer makers had been limited to a handful of niche markets or to emulation through cheap assembly. Europe's current and future growth has thus become increasingly dependent upon access to and rapid diffusion of American technology, both in computing and especially telecommunications, where every European 'flagship' telecomms company has formed one or more alliances with American partners. This American innovation 'advantage' flows from Europe's industrial structure, which is more skewed towards small and medium firms than in the USA and significantly lower rates of research and development (EC 1997: 3). Additionally, the creation of *de facto* standards based on American products means that Europeans are increasingly working with technologies and tools originally designed for the American marketplace and which are now carrying American 'best practice' throughout the world. Thus in the late 1990s even France's highly successful mass Minitel communication system lost out to the American-originated Internet. Product and performance standards have become increasingly measurable, increasingly comparable and, in consequence, increasingly international. This process of ruling the world according to American scientific and consumer standards is intensifying an already embedded process that is so pervasive it is hardly noticeable, as for example, the referencing system to which this book conforms. This occurs not necessarily because the 'best' products and standards always win out, but primarily because of America's impressive 'global reach' (Strange 1997).

The final effect of the accelerated rate of technological innovation is the erosion of local-national-international market distinctiveness within an increasingly deregulated international economy. This happens partly because local firms investing in new technologies require access to broader markets to recoup investment costs; and also because developments in communications (telecommunications plus air travel) put immense capabilities into the hands of intermediaries who can respond rapidly to small variations in consumer preferences for exotic products anywhere in the world. This exposes local producers and service deliverers to intense international competition, unless they can adopt similar strategies. In Europe this process has promoted the Europeanization of national markets and renewed moves since the mid-1980s towards European integration.

6.4   THE 'EUROPEANIZATION' OF BUSINESS

The factors so far considered in this chapter heightened competition within European product, service and labour markets, leading most employers and governments to support moves to dismantle the remaining internal European barriers to free capital mobility and free trade. There were also new right criticisms arguing that the economic impetus was shifting to Japan from the USA (Olson 1982). In fact, in the early 1980s more concern was expressed about the technological threat posed by the former than the latter. In 1963 Japan ranked as the world's fifth largest manufacturing nation behind the USA, Germany, Britain and France. By 1994 Japan had knocked Germany out of second place, and Britain had slipped into fifth position behind France (Dicken 1998: 28). Japan had succeeded less by technological innovation than by adopting flexible approaches to production and achieving continuous and rapid improvements in existing products. Europe's traditions of high wages, job controls based on union strength, and extensive social protection, were said by contrast to promote sluggish responses to changed market conditions, resulting particularly in lower growth and higher unemployment. Though such an analysis has enjoyed a wide currency, it is in fact problematic. Crafts (1999) suggests that an alternative explanation in the slowdown of European economies is the fact that the technological gap between them and the USA had largely closed by the early 1980s, and that European growth rates are still impressive in historical terms if the period 1945-75 is regarded as exceptional.

Whatever its merits the 'Eurosclerosis' thesis and concerns about falling competitiveness accelerated the pace of European integration, along a neo-liberal agenda of creating larger markets, liberalizing the economy, deregulating labour markets and 'modernizing' Europe's infrastructure. At the same time, however, there was ideological conflict about the extent to which this should be combined with measures to protect and promote a 'social Europe'. An important force for uniting both was the French Christian Social Democratic politician, Jacques Delors who, after becoming president of the EC Commission in 1985, persuaded both Margaret Thatcher and President Mitterrand of France to support the Single European Act (SEA) that came into force on 1 July 1987. This introduced qualified majority voting between governments on certain issues, gave a slightly more important role to the European Parliament within a system still strongly directed by the EU bureaucracy, and set 1 January 1993 as the date on which to get the Single European Market (SEM) up and running. Community competence was extended to include Economic and Social Cohesion, Research and Technological Development, and the Environment. The SEA also referred to a European Monetary System and laid down the process that led to the 1991 Maastricht Treaty on European Union. This established a timetable for the introduction of a single currency 'to maintain price stability and... to support the general economic policies in the Community, in accordance with the principle of an open market economy with free competition' (Article 3a). The Euro was finally launched by 11 EU members on 1 January 1999.

These renewed moves towards integration were partly generated politically by European federalists, and partly as a response to European multinationals that wished to operate in larger markets (Williams 1994). Large European employers are organized in two powerful lobby groups. The Union of Industrial and Employers' Confederations of Europe (UNICE) has been recognized as the official voice of European industry since 1958 and provides a constant critique on EU regulatory proposals. The European Round Table of Industrialists, comprising the leaders of the major European multinationals, was founded in 1983, and has been influential in promoting a neo-liberal vision of European integration. From the outset it has put special emphasis not only on the internal market itself, but also on heavy infrastructure investment in high-speed trains and cross-border motorways - Trans-European Networks - as profitable ventures in themselves which also facilitate rapid response to market conditions and accelerate the shift to associated 'lean' production systems (Balanyá *et al.* 2000).

Yet business interests alone did not deliver the framework for a pan-European federal state. Politically motivated federalism also played a key role. This emanated from both Christian democrats like Helmut Kohl of Germany and social democrats like Delors, from the new interventionist European environmental parties, and from the trade union movement. For some on the left and in the trade union movement the new federal state was a potential platform for a 'European Keynesianism' (Jefferys 1995). These forces started to forge new alliances in the teeth of continuing neo-liberal, nationalist and far left opposition, signing up to the broader social vision of European integration.

Table 6.6   Regional distribution of the world's largest companies by turnover, 1983-94

	Top 100 companies		Top 500 companies		Top 200 manufacturers	
	1983	1989	1983	1989	1990	1994
Europe	34	42	156	172	79	69
USA	46	35	224	153	68	64
Japan	9	17	75	119	40	53
Others	11	6	45	56	13	14

Source: EC (1991: 96-7); EC (1997: 46).

With the moves towards the SEM, intra-European trade became still more important than before. Boosted by transport developments such as containerization, improved European road networks, the construction of the Channel Tunnel, and falling costs and increased flexibility of air transport, virtually every local market was transformed into a potentially European one. By 1993 over 20% of all world trade took place just between EU12 countries (Cole and Cole 1997). The growing Europeanization of trade both reflected and encouraged the dramatic increase in cross-European-border merger activity of the 1980s and 1990s. This was both a response to the strengthening of the single European market and to the greater ease with which European deals could be financed and to the opportunities provided by the rising tide of privatization. In 1996 alone the value of European acquisitions and mergers grew to $253 billion, about two-thirds the level of American acquisitions, leading to predictions that Europe would overtake the USA in merger activity. As a result European-headquartered companies actually appeared more frequently than American-based MNCs among the world's top 100 and top 500 companies as measured by turnover at the end of the 1980s as shown in Table 6.6.

By 1991 22 of *Fortune*'s top 50 companies were European-based compared to 15 American and 10 Japanese, and with turnovers of over $21 billion a year they each had more cash go through their hands than did the national governments of EU members Ireland and Portugal (Humes 1993). The emergence of more large European firms in the 1990s is evidence of the greater importance of the Europe-wide marketplace as the regional backcloth to company growth. As this occurred more of these transnational firms adopted the multidivisional (or M-form) structure that we saw in Chapter 3 which is characteristic of large American enterprises and is often presented as essential requirement efficient business organization. As Mayer and Whittington (1996) point out, referring to seven surveys using different definitions of holding companies that were conducted in France, Germany and Britain between 1980 and 1993, between 8 and 31% of large European firms continued to use the holding company form. These firms were 'willing and able to resist the simple dictates of economic efficiency for long periods of time', confirming 'societal-choice' theory. More recently, however, many European transnational firms, like France's Michelin company in 1996, followed the logic of closer European market integration, and broke down their national structures into pan-European product line structures. Greater 'Europeanization' is therefore, paradoxically, leading to increasing adoption of American modes of business organization, undermining rather than strengthening a European model.

Europeanization is also leading to a shift in business psychology as strategic business interests become more significant than 'national' considerations. 'Today, for me, my country is Europe. One day it will be the world,' confirms Hans-Olaf Henkel, the anti-co-determination president of the German employers' association (*Le Monde*, 31 May 1999). This shift in business consciousness associated with the growth of multinationals has also been cited as an influence on the Swedish employers' 'breakaway' from the Swedish class 'compromise' (Pontusson 1997). Gray (1998) points out that the famous German firm Siemens will by 1999 have more employees abroad, though he emphasizes that German shareholder capitalism is still constrained by co-determination and the persistence of holding companies, ensuring that Germany's 'Social Market Economy' will adapt rather than succumb to globalizing pressures. Nevertheless, the pace of change has been rapid, and shows no signs of abating. In any case, many 'European' firms are in fact American, and a small but increasing number Japanese, lessening the constraints of national considerations. The effects of investment decisions by MNCs were particularly highlighted in 1993 by the American firm Hoover's decision to relocate production from its French to its Scottish factory, because of 40% lower wage and social costs (Garrison 1994: 1). Ireland, too, with extremely low rates of corporate tax, was enjoying an unprecedented boom created both by increased multinational and by EU infrastructural investment at the end of the 1990s. In already developed economies, however, Ericsson and other large corporations threatened in 1998-9 to close their Swedish head office unless the centre-left government lowered taxes, while in Germany business interests campaigned vigorously against the tax reform plans of the red-green government elected in 1999 (Balanyá 2000: 7-8). The notion that such 'purely' economic considerations should hold sway is, of course, a central ideological tenet of the neo-liberal right, whose remarkable resurgence we now trace.

6.5   THE POLITICAL RENAISSANCE OF THE RIGHT

Europe's two major political shifts to the left, at the end of the Second World War and again from the mid-1960s, were crucial in shaping the political economy of 'welfare capitalism' (see Chapter 4). Social democracy framed the rules within which the conservative and Christian right operated. There had however always been ideologues on the fringes, notably Hayek (1944) in *The Road to Serfdom*, who rejected the economist Polyani's (1944) judgement that the liberal market had failed. Then in the 1960s, the emergence of the 'Chicago school' of monetarist economics associated with Milton Friedman and the pamphleteering of the British Institute of Economic Affairs gave a more practical spin to this critique. This new movement borrowed the style and themes of the 1960s: it was libertarian, iconoclastic, and anti-establishment. It emerged on the backs of growing concern about the ability of Keynesian capitalism to contain the rising discontent of the 1960s and 1970s, and of a conservative concern to depoliticize social relations and undermine the collective challenge of the era through an assertion of individualism and the market against the state.

This new right was fundamentalist in the sense that it reasserted two complementary sets of 'ancient' truths: the seventeenth-century political philsophy of Locke which saw the prime aim of democracy as the protection of individual private property, and the eighteenth-century political economy of Adam Smith which argued that human welfare was best secured by allowing the 'hidden hand' of the market free play, relegating the state to a 'nightwatchman' primarily concerned with external defence and internal law and order. These truths were modernized by welding them together into a set of 'monetarist' economic principles and an approach to governance that involved, as far as possible, the 'rolling back of the state' from areas best left to the market, and its strengthening in areas such as defence and social discipline. In other words, combining 'the free economy and the strong state' (Gamble 1988).

The rise of the new right undoubtedly shows the influence of ideology, and the importance of mobilizing to win the battle of ideas through highly active conservative 'think tanks'. However this does not of itself explain why neo-liberalism has become increasingly mainstream. First, traditional forms of Keynesianism no longer seemed to work, neither in a narrow economic sense during the 'stagflation' of the 1970s, nor in successfully institutionalizing social conflicts. In Britain where the new right had its strongest European hold, full employment, the welfare state and neo-corporatist involvement in administering the state were projected as prime causes of economic decline. Welfare capitalism was also increasingly blamed for all kinds of social ills presumed to derive fundamentally from a lack of social discipline, such as increasing divorce, strikes, crime, general disobedience and rudeness by the young. The very presence of these problems provided a basic plausibility to the new right's critique, which in some ways also corresponded with Marxian critiques of the Keynesian compromise between state and the market, but which argued instead for its resolution by a fundamental shift away from the latter. For example, O'Connor (1973) argued that Keynesianism had produced a 'fiscal crisis of the state' in which people's demands for health and welfare provision exceeded the ability of capitalism to provide it by taxes within the free enterprise system, while Glyn and Sutcliffe (1972) argued that the enhancement of workers' power through full employment and strong trade unionism had significantly squeezed the profits of capitalist industry.

Although aided by growing electoral success from the 1980s, the growth of new right influence was primarily influenced by its ability to win support among Europe's ruling groups. The economic and social difficulties of Keynesianism had changed the tactical considerations of business and commercial interests. The new right agenda offered them a way of recapturing the power lost, and freedom to organize production, hire and fire workers, and above all to make money and profits, not just at the national level but by escaping the constraints of the nation state and 'going global'. A new right coalition of political and industrial interests started to form. While in Britain and more importantly in the USA, it triumphed politically in the early 1980s, in continental Europe its influence grew more slowly being mediated through Christian and social democratic parties who were often lukewarm towards it. In Britain the new right gained power in 1979 partly by default, a minority government (in terms of votes cast), aided by the Westminster electoral system, and a centralized form of governance which enabled it to launch its neo-liberal experiment. Britain was also more susceptible to the new right because of its relatively poor economic performance, and because, unlike on the continent, neocorporatism was weakly established. Low commitment to it by the labour movement was a factor behind the collapse of the 'Social Contract' incomes policy in the 1978 to 1979 'winter of discontent'. In Scandinavia, neo-corporatist social democracy was more solidly established and held firm through the 1980s. In 1982 the re-elected Swedish Social Democrats responded to the recession through traditional Keynesian reflationary measures. Nevertheless even in Sweden neo-liberal views gained ground, and neo-corporatism started to decay leading to the election of a neo-liberal government in 1991 (Boreus 1992). In Norway, Denmark and Finland the right also captured power or made political ground in the 1980s. Though policy shifts there were more gradual than in Britain, the right started to dictate a neo-liberal agenda (Ruysseveldt and Visser 1996). Conservatism also held sway in continental Europe. In Germany the Social Democrats were ousted by the Christian Democrats who ruled from 1982 to 1998. In Italy a right-left coalition of 'national solidarity' fell in 1979 and for the next 14 years it was led by a Christian Democrat centre-right coalition (Visser 1996). Between 1979 and 1992 the share of the communist vote declined from 30.4% to 16.1% (Allum 1995). Centre-right coalitions also dominated Belgium and the Netherlands in the 1980s.

At first sight, the Southern countries of Portugal, Spain and Greece seem exceptions to this rightwards shift. With the overthrow of authoritarian governments, parties were voted into power with radical commitments to modernize their countries through the adoption of social democratic and Keynesian measures, including extensive state planning. In Portugal, for example, the 1974–75 revolution saw the nationalization of the whole of the domestic finance sector. Soon, however, their policies also started to drift rightwards. Ruling at first in coalition and then alone between 1985 and 1995 the Portuguese conservatives reversed virtually all the earlier nationalizations (Sassoon 1996). In Spain the Socialists held office from 1982 to 1996, but their policies became scarcely distinguishable from those of the European right: 'inflation control, economic restructuring and rationalization, and flexibilization of industrial relations' (Meer 1996: 316). In Greece a Socialist Government ousted the conservatives in 1981, but its failure to deliver an effective left reformist programme led to the election of a neo-liberal conservative government in 1990. Within a few years the Socialists regained power, but did not radically change the policy turn to the right (Kritsantonis 1998).

Nowhere were the problems of the left more apparent than in France. François Mitterrand was elected as Socialist president in 1981 at a time of growing recession and he responded initially with a major nationalization programme and the extension of the welfare settlement to 'catch up' with the rest of Europe. Isolated in a rightwards-moving Europe and faced with an outward rush of capital, he had by 1983 abandoned Keynesianism and the core of his earlier reforms. Between 1986 and 1988 the right again secured a parliamentary majority creating a period of 'cohabitation' that was to be repeated between 1993 and 1995. Mitterrand's spectacular about turn is often seen as either marking the triumph of neo-liberal commonsense over leftist ideology, or the new power that international finance markets could exercise over governments of the left. This is very far from the case. It remains an economy with one in four employed in the public sector. At that point during Delors' presidency of the Commission some French socialists shifted their focus to the European level. Delors' project was to create a single market with a significant social dimension. His socialist ambitions were tempered by Germany's fiscal conservatism, and by remorseless neo-liberal pressure from the Thatcher government. Nevertheless Mitterrand, Thatcher and Delors shared a similar diagnosis, that 'Eurosclerosis' was impairing Europe's ability to compete economically against Japan and the USA thus requiring a radical shift towards a single, liberalized market. Initially this shift was seen by European leaders - Thatcher apart - as being compatible with European neo-corporatist traditions, as Japan's success was seen as linked to its tight business-financial linkages. However after the communist collapse of 1989 and the revival of American capitalism in the 1990s, the project shifted to a more undiluted neo-liberalism (Williams 1994). This was exacerbated by the fact that Europe itself went into recession in the 1990s, partly in fact due to the monetarism associated with the Maastricht Treaty. The chief victim was, as we shall see in Chapter 9, a scaling-down of ambitions for a 'social Europe'. At the same time, however, recession also brought growing popular disillusion with the neo-liberal project, and led to the election of centre-left governments throughout much of Europe, who then became caught between domestic expectations and the monetarist requirements associated with the build-up to the launch of the Single European Currency in 1999 and the EU discourse of 'competitiveness'. These tensions came to be managed in several European countries by tripartite 'pacts' between the state and the 'social partners' of capital and labour, with mixed degrees of success (Fajertag and Pochet 1997). Certainly there was substantial resistance to the wholesale shift to labour market flexibility advocated by the OECD.

Thus power and influence of new right ideas in the 1980s and 1990s owes more to its political dominance in the USA, and the subsequent adherence to its basic principles by political elites in Europe, than to any demonstrable popular enthusiasm. Even in the USA the new right's triumphant success was partly due to circumstances, particularly the Iran hostage crisis of the late 1970s, which largely won Reagan the presidency in 1980 (Ambrose 1988). Doubtless the political drift would have been in the same direction since in 1979 the Federal Reserve restricted the money supply to reduce American inflation and deepened emerging recession round the world (Grahl 1997). Yet the shift to the right might not have otherwise occurred at such a gallop if Reagan had not won. The prime aim of the American new right was to restore America's position in the world politically, militarily and economically after the humiliation of defeat in Vietnam in 1973. It reasserted American values in the world with a missionary zeal and intensified the Cold War through the 'Star Wars' programme. It also made less overtly visible attempts to 'discipline' the world through its indirect influence over the international money markets and its very strong presence in 'international' institutions such as the OECD, World Bank, IMF and GATT (subsequently the World Trade Organization (WTO)). In the 1990s the USA also increasingly flexed its neo-liberal muscles within UN agencies such as UNCTAD, the WHO and the ILO, threatening to withhold or withdraw funding unless they followed more distinctly neo-liberal agencies. By the 1990s America had accumulated an impressive amount of 'regulatory power' (Strange 1997). Thus what occurred was not an autonomous process of globalization, involving a 'natural' shift to the right, but one that was politically made to a considerable extent by the exercise of American political and economic power (Martin and Schumann 1997).

Table 6.7 'Economic freedom' ratings between no freedom (1) and total freedom (10) between 1975-95 (ranked by initial rating)

	Initial rating		1995 rating
	Year rated	Initial	
Switzerland	1975	7.0	7.4
USA	1975	6.1	7.9
Germany	1975	5.9	6.4
Belgium	1975	5.6	6.3
Netherlands	1980	5.5	6.5
Austria	1980	4.7	6.0
UK	1980	4.6	7.3
Ireland	1975	4.1	6.5
Finland	1975	3.9	6.1
Spain	1975	3.9	5.9
Denmark	1985	3.7	5.9
France	1985	3.6	6.1
Italy	1985	3.6	5.5
Sweden	1980	3.5	5.9
Norway	1980	3.3	6.1
Portugal	1975	2.5	5.9

Source: Henderson (1998: 40-41).

America's influence increased within continental Europe partly as a result of Britain joining the EEC in 1973. Thatcher undoubtedly spearheaded European neo-liberalism in the 1980s, while after 1997 Prime Minister Blair campaigned to merge social democracy with neoliberalism through the so-called 'Third Way'. His close affiliation with Clinton's 'New Democrats', from which much of the political style and substance of 'New Labour' can be traced, provides a powerful conduit for American influence on centre-left governments in Europe. This is not limited to the economic sphere, as NATO's 1999 war with Serbia demonstrated. Yet American market assumptions and managerialism have still been resisted. Scandinavia has not yet fully renounced social democracy, conservative central Europe is still saturated with neo-corporatist institutions, and France is far from abandoning statist *dirigisme*. Neither have employment rights and welfare been eroded in the name of flexibility on the same scale as in Britain. Nevertheless in November 1998 Europe's 13 social democratic finance ministers adopted a common European Socialist Party position that confirmed their acceptance of market social relations and redefined their goals as 'a just, humane and decent society' rather than as a more equal society (*Le Monde*, 22 November 1998).

The achievement of the new right lies in its having legitimated American political, economic and military hegemony with the common sense argument that the power of global markets cannot be challenged. Thus the Friedmanite indices of 'economic freedom ratings', covering 17 weighted attributes of an 'open' economy, not only boasts a huge accretion of European neo-liberalism between roughly 1975 and 1995, as shown in Table 6.7, but also display a surprising degree of convergence, with a Western European spread of just 2 points in 1995 compared to 4.5 points at the start of the period. It is little wonder that the 'Freedom Ratings' advisor Milton Friedman and his collaborator Rose Friedman feel able to write in October 1998:

> We are in the mainstream of thought, not as we were 50 years ago, members of the derided minority (cited in Henderson 1998: 9).

One of the most significant consequences of Europe's adaptation of neo-liberalism is what Crouch and Streeck (1997) call 'symbolic politics', the pretence that national decision making is shaped by domestic democratic politics rather than international finance markets and requirements of multinational companies. Yet electorates still aspire to prosperity, employment rights and welfare protection, and look to governments to provide them. It was the political failure of most sitting new right and Christian Democratic Conservative Governments of the early 1990s to tackle high unemployment, and the spread of insecurity to professional and managerial layers, that led to their replacement in the mid-1990s, but without any real political renewal having taken place. Thus although reflecting popular discontent with right strategies, the temporary reduction of the number of right governments within the EU to just two by 1998 did not represent a groundswell to the left even remotely comparable to those after 1945 or in the 1970s.

Thus Europe's 'modernizing' centre and centre-left *fin du siècle* governments have largely and uncritically accepted the constraint of implementing the legacy of American managerialism and material values bequeathed by the new right and the Maastricht criteria. For the European Socialist Party the 'response of socialists and social democrats to the challenge of globalization is... to maintain a strong commitment to social stability while at the same time ensuring that European workers can adapt themselves continuously to a world undergoing rapid change' (*Le Monde*, 22 November 1998). In this context, where mainstream politics faces a crisis of credibility, significant anti-political elite protest votes have taken place for nationalist and neo-fascist parties, such as the Northern League in Italy, the National Front in France and the Freedom Party in Austria, which in February 2000 became part of a right coalition government in Austria. These protests have led to a general tightening of national immigration laws and increased harassment of minorities. The decay in credibility of traditional collective politics further heightens an existing tendency towards individual consumerism as a means of self-identity and expression, an issue to which we now turn.

6.6   THE INDIVIDUALIZATION OF LIFESTYLES

A key component of Europe's political economy since the 1970s has been an accelerated shift towards individualist ethics of consumption and self-fulfilment, which has been overlaid by a significant growth in the range of mass-produced products like Walkmen, PCs and mobile telephones, that are essentially consumed individually rather than collectively. Although a hi-fi or television set may be used by the whole household, these too heighten the decline of a public civic culture, while car culture effectively privatizes public spaces. The process of 'individualization', as Beck (1992) and others describe it, is a complex process that has a range of causes. It does not always sit comfortably with new right ideology because of the inherent tension within it between asserting authority and allowing freedom. Feminism is one ideology that has undoubtedly fed into individualization, yet neo-liberal ideology is often informed by moral panics about the demise of traditional patriarchy. Individualism is also associated with the assertion of rights to express one's own sexual orientation which often causes concern for neo-liberals, especially when allied to the conservatism of the Christian right.

Individualism cannot be reduced to the changes in production and available commodities that have occurred since the 1970s and the growing importance of consumption and consumer politics. Individualism should rather be seen as both part of the radical agenda constructed from below since the 1960s, and also as moulded from above and channelled into forms of consumption by the changing capitalist requirements. One effect of shifts in labour markets and services and polarization is that, particularly for those knowledge workers whose labour is in demand and skills are in short supply, it is possible for them to bargain effectively as individuals. However, changes in business organization towards fragmentation are also, at least in part, attempts to weaken worker collectivism by strategies of fragmentation. Yet the extent to which classes have been definitively fractured should not be exaggerated since while consumerism is becoming a more important form of self-expression, hierarchical work relations are being reinforced and the collective experience of insecurity is becoming more general, trends which are not necessarily in contradiction.

For those who can afford it, there has been a considerable expansion of consumer choice since the 1980s, even if much of it may be illusory when, as the Bruce Springsteen song puts it, there are dozens of television channels 'and nothing on'. So while the consumer is still far from 'sovereign', intensified capitalist competition has driven the rapidity with which products are brought to the market and forced manufacturing firms to rely increasingly on marketing and retailing intermediaries to get their goods sold. They are heavily promoted in similar (though not always identical ways) across Europe through the burgeoning mass media - television, cable, video, radio, the Internet and newsprint - which, with the advertising revenues on which it relies, is now a major part of every Western European economy.

Patterns of consumption and leisure in urban and even rural Europe are thus converging, if unevenly, towards a transatlantic 'lifestyle'. This starts with viewing television advertisements, passes through the act of purchase in a huge supermarket, makes the journey home in a private hatch-back car (whose rear window opens to conveniently transport a week's shopping), storage in a freezer compartment, and finally the ceremonial ripping open of the elaborate packaging, before microwaving and eating. Between two-thirds and three-quarters of all groceries bought in Britain and Germany are now purchased from just five supermarket groups, and France is fast catching up with this degree of concentration. More often than ever before,

European consumers may also take a meal at a fast food chain, Western Europe's fastest-growing niche market. If advertisements have prompted them to think about buying new clothes, they are also quite likely to stop at a shop owned or franchised across Europe, such as Marks & Spencer, C&A or Benetton. For furnishings they may drive to an IKEA with franchises in all West European countries (*European*, 30 October 1997).

While people's behaviours have changed and their social relations have become more privatized, it is important not to overlook the considerable continuity with the previous era. Most consumption is still of standard, mass-produced or distributed goods or services (such as lottery tickets, insurances and television programmes) rather than of 'post-Fordist' products closely tailored to the tastes of small groups of discriminating consumers. Cars and televisions are virtually universal. Between 1978 and 1989 the numbers of passenger cars per 1,000 inhabitants continued to rise at the rates they had done in the 1970s. Overall Western European car density levels rose to nearly one car per two inhabitants. Similarly, between 1980 and 1990 the density of television sets rose rapidly across Europe (Wegs and Ladrech 1996). Mass-produced industrial goods are still being consumed, and mass-delivered services, from pizzas to portable telephones, dominate consumption. It is true that more of these consumer products and services are now delivered by non-European headquartered firms or franchises. Nevertheless, those Europeans in regular work who had not previously been a part of the wealthy classes have enjoyed a significant expansion in access to a wider range of goods and services than was possible before. This is, however, of little comfort to the growing ranks of Europe's excluded poor, whose situation is examined in Chapter 9 and who, in Bauman's (1998) memorable phrase, are increasingly likely to be stigmatized as 'flawed consumers'.

The new right is not the only ideological challenge of significance in the last 30 years: the renewal of the feminist challenge is having an enduring impact on relations between men and women. This is coinciding with the structural economic shifts, which are also hastening the decline of the male manual worker 'culture' that still dominated whole communities in the 1970s. The trend away from work based on manual strength or skill, towards service work in which interpersonal skills or 'emotional labour' figures (Hochschild 1983) is leading to a decline in demand for weakly skilled but physically strong men, and is offering new opportunities for women to enter the labour force. Thus more 'feminine' expectations of higher levels of education provision for their children and of better quality living have become more important. This shift also contributed to a major demographic transformation. While life expectancy continued to advance in the 1980s and 1990s, Europe's fertility rates fell below replacement levels, reflecting both women's wishes to live out more personally rewarding lives than is generally possible in large family settings and their economic anxieties about the future. Except in Southern Europe family structure, too, changed significantly. There has been a considerable increase in the proportions of both old people living on their own and of working-age households living without children. At the same time, divorce has increased and more children are being brought up in women-headed single parent families (OECD 1998). People's lifestyles are shifting perceptibly away from the earlier 'norm' of the nuclear family.

6.7   DEBATING 'POST-FORDISM'

In this chapter we have reviewed the political economic and social changes that have occurred since the 1970s. We now wish to focus on the argument that they amount to a systemic shift from a 'Fordist' to a 'post-Fordist' form of capitalism. Although we ultimately find this analysis wanting, we nevertheless concur with Rustin (1989) that it does focus attention on important social changes, and shows the continuing relevance of a holistic Marxian political economy to an understanding of what is going on.

The essence of this argument presents 'Fordism' as a set of employment and social relationships built around mass production technology, dependent on the particular 'regime of accumulation' or economic system of making profits that reached its maturity between 1950 and 1975. Capitalism is, however, always crisis-prone and needs an appropriate 'mode of regulation' to stabilize it. This was provided by the 'Keynesian Welfare State', which integrated government economic management, pluralistic industrial relations and universal access to state welfare in order to create a stable environment for profits to expand. Fordism, it is argued, had developed Taylorism into a full-fledged factory bureaucracy, paying high wages to workers whose mass demand would then buy the Fordist products. It matched mass production techniques and deskilled jobs to produce long runs of standardized goods. Capitalists in that period needed to ensure a return on their massive investment in plant and machinery primarily by ensuring a market for goods, but also by a welfare state that would help maintain consumption, ensure social peace and assist in the wider tasks of social reproduction. Thus while this analysis recognizes that class conflict exits, it views the main initiative for the construction of national welfare states as coming from above, from the functional 'needs' of capitalists, although national politicians, and to a lesser extent working class publics, did retain some power because markets were nationally based (Jessop 1990).

Subsequently the difficulties of the 1970s are viewed as the result of the breakdown of this productive and regulatory system. Thus Aglietta (1979) argued that by the early 1970s the possibilities of Fordism had been exhausted: markets were saturated, workers were resisting further Taylorist changes in production, productivity had slowed and profits were being squeezed by the 'stagflation' described earlier in this chapter, and exacerbated by external oil shocks. He predicted that there would be either a transition to socialism, or that the crisis would be resolved by an intensified application of 'neo-Fordist' methods to the service and state sectors and an attack on the power of manufacturing labour. Other writers in the same tradition added that in a period of economic difficulty, the internal inflexibilities of the Fordist system were exposed by competitive pressures in the world economy, particularly from the rising 'tiger' economies of the East. Lipietz (1987) suggested that these problems were leading to the relocation of Fordist production from the European and North American 'centre' to the 'periphery' in the developing world, taking advantage of cheap and poorly organized labour, and lower social costs.

However, other post-Fordists such as Piore and Sabel (1984) use the same analysis to underpin less pessimistic arguments, focusing on the role of markets rather than social relations between classes, suggesting also that global capitalism itself can resolve long-standing problems such as worker alienation by new methods of production. These involve labour requirements shifting from 'low-trust' semi-skilled repetitive labour to 'high-trust' multi-skilled and more satisfying work, with less emphasis on hierarchical control and more on teamwork and initiative. They suggest that 'flexible specialization' represents the emerging form of accumulation and is leading to a 'second industrial divide'. This is replacing bureaucratically inflexible Fordism with a decentralized production system that can swiftly respond to consumers' increasingly shifting and differentiated tastes. They maintain that a critical shift is occurring from mass production of long runs of standardized goods, to small batch production of a wide variety of changing products and that Fordism was equally inappropriate for the increasingly important service sector. These arguments are linked to theories of globalization which predict that in increasingly competitive market conditions firms will have to seek out consumers across frontiers and find market 'niches'. Thus decentralized production is flagged as having a key role in particular regions such as the 'Third Italy' districts specializing in engineering, clothes and footwear, as in Austria around Salzburg, parts of Baden-Wurthemberg in Germany, and in California's Silicon Valley.

If the implication is that the 'productive base' drives social change, then the regulatory system is seen as a dependent variable, and must respond accordingly. Thus Sabel and Piore suggest new 'modes of regulation' are emerging, involving some kind of return to pre-industrial traditions in which regional political institutions must balance local forces of competition and cooperation, and provide the necessary infrastructure to attract transnational capital. Inasmuch as both national industrial relations systems and national welfare states were the product of national markets made possible by Fordism, it is predicted that the twin forces of globalization and decentralization will 'hollow out' the nation state from above and below, leading inevitably to their decay. It will also be harder to sustain consumptionist welfare states, which will shift increasingly in the direction of 'Schumpeterian' or conditional welfare aimed at reintegrating people back into the labour market (Jessop 1990, 1994).

These theories are also consistent with theories of the evolution of a 'post-industrial' society where 'information technology' or 'knowledge' becomes the basis of a new elite of professional and technical 'knowledge workers' (Bell 1973; Castells 1989). Only fully 'flexible firms' will have committed workforces capable of accessing the detailed and up-to-date information on costs and market intelligence necessary in the new competitive environment (Berggren 1993). They tend to view 'knowledge' and expertise as being more important than the ownership of capital in exercising power, a line of thought that can in fact be traced back to the 'managerial revolution' identified in the Fordist era by Burnham (1945). There is also a fit with the arguments of Lash and Urry (1987), who suggest that the new competitive conditions are associated with the decay of the stable, national 'corporatist' bargains between workers and employers brokered by the state during the boom years, The shift to 'disorganized capitalism' in line with the interests of transnational corporations, undermines these nationally based arrangements. They also see the growth of the managerial and professional service class as a significant factor in the ideological shift towards individualism, and associated political influence of the new right.

Post-Fordist theories outlined have been widely discussed and criticized (Rustin 1989; Navarro 1991; Clarke 1992; Kelly 1998). While it should be acknowledged that the tradition represented by Aglietta and Lipietz is more cognizant of social and political influences than the emphasis of the Piore and Sabel tradition on the autonomous actions of markets, there are serious shortcomings with both traditions. First there is the error of assuming that a particular kind of state regulation, that is, 'organized' and 'disorganized' capitalism, respectively, are 'naturally' associated with particular forms of accumulation. While sophisticated approaches do recognize that political and cultural influences mitigate these influences, these are still viewed as variants from an 'ideal type' of Fordism or Post-Fordism, that can never be shown to exist as a concrete society (Clarke 1992). Second, even where some of the trends can be shown to be real, there is a tendency to mistake cause and effect, because so much is read off from the productive system, and particularly shifting technological imperatives. We argue that the postwar expansion and the creation of welfare states were shaped by both the political-military context of the postwar American-European compromise, and social struggle from below, and we will shortly construct a similar outline 'political' account of the changes affecting Europe since the 1970s. A third problem is the depiction of a sharp 'break' and exaggerated contrasts between past and present eras. Many of the features claimed for post-Fordism, such as production based on 'scope' as well as scale were present in an earlier era. Similarly, many of the changes, such as the shift to services, expansion of knowledge workers, the globalization of production and internationalization of finance, are not new, but merely an intensification of well-established processes (Hirst and Thompson 1996). A fourth and very real problem is that no stable system of regulation appears to be emerging, with three major recessions and two serious crises in the world's financial system since the 1970s. If 'disorganized' capitalism is to be brought to some state of order, it will not happen automatically and a new 'mode of regulation' will require conscious political intervention.

The final criticism is about the way that post-Fordist theory can restrict our choices and devalue our heritage. If the pluralist industrial relations and welfare states are seen as obsolete features associated with an earlier productive system, then of course it will not be possible to preserve them. Yet it is also often implied that we should not *want* to preserve them, since welfare capitalism reflected the interests of capital, rather than being seen as a prized possession won by struggles from below that should therefore be defended. We do not deny that pluralistic industrial relations and welfare states are at best only partial reforms of class relations which do not deal much with gender and 'race' issues, and are insufficiently sensitive to individual preferences, and may operate in negative and controlling ways. However we cannot see why these problems should not be addressed in evolutionary ways, building on their current universalist and collectivist frameworks.

6. 8   AN OUTLINE POLITICAL ECONOMY OF CONTEMPORARY EUROPE

In seeking to construct an outline account of trends in European political economy since the 1970s, there is a need to overcome both the unhelpful polarization between 'institutional' theory that exaggerates the cultural influence of 'path dependent' national difference, and the excessive determinism of the 'new' convergence theory (Strange 1997). While the first encourages complacency and ignores the fact that 'something is happening out there' (Dicken 1998), the second engenders a sense of powerlessness in the face of the inevitable juggernaut of 'globalization'. Explanations are therefore needed that satisfactorily combine structure and process at all levels of analysis. In the period 1945-75 there was diversity, but it occurred within a framework of growing regulation, just as the shift to deregulated capitalism will not eliminate all national diversity.

Our argument is that while the European model is slowly being eroded and replaced by an American one, the process is being politically mediated and can therefore be challenged. It is not 'convergence' towards a single 'functionally necessary' post-Fordist model, but rather towards several elements of the American weakly restrained model of market capitalism. These are partly being levered into place through American economic and political power, but they are also being ideologically 'sold' within Europe by the new right, management schools, and 'realists' of the left (who often in fact lean on post-Fordist arguments). However, there is still considerable resistance to these processes by labour movements, environmentalists and other social groupings which, though weakened, are still making an impact at local, national and EU levels, and occasioned the reversal of right government in much of Western Europe between 1995 and 1998.

Twenty-five years of very rapid European expansion ended in the 1970s and, as time goes on, that decade seems more and more like a watershed. However contemporary neo-liberalism has been built on, rather than been discontinuous with, the foundations of the post-1945 world economy. Political events and processes have also had an important contextual influence throughout, including: the defeat of the USA in Vietnam, the 1973 Arab-Israeli war and 1979 Iranian revolution, the oil-producing countries' decision to raise the price of oil in response to these events, the political triumph of the American new right with the election of Reagan, the collapse of the communist bloc in 1989, the reunification of Germany in 1990 and the Gulf War of 1991. Within this political framework, capitalists have been encouraged to search for new sources of profit, to use increasingly efficient technologies, and to compete more intensively. They have not been encouraged to put people first. By the 1980s the expectations of ordinary Europeans for job security and greater social equity have come to be increasingly seen as obstacles to the realization of these projects. To counter the previous decade's new welfare and industrial relations settlements and the developing world's growing clamour for greater justice in the world economy, a more aggressive form of international finance capitalism was unleashed while MNCs were given the green light to extend further their activities across national boundaries (Ikeda 1996).

As developing countries were first told to borrow and then slipped into debt, the major American-dominated world economic institutions, the World Bank and the International Monetary Fund, curtailed their aspirations through dictating neo-liberal 'structural adjustment' conditions involving privatization, cuts in welfare and the opening of their markets to foreign multinationals, in exchange for the continued servicing of their debt (George 1988). Thus the pressure to liberalize regulatory regimes for foreign direct investment (FDI) by multinational companies has mounted consistently through the 1990s. According to UNCTAD (1999: 9) whereas in 1991 35 countries introduced 80 regulatory changes that were more favourable to FDI ('including liberalizing changes or changes aimed at strengthening market functioning, as well as increased incentives'), by 1998 60 countries introduced 145 such changes.

Less direct and more gradual means were used to discipline European countries, through the exhortations of the OECD, the operation of money markets, and the pressure brought to bear by American and other multinationals upon national and EU decisions. Hence American support for the shift to the Single Market and the Single Currency. Rather than 'disorganized' capitalism naturally creating space for neo-liberalism in the world economy, American neo-liberalism consciously constructed the new world order. The deregulation of financial markets, the privatizations of publicly owned industries and services, and the successive attacks on economies that have tried to protect their industries behind trade barriers or through devaluations have followed a script largely written in the USA. In this drive even its 'allies' are not allowed to stand in its way. Thus because the USA is a more open economy than Europe or Japan, it is increasingly insisting that the World Trade Organization (WTO) acts to break down barriers elsewhere. This explains its drive to give MNCs rights over national governments in the temporarily failed (thanks largely to NGO and French socialist opposition) negotiations on a Multilateral Agreement on Investment in 1998, but also the American victorious 'war' in 1999 against European import restrictions on bananas sourced by the major American food multinationals (*Economist* 1999a).

In the 1990s America's 'organizing' power within the global marketplace has thus become still stronger. The collapse of communism, the economic slowdown in Western Europe resulting from application of post-Maastricht monetarism and the monetary crisis of the former 'Tiger' economies, have all reinforced its political power and economic success at the close of 'America's century'. The all-encompassing character of American-led market capitalism should still not, however, be exaggerated. Globalization is better seen as 'a complex of interrelated processes, not an end-state' (Dicken 1998: 5). Within this complex, European nation states remain very important actors, rather than mere ciphers and continue to shape the distinct ways in which their national economies are located within Europe and the world economy (Smith and Elger 1995).

The power of the American market model is not the result of any inherent economic superiority. For while the American economy is good at generating short-term profits, with a premium on innovation that serves it well, it is less good at enhancing product quality in the longer term. Equally, while American labour and capital markets are 'efficient', Germany with its better vocational training system and public infrastructure has actually achieved higher levels of productivity in the 1990s (*Economist* 1999b). The USA runs on millions of low-paid, low-productivity workers. It also pays huge social costs in terms of social inequality, poverty, crime, racism and urban decay (Sassoon 1996). That the American model works cannot be denied. That its more extensive adoption and implementation in Western Europe and the removal of the remaining extensive Christian and social democratic restraints will entrain major *dysfunctional* consequences is equally undeniable.

The next three chapters elaborate the extent to which Europe is converging towards such a model in relation to the spheres of management, work and welfare, before the final chapter considers whether distinct European models can survive the current pressures being mounted against them.

7. Management in Contemporary Western Europe

The 1980s and 1990s witnessed the growing power of an expanding managerial class, alongside the elevation of many aspects of American managerialism into a dominant organizational and political credo, a process closely linked to the rise of the neo-liberal right, even if it cannot be simply equated with it. Even taking into account significant variations in its impact across Europe, the increasing adoption of American managerial ideologies and methods is one of the most striking developments of the contemporary period, and is accelerating rather than abating. We saw in Chapter 5 that the adoption of American-originated technologies up to the 1970s only led to a partial transformation of European managerial relations which were strongly influenced by European traditions and worker mobilizations. Indeed renewed moves to 'workers' participation' and co-determination in the context of the second wave of 'settlements' in the 1970s was even a powerful counter-response to managerialism. Why then has there been this dramatic turnaround in the 1980s and 1990s?

In exploring this question we again seek to avoid technologically determinist and economic reductionist explanations. Since the 'requirements' of mass production do not adequately account for managerial developments during the boom years, we also question the neo-functionalist notion that a shift to 'flexible accumulation' has been the prime mover in the ascendency of managerialism. The spread of American managerial approaches has often facilitated technological and organizational change, and cannot simply be regarded as a product of it. This chapter therefore extends the political economic framework developed in the last chapter to show that managerial power has increasingly impacted on the productive sphere and political cultures in ways that increasingly correspond to American cultural preferences or 'peculiarities'. 'Management', confirms Locke (1996: 1) in an overly optimistically entitled study of its 'collapse', 'is an American term and an American creation. Although American management has always hankered for universalism, it is nothing more than a cultural peculiarity'. We see its slowly growing influence in Europe as substantially shaped from the outside, by the American political-economic leverage over the global economy and regulatory institutions which has shaped the competitive conditions eroding worker influence and strengthening managerial power. This has often been reinforced by the increasing number of American corporations and financial institutions operating in Europe, which have enormous influence over their workforces and also mount significant pressure on national and EU governance. It has also been underlined by the growing number of European firms operating with 'American' methods in North America. We also argue that the spread of managerialism has been significantly assisted by the extraordinary recent growth in management education and publishing, largely transmitting applied knowledge from American-derived principles to growing numbers of Europeans.

However, we do not see this evolution as engineered wholly from above or from the outside. Without attributing them a determining role, shifts in productive processes, including technological changes, have increased demand for 'knowledge' workers and the need for larger numbers of coordinating agents. The accelerated transmission of American managerialism was facilitated by receptive constituencies in Europe. These naturally include many of the 'captains of industry' who have become increasingly convinced that it meets their strategic interests. However, managerial discourses have also embedded themselves lower down among the growing numbers in the 'new' managerial and entrepreneurial layers, who we suggest may have embraced it as a form of 'credentialism' opening up avenues for social mobility and enhanced status. While this helps to make managerialism a 'mass movement' allied to the new right, we also suggest that its hold has often become precarious among the middling groups, particularly in the context of the recessions of the 1990s and the acceleration of the managerial revolution. First, significant numbers of middle managers in the public services (and in fact beyond) may be ambivalent towards or even opposed to its associated political project to run down the welfare state. Second, growing numbers of people in the middle layers and the self-employed have latterly themselves become targets of managerial rationalization and accelerated technological change, or victims of recession. Thus though we argue that the growth of managerialism assisted the new right politically in the 1980s, growing 'unease' among middle layers has contributed to the revival of the centre-left across Europe from the mid-1990s.

American managerialism itself we see as an influential set of competing but complementary discourses that have changed over time rather than as a single dominant fixed technique or concept. These discourses are currently expressed through the world views of senior executives of America's large, generally non-union firms, and are taught to the 200,000 students who in the 1990s each year received American MBAs (Locke 1996). They stress that managerial leadership is the key creative 'productive force' in capitalism, and that any constraints over it associated with workplace and social democracy must be swept away. One early textbook (Brooke and Remmers 1978: 52) summarized 'American managerial philosophy' as having 'five major traits':

- One is the belief in growth as a vital need in its own right.
- Another is the belief in profit as a mark of efficiency and performance, and as a producer of social benefits.
- The third is a belief in free initiative and private enterprise as a system which, in spite of its imperfections, has hitherto performed more effectively than any other.
- The fourth element in this philosophy is that hard decisions must be accepted for the sake of the well being of the whole organization. Such decisions include the elimination of inefficient businesses, the dismissal of weak executives, and the downgrading of conventional status symbols.
- The final feature is that change must be accepted in every aspect of the working existence.

The 'Americanization' of management, then, is the piecemeal, incremental adoption within the Western European political economy of this project and the priorities associated with it. For Western Europe the applicability of all five traits would have been disputed both by most right and left political parties in the 1960s and 1970s, and also by many managers: growth was important, not as an end in itself, but as a means to providing full employment and greater equality; greater profits might mean greater 'efficiency' yet also signalled greater exploitation; private enterprise was largely incapable of delivering social benefits; the social consequences of hard decisions should always be taken into account; and stability and security were still seen as important European social aspirations. Today, however, despite significant national variations, most mainstream political parties and virtually all management pronouncements are expressed within the discourse of this new project. Thus the Lisbon EU summit of March 2000 could comfortably commit itself to becoming 'the most dynamic knowledge-based economy' and to accelerating the liberalization of the internal market, but omitted setting the targets trailed in advance by the Portuguese presidency of reducing unemployment by 2010 from 8.8% to 4% and the poverty rate from 18% to 10% (*Le Monde*, 26-27 March 2000).

In tracing this remarkable socio-political evolution, we first set the scene by charting the growth of the European managerial labour force and the evolution of its functional tasks. Next we examine the education and training processes that have helped to shape managers' perspectives. Following this we consider some of the managerial practices that have become commonplace in Western Europe over the last 20 years, and are helping to undermine the earlier more 'pluralist' or power sharing traditions. Finally, we consider the wider political influence of managers and managerialism as a force within society and politics.

7.1   THE EXPLOSION IN MANAGERIAL NUMBERS

In the 1980s and 1990s the growth in the numbers of European managers traced in Chapter 5 continued unabated. Part of this can be detected in the rising proportions of 'employers and self-employed' within the labour force. In 1979 an average of 12.4% of the labour force in the EEC's nine member states fell into this category (Eurostat 1981) but by 1996 the equivalent figure for the EU's 15 members had risen to 15% (Eurostat 1997). Not all included in this category were 'managers': in the more agricultural countries the overwhelming majority were independent farmers. But we can get some idea of the trend in Table 7.1 comparing the 'employers and self-employed' data for eight EU members between 1979 and 1996, with 1996 Eurostat Labour Force Survey occupational data on 'legislators and managers' for these same countries.

Table 7.1   'Employers and self-employed' and 'legislators and managers' as a % of the total labour force in selected European countries, 1979-96

	Employers, self-employed		Managers, legislators
	1979	1996	1996
UK	7.5	12.6	14.6
Netherlands	10.2	11.2	12.5
Belgium	14.6	15.4	10.8
Ireland	23.1	19.8	9.0
France	12.5	11.3	7.6
Denmark	12.8	8.3	7.1
Germany	8.8	9.6	5.8*
Italy	22.7	24.8	1.1

Sources: Eurostat (1981, 1996, 1997).

By 1996 there were more 'legislators and managers' in Britain and the Netherlands than 'employers and self-employed'. As the strangely small occupation of 'managers and legislators' in Italy suggests, a lot clearly hangs on the definition of 'manager'. Thus if the British definition is widened to include both 'management' and 'professional and related supporting management and administration' occupations, their proportions rose from 12.3% in 1979 to 17% by 1988 (HMSO 1981: 31, 1991: 38), and in 1998 were still at 16% after a decade of supposed 'managerial delayering' (ONS 1998: 22). The managerial explosion is also a feature of Scandinavian countries such as Denmark where, according to official statistics, between 1983 and 1992 the numbers of Danish managers actually rose by between 30% in central government, 70% in local government including the health service, and by around 50% in the private sector (Kvinder 1995: 67-8). Despite the imprecise definitions of 'management', 'employers' and 'administrators' and many national variations, by the early twenty-first century at least 10% of working Western Europeans - or over 16 million of us - are working as 'managers'. This management explosion is the result of three interrelated developments which are considered in turn: (1) a continued broadening of the definition of 'manager'; (2) an increase in subcontracting, 'outsourcing' and the like, associated with the so-called 'flexible firm'; and (3) a shift in the key locus of competition downstream from the production process to sales, marketing and post-sales services.

In most European organizations a wider definition of management became increasingly common in the 1980s. This involved all those engaged in *coordinating* the work of others, even if this did not always involve a disciplinary or hiring function. The earlier definition of European managers as *representatives* of the employer-owner with attendant power and autonomy increasingly came to be reserved for *senior* managers. Thus while British bank managers in the 1970s were significant local sources of (male) power, by the 1990s they had often become plug-in 'business development' managers with very limited autonomy (and were more often women). Their new responsibilities were mainly coordinating the tasks of more junior cashiers ('personal advisors') to ensure they reached their sales targets (Thornley *et al.*1997). The broadening of the definition of 'management' has left the same term including 'senior' executives, 'low-grade' office coordinators and Pizza Hut supervisors. In France a continuing statistical occupational distinction is drawn between *cadres moyens* and *cadres supérieurs*, and from a sociological viewpoint the European managerial 'service class' can be seen as having upper and lower substrata. This blurring of definitional and functional distinctions between a small managerial elite and a larger but less powerful 'middle' and 'junior' managerial group created new opportunities for upward mobility and enhanced status, in ways which made the latter potentially receptive to American managerial values.

The evolution of capitalist organizations has also contributed significantly to the growth in management. The development of computer and communication technologies has enabled many sectors to reverse Coase's 1937 maxim that the higher cost of transactions involved in doing business externally made it more cost efficient for that business to be brought in-house, while the slow-down in economic growth and the greater competitive pressure exerted on firms since the 1970s gave an impetus to attempts to lower costs while simultaneously raising quality. Since the central production process in most industries is now fairly standard across the world, competitive product differentiation has become critical for firms wishing to raise prices above the industry average. This has enhanced the role of the high-density professional pre-production 'upstream' processes of research and development, design and the purchase of raw materials and components. But it has particularly prioritized the post-production 'downstream' processes of marketing, distribution and sales and post-sales service. Both upstream and downstream processes are now capable of being independently and more profitably organized if kept 'independent' from the longer bureaucratic procedures of the core organization (Porter 1985). Competitive advantage has thus increasingly come to lie in differentiation through advertising campaigns and post-sales services, areas where the new communication technologies enable organization by structurally independent or semi-independent firms. Under these pressures growing numbers of European firms are now following American practice and choosing to outsource both 'non-core' work and even certain 'core' tasks, ranging from market research to personnel administration and from component parts manufacture to warehousing, and occasionally even final assembly. At the extreme, a company like BP has transformed the status of virtually all its headquarters staff into 'self-employed'. The claimed benefits of outsourcing are cost savings, improved service from a specialist supplier, freeing up managerial time, greater flexibility, a switch from *fixed* to *variable* costs, reduced exposure to government regulation and the avoidance of headcount controls.

Whatever the actual benefits the consequence of firms choosing outsourcing strategies is to expand the numbers of managers. This occurs partly because these processes require coordination, both by managers at the core who assume responsibility for communicating orders and ensuring deliveries 'just-in-time', and those at the subcontracting periphery to coordinate matters at their end. In addition the fragmentation of production multiplies managerial positions as the numbers of small- and medium-sized businesses and consultancies has mushroomed. The expansion of firms selling specialist managerial skills has thus fuelled the continuing growth in the numbers of managers. It is also the case that services capitalism tends both to be organized in smaller units closer to the customer than industrial capitalism, and to require greater coordination between different phases of delivering services. Already by 1988 out of 107 European industrial sub-sectors the value of the output of advertising was ranked 23rd and software and computing services 28th, while the new areas of management consultancy (92nd) and market research (101st) had just made their mark (EC 1991: 28-9).

However, as the numbers of managers rose, so their relative status declined, and their degree of autonomy often narrowed. They became less remote, and the overlap between their functions and those of professional and other non-managerial employees has tended to grow (Moody 1997, Warhurst and Thompson 1998). This growth in managers was also superimposed on existing patterns of discrimination. By 1988 just 5.9% of EU-14 (excluding Ireland) women were company directors or senior managers compared to 14.9% of men (Eurostat 2000: 66-7). The UK Labour Force Survey, for example, showed that in 1979, among over-16 year olds in employment, only 5.6% of women were employers and managers compared to 14.6% of men. But racial discrimination was even more dramatic. If they had West Indian ethnic origins only 2% of women surveyed and just 4.1% of males were managers (HMSO 1981: 22). By 1988 the proportion of women employers and managers had risen to 10% compared to 20% of men, and included just 6% of West Indian women and 8% of West Indian men (HMSO 1991: 28). Thus a slight blurring of the dominant white, male picture occurred in the 1980s, but as women and black workers took up disproportionately more of the new 'manager' posts, they also found themselves increasingly subject to a segmented managerial labour market. In the private sector they were largely confined to a junior managerial substrata, and their jobs were increasingly subjected to close supervisory inspection and offered little prospect of further promotion. The greatest advance of women in management was recorded in the state sectors of Europe's economies, paradoxically at the very moment that the growth of these state sectors slowed down, ended or went into decline. For example, in Denmark, where between 1983 and 1992 the proportions of women in management as a whole rose much faster than the already high rate of growth in managerial numbers (Kvinder 1995). In the state sector, however, the 'new' managers still found themselves with comparatively low pay and status compared to equivalent levels of managerial responsibility in the private sector.

Despite the opening up of new avenues of mobility in the wake of managerial expansion in the last 20 years, the manager occupational grouping thus remains solidly white and masculine, particularly so at senior levels. This, alongside the more competitive conditions, arguably made it easier for the 'masculine' American management culture of ambition, materialism and aggression to dominate and weaken what Hofstede (1980) describes as the 'feminine' culture of cooperation, relationships and quality of life. In those European business cultures Hofstede identified as having comparatively high 'femininity' scores (France, Spain, Portugal, Denmark, Netherlands and Sweden) the conjuncture of highly competitive economic conditions with the growth of a manager stratum whose most senior ranks remain male-dominated, has arguably reinforced the receptivity of 'middle' and 'junior' managers to these American 'masculine' managerial characteristics. We will now argue that the 'socialization' processes contributed by management training and education has made a key contribution to this process of identification with these values.

7.2 MANAGEMENT TRAINING, EDUCATION AND CULTURAL DIFFUSION

The 1980s and 1990s saw an immense expansion in management and business studies training and education throughout Europe. The demand came from the growing need for better trained and educated coordinators, but the supply, we shall argue, comes from educators increasingly influenced by the 'knowledge base' of American management values. This movement had its own prophets: the 'born again' evangelism proclaimed by American business gurus set upon transforming the globe into their 'village' (or shopping mall). This in turn can be seen as linked to the tested and survived strength of American capitalism in the last two decades of the twentieth century, when first its 'Communist' and then its 'Far Eastern' competitors effectively acknowledged the superiority of its ways. The business academy was also a constituency seeking to ride on the crest of these waves, who saw in them an opportunity to expand influence and careers. In the 1960s and 1970s business educators in Western Europe were largely concerned with refining a small elite of already successful managers. By the 1980s and 1990s, not only had they extended their reach down into the middle and lower ranks through expansion of undergraduate degrees and diplomas, in Britain they had even entered secondary schools to offer standard *pre-experience* courses. At this rate, before long entrepreneurship and time-management will become prescribed elements of primary and even nursery education! Alongside this, managerial publishing has become a major international business in its own right, with dozens of American or European versions of American management texts and 'how to' books selling millions of copies throughout Europe. These do not just address the formal student market but increasingly offer populist and 'cut-down' versions to the general public, making managerialism one of the major self-education movements of our time. Increasingly such books blend with pop psychology to offer 'total' advice on how people can 'liberate' themselves, reinforcing the universalistic message that American managerialism is not just a guide to doing things, but to life itself.

The transformation of American management education in Europe from what was a small 'cult' to what is almost a 'mass religion' involved changes among the American 'high priests' as well as among the prospective believers. The onset of the slower growth rates and heightened international competition of the last quarter of the twentieth century created the dynamic for modifications to the catechism, and American capitalism showed considerable resourcefulness in borrowing back successful management methods from its Japanese competitors. By the 1990s American and American-influenced business schools began introducing 'international management' as a major curriculum subject and product. It is at first sight surprising that this was not already happening, for capitalism has been international through the whole of this century. Jacques (1996: 171) suggests the recent internationalization phase of American business schools began in recognition 'of the passing of centralized control and profit accrual from the USA to other countries'. In other words by becoming more integrated into a global market American managers increasingly required their methods, tools and assumptions to become the common currency of all the economies within which they operated. He goes on to argue that:

> Beneath the addition of a little international case material, however, what is exported worldwide is a curriculum with a knowledge base developed on a primarily US work force, embedded values reflecting the American Dream of freedom, competition and individuality, and a discipline still geared to the core problems of an industrializing US.

Prentice Hall's 'International Edition' of their big-selling *The Strategy Process* by Mintzberg and Quinn (1996) is perhaps a classic example of this type of approach.

Only rarely did European managers become directly converted to a transplanted 'American Dream' by ideologues like Milton Friedman who personally and through close disciples had begun to exercise growing influence over the World Bank and International Monetary Fund in the 1970s (Van der Pijl 1989). More commonly conversion followed the combination of the narrowing of choice created by more intense global competition, personal experience of the success with American methods, and the continuous and repeated exposure of Europe's managers to the voluntarist assumptions of American academics like Michael Porter, whose universal recipes for developing new management strategies became the staple diet of corporate strategy departments. In the 1980s the free market ethos was advanced still more aggressively by an expanding cast of American business experts, starting with *In Search of Excellence* by Peters and Waterman (1982), which was translated into nine European languages and sold more than one million copies.

In marked contrast to the 1950s and 1960s, when management theory pictured a stable and increasingly predictable world that was gradually coming under control or being successfully 'managed', the new American management literature of the 1980s saw a chaotic, unpredictable world where opportunities had to be seized rather than taken for granted. In particular, the new American management literature of the 1980s dwelt on American corporate weakness and reflected on how to respond to the success of Japanese capitalism. For a brief period in the 1970s and 1980s it even appeared as if Japanese capitalism might overtake American as the main global source of management thinking and capitalist dynamic. Building on strong pre-capitalist foundations of collective obedience and 'clan' loyalties, a crushing defeat of adversarial trade unionism in the 1950s and the direct promotion of industrial expansion by the state, and in the context of enforced demilitarization Japanese capitalism has become enormously powerful. In the process certain of the organizational methods it had honed from American practices and ideologues became seen as ripe for retransmission to the USA and wider emulation. The most important of these were: (1) 'just-in-time' (JIT), which seeks to speed up production, eliminate waste and make production more sensitive to rapidly changing market conditions, consistent with so-called 'lean production'; and (2) 'total quality management' (TQM), 'a US-inspired quality management method' which aims to improve customer satisfaction through providing 'better quality of product and service; faster response to customer needs; greater flexibility in adjusting to customers' changing requirements and lower costs through improvement in quality and deletion of non-value-adding work' (Prasad and Sprague 1996: 82, 71). These approaches were particularly suited to Japan's corporate traditions, its dualistic industrial structure of large powerful firms and dependent suppliers, weak company unions and subordinated workers. While both the efficiency and desirability of the Japanese 'model' have been questioned (e.g. Woronoff 1996), in the 1980s JIT and TQM were abstracted from their Japanese culture and political economy and popularized as bywords for 'modern management' approaches, first in the USA and then in Europe.

The dominant managerial paradigm remains American, albeit revitalized by absorption of 'foreign' elements. Indeed, this model is increasingly being reabsorbed in Japan and the Far East, especially as the Asian financial crisis since 1998 has partly undermined the material basis for Japanese paternalism. Thus the years 1999 and 2000 witnessed the nearly unthinkable of ten years ago: Renault and DaimlerChrysler taking controlling shares of Nissan and Mitshubishi. Of course Japanese 'clan' and Chinese 'family' capitalisms continue as a whole to operate on quite different bases than does American. Richard Whitley's work (1992, 1999) convincingly points to the strong interdependence between business systems and work patterns and the structuring role of nationally-based social institutions. Further, he states the obvious in writing that 'the ways in which economic activities are organized and controlled in, for example, post-war Japan, South Korea, and Taiwan differ considerably from those prevalent in the USA and the UK', and in declaring that:

> Convergence to *a single most effective type of market economy* is no more likely in the twenty-first century than it was in the highly internationalized economy of the late nineteenth century (*our emphasis*, 1999: 3).

Part of our argument, too, is that the mediating effects of politics, institutions and resistance have resulted in different capitalisms between Western Europe and the USA. Yet while no single model is emerging Whitley arguably underestimates the significance of long-term pressures towards convergence. We would suggest that both globally and within Western Europe there are today significantly fewer differences between market economies than existed a century ago. Equally, it appears that national management structures and strategies, far from being increasingly distinct from each other (as Whitley's 1999 book title, *Divergent Capitalisms* implies), are everywhere being modified and reshaped and through pressures generated by increasing integration in a global economic order strongly influenced by the world's dominant American economy and international institutions like the WTO and IMF which share its world-view. This may not be convergence to a single point or model, but nevertheless market economies are all moving in an increasingly similar direction.

In part it was the emergence of a 'critically reflective' American new managerialism in response to the sense of being 'overtaken' by Japanese and German capitalism at the end of the 1970s (Locke 1996) that has enhanced its legitimacy in Western Europe. No longer simply laying down the law the revised core message stresses the key role of senior managers in meeting new challenges, in mapping out change, in exercising greater levels of control and in extracting new levels of commitment from employees through more effective motivation. 'The American business hero', writes Humes, whose book was hailed as a 'modern bible' by the head of Fiat's Brussels lobbying team, 'has been the individual achiever, taking risks, acting quickly and decisively, and reaping rewards' (1993:115). As competition intensified in the 1990s American management further taught that managers must take on greater and more flexible responsibilities, while simultaneously responding more sensitively to customers (Clarke *et al.* 1994). Jacques (1996) argues that this continues the philosophy of perfectionism, individualism and faith in progress that are embedded in the American Puritan and Quaker tradition, with success in business as the 'God' that managers much serve rather than promotion of workers' or community welfare. The firm is thus transformed into a quasi-religious community with its own holy writ, or 'mission statement'. As Guillén puts it, a new paradigm has emerged in which:

> The business firm is seen as a community, almost to the exclusion of all other possible group memberships that workers may have. The buzzwords of the organizational culture paradigm include *sense of belonging, integrative leadership, organizational climate, involvement, participation, loyalty, commitment, harmony, interdependence, cohesiveness, and team spirit...* The echoes of the human relations paradigm could not resonate louder. The overall tone is strongly paternalistic (*original emphasis*, 1994: 289-90).

In practice Guillén argues, these buzzwords are mantras which represent an amalgam of at least two core American organizational models: scientific management and human relations, the former fitting more easily within Protestant cultures which have 'emphasized individualism, instrumentalism, independence, and contractualism' and the latter among Catholic, stressing 'the community, self-actualization, paternalism and organicism' (*op. cit.*: 297).

The role of the educational transmission belt of American managerial ideologies in reshaping the European managerial hierarchy should not be underestimated. By 1988, for example, nearly half the volumes in the French Grenoble University Business School's library were American. Almost all of these textbooks are prescriptive. They are directed at raising 'economically defined' productivity, and assume that managements have or are given 'the right to manage' in order to achieve that goal (Pollitt 1990: 2-3). What is being taught are on the whole the narrow philosophies and practices of what Ritzer (1996) calls 'McDonaldization', whose emphasis on 'calculability' tends to reduce quality to quantity, and whose 'predictability' requirement combines with 'greater control over work-related processes as well as the finished product' to eliminate 'the uncertainties created by employees' (1996: 120). American management textbooks mainly offer patient, step-by-step, technical accounts of how managers should get these results. If they are not yet facing a totally free market, the assumption is that inevitably they will do soon - a future that becomes much more likely if those reading these texts then follow their prescriptions.

However, the dominant prescriptive messages are not entirely uniform.

At least two main alternative variants of the new managerial discourse coexist within the American management literature (Sparrow and Hiltrop 1994), representing differing versions of the 'human resource management' (HRM) paradigm. This often involves more than a terminological shift from 'personnel management'. The latter emerged partly because trade union influences on the wider labour market meant that 'labour questions' such as recruitment, retention and industrial relations became relatively autonomous from production, and partly to implement the paternalistic 'company welfare' tradition of European management. HRM, by contrast, though variable in impact, not least in who carries out these functions, typically involves the reintegration of personnel functions into line management, an added focus on achieving superior quality, output and profits and a stress on the central role of people management within business strategy. Overall it is strongly unitarist and its essentially exploitative paradigm of labour as a commodified 'resource' is consistent with the precepts of American managerialism and the growing dominance of accountancy (Armstrong 1988). The 'harder' version of HRM is 'neo-Taylorism', or Ritzer's 'McDonaldization', emphasizing the manipulation of inputs and outputs to engineer higher productivity and competitive advantage. It stresses 'resource' efficiency allocation as being the most critical element within the term 'human *resource* management'. Managers are essentially inspired controllers. Under this *'efficiency scenario...* effective competition is only possible on the basis of less regulation, greater flexibility and lower (wage) costs' (Visser 1996a: 41, *original emphasis*). A 'softer' 'Harvard' HRM variation stresses the 'humanity' of *'human* resource management'. Starting from human relations theory, people's needs and motivations are put at the centre of organizational structure and business strategy. Bureaucratic management must be uprooted and replaced by a common culture of commitment to wider organizational goals. From this viewpoint managers are essentially inspirational leaders, and the firms they lead have the option of adopting a 'quality scenario'. Guillén (1994: 287) points to a long history in twentieth-century America of oscillation between:

> rational and natural approaches, mechanistic and organic solidarity, and individualism and communalism that has haunted employers and managers in the attempt to establish and maintain authority and control in the workplace.

Despite these differences in discourse, there is nevertheless consensus on the core philosophy on the need to restore the 'right to manage'. Their common enemies are 'overmanning' of businesses and 'overintervention' by the state (Clarke *et al.* 1994), and their common aim to promote behavioural consistency among employees. Lean production (TQM), the two dominant organizational approaches of the 1990s combine elements of both traditions (Guillén 1994); and both place significantly less emphasis upon pluralism and societal effectiveness than is usual within contemporary Western Europe, and significantly more upon unitarist values and the benefits of the resource allocation delivered by managerial authority operating in 'free' markets.

In summary, the American message became more critical and sophisticated, at the point at which European managers were also becoming more receptive to it. This was partly due to the end of the '30 glorious years', and to European managers' realization that they needed to consider new ideas to meet intensified competition and shrinking profits. It was further reinforced by the growing two-way exposure of Europe to American business, and the financial reach of an American-centred global finance market and American-based multinational business organizations discussed in Chapter 6 (Strange 1997). In the early decades of the twentieth century American firms like Standard Oil, Ford and General Electric began to directly invest overseas, accelerating after 1945, with Britain serving as the most important portal into the European market. Over half of all American FDI was now invested in Europe, with just over half of that shared nearly equally by Britain (still just ahead) and Germany (Dicken 1998). The 'American challenge' was by the late 1960s seen as 'a war' that:

> is being fought not with dollars, or oil, or steel, or even with modern machines. It is being fought with creative imagination and organizational talent (Servan-Schreiber, 1968: xiii).

Dollars, oil and technology have, of course, played a significant part in making Europe more open to American business today than 30 years ago.

Yet Americanization should not today be solely equated with direct American ownership. Europe's largest businesses have also been increasingly adopting American management 'knowledge' and values as they have traded and invested in the USA. Europe had its own 'world players' in the international economy restored after 1945, such as the Swiss giant Nestlé, the Dutch electrical firm Phillips, the Anglo-Dutch Unilever and oil companies like Royal Dutch/Shell, British Petroleum and ICI (Sparrow and Hilltrop 1994). However by 1959 all but six of the world's 50 largest multinationals were still American-owned. It was only when large German firms like Siemens (electrical equipment), Daimler-Benz (automobiles, electronics), Volkswagen, and chemical firms like Hoescht, Bayer and BASF, the Italian Fiat company and the French nationalized firm Renault joined the top Global 50 in the 1960s and 1970s that European firms began to develop on the same scale as American firms. It was then that significant European capital investment into the USA began to take place, and by 1989 Western Europe had 42 firms among the world's 100 largest multinationals compared to 35 American and 17 Japanese firms (EC 1991: 96). In fact, as early as 1985 the USA had become a net importer of European capital and the gap has widened considerably since (Hirst and Thompson 1996, *European*, 10 August 1998)

In 1998 when Daimler-Benz, the German company that had been the 12th biggest company in the world by turnover in 1989 took over 57% of Chrysler, the unthinkable happened. The world's biggest-ever industrial merger occurred leaving a European company, whose principal shareholder is the Deutsche Bank, in the driving seat. It confirmed the survival of German industrial muscle, but it was the very reverse of a 'victory' of European over American managerialism. For Jürgen Schrempp, the chairman of Daimler-Benz due to become chief executive officer of DaimlerChrysler in 2001, cut his industrial teeth in the USA in the early 1980s running the German firm's Cleveland, Ohio truck subsidiary. One observer commented that Schrempp 'has clearly absorbed and taken on board the American management values of the 1990s' (*European*, 11 May 1998). Schrempp himself boasts that:

> We were the first German company to go to the US Stock Exchange and to adopt American accounting rules, which made for much greater transparency of our financial results...We had to change over to a culture where the stock price was the first priority...I love the entrepreneurial spirit, I have read many books about how American companies are run. Investors must be the first priority; after all, they own the company' (*European*, 10 August 1998).

The DaimlerChrysler merger confirms it is no longer necessary to have American nationality to embrace 'American management values'. As if to prove the point, one of Daimler-Benz's directors, Sir John Browne, the English chief executive of British Petroleum, promptly signed up to merge BP with the American oil giant, Amoco. Browne, a graduate of Cambridge and Stanford, California, who worked for years for BP in the USA, will become chief executive of the joint BP Amoco in 2000 (*European*, August 10 1998).

Both European-based and American-based MNCs played significant roles in the development of mass business education in the 1990s. These firms tend to be the most interested in promoting managerial professionalism and the transferability of managerial skills within European management labour markets. Partly this has occurred through the natural exposure of individual managers to new international experiences, but partly too these companies have increasingly tended to recruit new managers on the basis of matches between their qualifications and some form of standardized managerial job descriptions. Since management training is intended to increase the marketability of the trainees, these job requirements are often used as guidelines for the content of management courses. Thus feedback from Nestlé was and is a major component in developing programmes at the Lausanne-based IMD (International Institute for Management Development) it founded in 1957.

The companies that recruited from management schools in the 1960s and 1970s were almost exclusively big firms as shown, for example, in analyses of intakes at INSEAD, the French international business school, of graduates of the London and Manchester Business Schools' MBA programmes, and of the Swiss St Gall business school. The multinationals and larger national firms also came to be the subject of most academic research. However, by the late 1980s most European governments started to respond to evidence that small- and medium-sized firms were often more dynamic than larger ones. They began pressing higher education to become providers of management education and training directed specifically at small- and medium-sized businesses. New short courses were introduced in both West Germany and Belgium, and this format was also adopted as the appropriate delivery vehicle for new courses for start-up companies launched in Denmark, West Germany and Britain in the 1980s (Holzer 1989).

No sector of the European political economy has been left untouched by the spread of management education and its core set of free enterprise values. This is particularly evident in the state-owned or funded sector. Following the tearing down of the Berlin Wall, the free market critique of public sector service delivery intensified. In the 1990s the reality or threat of privatization has become ubiquitous throughout Western Europe's publicly owned industries and services. State-sector managers, accordingly, joined the trek towards management education. In countries where in-service training traditions made it possible, managers in central government, the health service and even teachers, queued up to study specialist management skills. In other countries where pre-experience qualifications were traditionally more important, the initial recruitment of public sector managers has been skewed towards those with business qualifications. Throughout Europe countries the 1980s and 1990s witnessed a huge increase in the use of private management consultants and trainers by the public sector.

From the late 1980s as unemployment rose across Europe prospective managers increasingly opted for more 'vocational' degrees. Virtually all Europe's universities began to offer professional management programmes, ranging from generalist MBAs to specialisms like marketing. In the early 1990s a survey of Spain's 1000 largest firms found that two-thirds of their senior managers and over half of their managers had university degrees

(Baruel 1996: 104), against an average level of 19% of Spanish men aged between 15 and 59 in or having completed 18+ education (Eurostat 1997: 78). By the mid-1990s the continuing demand for managerial qualifications meant that across Europe the numbers of business studies and management students, or students on engineering and law courses who took those subjects in addition to their main courses, rose dramatically. While there are no precise figures available we estimate that up to one fifth of all Western European students aged 18-24 are currently undertaking one or more business-focused modules as part of their studies. Management training in American knowledge or methods is also directed at a significant proportion of managers already in post. European company training budgets have been rising continuously in the 1990s. Management training comes from both in-house and external providers, but it is the latter who are more likely to follow the 'latest trends' and act with greater evangelical zeal. In the survey of Spanish firms just referred to, the senior managers were twice as likely to receive training provided by external private providers as they were by in-house trainers.

Of course the specific character of each managerial labour market varies between different European countries, and each nation's certification process is not equally open to external influences. Thus the German managerial labour market remains largely defined by the acquisition of both apprenticeships, and university qualifications in engineering and economics, thereby inhibiting American managerialism from becoming the explicit organizing centre of its managerial labour market. Lawrence (1980) reported that there were no specialist undergraduate courses in management or business studies in German universities, although *betriebswirt* and *kaufmann*, business and commercial economics, were widely sought after qualifications at apprentice, degree and doctoral levels, that led to jobs in sales, administration, finance (where they do work done by accountants in Britain) and personnel (a function more likely to be fulfilled by someone with a law degree). It was only in the late 1990s that a growing group of German senior executives began to appear at the helm of the largest German companies with American or European business school backgrounds on their CVs (*European*, 1 June 1998). In France the most senior managers continue to be largely educated within the elite *grandes écoles* system. Yet over the last 20 years the expansion of university business-oriented degrees has provided an increasing number of students who have (often unpaid) 'work experience' in firms as part of their studies, which then provide the core of mass recruitment to junior manager positions. The pull of American business schools has also become strong. Not only is there quite intensive advertising for MBA programmes, but senior career patterns are being to change. Thus the latest member of the

Michelin family to head up the (family-owned) tyre multinational was educated at American business schools.

Table 7.2 Typologies of Western European and American management styles

	Western Europe	USA
Group values	Personal relationships	Individualism
Decision criteria	Personal trust	Structured systems and standards
Job roles	Quasi-generalists, loosely and ambiguously defined	Specialists, well-defined
Results orientation	Middle term	Short term
Government	Supportive	Confrontational
Trade unions	Negotiate	Oppose/undermine
Managerial hierarchy	Steeper	Flatter
Organizational commitment	Longer duration	Shorter duration

Source: adapted from Humes (1993) and Hampden-Turner and Trompenaars (1994).

The absence of the MBA postgraduate qualification from a particular country's managerial entry routine does not mean managers in those countries are not exposed to the same or to strongly derivative teaching. This is in part because of the international significance of American management thought, but also because English has become Europe's *de facto* business language. In Sweden English is a compulsory two-year subject at the *gymnasium,* attended by 80% of 16-year-olds. Since all Swedish managers have taken HNC/HND-type *gymasiumingenjör* (engineering) or *gymasiumekonom* (economics) exams or have been to university, this means all Swedish managers have had considerable exposure to American management approaches, whether or not they have formally studied them. As in Germany, the university degrees of Swedish managers are overwhelmingly in engineering, economics and law. Production and technical function managers tend to have engineering qualifications, while commercial managers generally come from an economics background, and personnel managers from law. Many senior Swedish managers have degrees in both engineering and economics, while the latter have a strongly business or 'applied' character (Lawrence and Spybey 1986).

In all these ways as they grew into a mass social stratum European managers have been increasingly exposed to what was at core a common form of management knowledge and assumptions. Europeans were used to more restrictions upon their rights to hire and fire, and placed less stress on the market and individualism and more on social rights. While there were and are differences of degree between different countries and different sectors, generally they placed some importance on workers' views, bargained more with the trade unions, and expected - even if they did not always welcome it - the state to intervene in industrial and social issues (Sparrow and Hiltrop 1994). Yet the challenge to these traditions from American business education has been unrelenting and its impact should not be underestimated. Despite important intra-European differences, two broadly distinct management traditions clearly coexisted during the last quarter of the twentieth century, one rooted in the complex political economies and historical choices of Western Europe and the other in those of the USA. The crude contrasts shown in Table 7.2 between these management styles reflect at least a partial reality. Our argument is that at that start of the twenty-first century European management is pulled in both directions, but that there is clear evidence that it is tending to move towards accumulating more of the attributes associated in Table 7.2 (admittedly in schematic ways) with the full-blown American model.

7.3   THE SHIFT IN MANAGERIAL PRACTICES

While acknowledging the continuing differences between European and American management, shifts to methods such as HRM and TQM are eroding them. Innovations are occurring in key areas of 'management practice' such as the recruitment and selection of employees, the training of new and old employees, and the 'engineering' and 're-engineering' of the workplace. The search for enhanced worker 'efficiency' has led to increased monitoring, discipline and individualization of reward systems. Allied with this has been the been the full or partial decay of traditional formal communication channels, such as through trade unions, in favour of a strong preference for unmediated formal and informal communication between individual workers and managers in both directions. The ideal is American non-unionized industrial relations, but since this has not always been possible a reduced trade union role has been pursued. Over the previous 20 years structural shifts in the American economy and labour markets have increasingly permitted managers to exclude unions, so that by the early

1990s less than 12% of its private sector workers were trade unionists, with unions virtually absent in the new industries, firms and occupations that had grown up since the mid-1970s. Leading the way were firms such as Hewlett-Packard, McDonald's and Toys-R-Us that have become household names in Europe. As they entered Europe they popularized the methods originally developed from the 1950s and 1960s by America's anti-union 'pioneers', IBM, Motorola and Delta Airlines (Kochan *et al.* 1994). The new global standards of production and service delivery these companies generated were increasingly based on the assumption of a pronounced power imbalance between employer and employee in the workplace. Their success encouraged European emulation and generalisation of the methods, which over time has begun to wear down any employee resistance.

One study carried out in 1990 revealed the role played at that time by foreign-owned multinationals in spearheading management changes. Hiltrop (1991) found that foreign-owned firms in Belgium managed differently from Belgian-headquartered firms. Table 7.3 confirms that these foreign-owned Belgian firms used new managerial methods much more frequently than did the Belgian-owned firms.

Table 7.3   Take-up of new management methods in Belgian foreign-owned multinational firms compared to domestically owned firms

Management practices	Variance from domestic (%)
Work and personnel allocation:	
Creativity assessment in selection process	+82
Internal promotion policy	+200
Formal manpower planning	+112
Ensuring performance:	
Performance appraisal interview	+89
Performance-related pay	+287
Job evaluation	+473
Communication:	
Corporate goals and priorities to all workers	+114
Employee shareholding scheme	+89

Source: adapted from Hiltrop (1991).

Acceptance of 'best practice' was rarely left to chance. At the end of the 1980s the American-owned multinationals Goodyear and American

Standard also required their French subsidiaries adopt practices such as 'Total Quality culture', teamwork and flexible work assignments together with a more central role for the human resource function (Prasad and Sprague 1996). Many multinationals consciously practise senior management rotation between their subsidiaries in order to encourage the spread of their preferred methods. Transmission to 'native' firms of successful experiments, however, follows quickly. A comprehensive survey of European HRM practices carried out in 1992 pointed to a general tendency in most European countries for line managers to take more responsibility for human resource issues and for most personnel departments to prioritize training and staff development (Brewster and Hegewisch 1994). Line managers throughout Europe also either had their responsibilities in the recruitment and selection of staff confirmed or increased (Dany and Torchy 1994). On performance management, in most of Europe 'there is a clear trend away from central, large group pay determination towards decentralised, variable and more individually related pay' (Filella and Hegewisch 1994: 103). In communication 'the main trend is towards an increase in communication practices with employees, particularly marked in the case of individual communication but not excluding collective channels' (Brewster *et al.* 1994:166).

Jones and Cressey (1995: 5) argue that the 'newer decentralized, employee-centred systems of quality management, human resource management and flexible production systems, imply a *common organizational basis* for European industrial firms' (our emphasis). Locke *et al.* (1995: 359) state more explicitly that many firms 'have sought to adjust to increased competition by subcontracting work to lower-wage workers and firms, downsizing, and seeking to compete on the traditional bases of cost and price competition'. Their review of world employment relations concludes that the enterprise has become the focus for managerially driven changes in work organization and pay systems to achieve greater flexibility, enhanced skill and improved worker performance. 'Everywhere', they claim with just a little exaggeration, 'unions are in decline and management is resurgent' (Locke *et al.* 1995: 365). Of course the impact of these forces varies within and between European societies, but the trend is clear. Yet though the enterprise may be the prime site within which the new managerialism operates, it also has a more general impact on politics and society, which is now analysed in the last section of this chapter.

7.4 RESURGENT MANAGERIALISM, POLITICS AND SOCIETY

The rise of the new right, already analysed in Chapter 6, and resurgent managerialism are so closely allied that it is hard to see where one ends and the other begins. The need to assert authority through the 'need' to manage, and to allow the market 'free' play is common to both. Managerialism asserts that individual leaders require freedom from constraints in order to achieve society's productive potential; only acceptance at work of this principle will both engender social cohesiveness, while delivering a material abundance of constantly improving 'quality' goods to consumers. New right thought endorses this by seeing managers as *the* critical agent determining the success or failure of society, the only group capable of creating new wealth and uprooting the old failing state and industrial bureaucracies. While they go on to articulate a more explicit attack on the state for stifling wealth production, and for undermining individual and family-based incentives and responsibilities, a Lockean suspicion of government is common to both.

However one strength of managerialism derives from its apparent independence from the new right. Its ideological influence is the stronger for appearing to be a politically neutral set of principles and practical technologies. Thus while the right may have lost ground in terms of formal political power across much of Western Europe in the late-1990s, its managerial principles and free market individualism continue to hold sway, with only limited modification by European centre-left governments. Part of this has been due to the ideological 'hegemony' of managerial politics. Increased unemployment, weaker trade unions, lower levels of worker combativity, and the state's premium on international competitiveness rather than social objectives have all enhanced managerial power. They also give managers a key bargaining lever: cooperation is demanded in return for inward investment or to prevent capital flight. Although we are cautious about deriving political behaviour from productive relations, the absorption of American managerial beliefs by many of the expanding ranks of European managers helped to shift Western Europe politics to the right in the 1980s and 1990s. This has taken several forms: the capture of many 'old' conservative and Christian democrat parties by interests prioritizing tax-cutting and managerial 'freedoms', the demise of the traditional agenda of redistribution among social democratic left parties, and the rise of a new centre, the 'third way', or managerial politics with a 'social market' face.

This appears to fit Goldthorpe's argument that 'as the service class consolidates, it will become an essentially conservative element within modern societies' as the structural consequence of 'employment relationships and associated returns from employment that are of a relatively privileged kind' (1995: 322-4). Managers' jobs are often better than the alternatives and newly posted managers often experience some increase in salary and enhanced employment benefits such as pensions and health care. While Goldthorpe may be broadly correct, his argument is too sweeping, as members of the lower reaches of managerial strata may be pulled in more than one direction. The work of many 'managers' and 'knowledge workers' may only involve a limited degree of autonomy, 'trust' and enhanced rewards (Warhurst and Thompson 1998). Goldthorpe's structuralism also plays down the fact that managerialism is a political phenomenon whose appeal was always likely to be strongest in the growing 'service class'. In these terms it has also been promoted as a 'neutral' set of discourses beyond the managerial stratum to workers as a whole, and wider still as in the interests of consumers and the 'community' as a whole. All these factors helped to broaden the appeal of managerialism beyond political ideologues and business leaders. Another element was the argument that far from undermining public provision, it was potentially a means of *improving* it. It was thus proposed as an urgent general political task or, as Michael Heseltine leading businessman and Environment Minister of the newly elected British Conservative government, declared in 1980:

> Efficient management is a key to the [national] revival... And the management ethos must run right through our national life - private and public companies, civil service, nationalized industries, local government, the National Health Service (quoted in Pollitt 1990: 3).

The argument from the right, and increasingly accepted by the new centre-left (Blair in Britain, Schroder in Germany etc.) has therefore been that managerialism's unrelenting pursuit of 'excellence' (Peters and Waterman 1982) was also suited to Europe's public sector. In making this claim it sought to exploit dissatisfaction among users of public services with the results of social democratic and professional dominance (Carpenter 1994).

Goldthorpe's analysis is finally not sufficiently sensitive to the fact that managerialism heightened tensions within the service class itself, most pronounced in the public services such as health, education and social services, where managerial leadership was being imposed on workforces used to exercising some professional autonomy, and where there was traditionally an ethos of public service. In France the resistance of many public sector professionals was exemplified both by their degree of participation in the 1995 strike wave (Jefferys 1996), and by the widespread strikes among health workers and teachers in the winter of 1999-2000. This resistance saw over 60% of all teachers strike and 200,000 teachers demonstrate on 16 March 2000 eventually bringing the downfall of the Education Minister (*Le Monde* 29 March 2000). In Britain, as Clarke and Newman (1997: 76) point out, attempts to subordinate professionals have also been combined with a range of 'cooption' strategies. These include opportunities for enhanced mobility, power and rewards involved in shifting from 'administration' to 'management', which put senior public sector managers on a par with 'reference group' colleagues in the private sector.

In many ways, however, it can be seen that the neo-liberal and managerial constituencies have operated in mutually reinforcing ways. Once 'efficient management' is seen as the priority (and who could reasonably disagree with it?), then a whole basket of policy measures were dictated, which involved either the enthusiastic or reluctant adoption of the programme associated with the new right. The first 'constraint' to be abandoned almost everywhere in Western Europe with the right turn of the 1980s was central government's major postwar macroeconomic aim of full employment of the whole population in full-time jobs. In its place was increasingly erected the neo-liberal orthodoxies of 'low inflation', 'flexible labour markets' and the 'right to manage'. Without any reference to employment and equality goals they enjoin governments to 'set macroeconomic policy such that it will both encourage growth and, in conjunction with good structural policies, make it sustainable, *i.e.* non-inflationary' (OECD 1995: 15). For the OECD's economists 'good structural policies' include cutting government expenditures through 'increasing public-sector efficiency... strengthening links between performance and pay, rationalisation of work within the public administration... charging for the provision of services, and from contracting-out the provision of services to the private sector'. In addition as a bastion of neo-liberal orthodoxy the OECD calls for reduced industrial and agricultural subsidies, and 'a fundamental reassessment of social transfers'. These include reducing the 'generosity' of pension benefits, and 'accelerating the implementation of health-care reforms' to 'reduce demand for unnecessary and low-value medical services and the facilitation of medical innovations which can improve the health status of the population at lower aggregate cost' (OECD 1995: 17).

The shift to managerialism has therefore increasingly been allied to a neo-liberal political economy, involving policy proposals which by the 1990s were imposed to a greater or lesser degree on virtually every Western European economy. Finland, Sweden and Britain established explicit inflation targets; France, Greece, Italy, Portugal and Spain announced medium-term inflation objectives. Privatization of publicly owned industrial companies, public utilities, public services and even government services has been extensively implemented both by right and centre governments.

Substantial cost saving in Europe's public sector was required by the Maastricht Treaty's criteria for monetary union. This too had the effect of initiating 'reviews' of social security and pension provision in most European countries (see Chapter 9).

The strength of the 'new managerial' consensus is to be found as much in its influence on left and centre governments. Most markedly of course in Britain, where the advocacy of the 'third way' (Blair 1998) involves a managerial approach to politics and statecraft, as well as efficiency within the state itself, and a reassertion of (undemocratic) leadership within parties, whose rank-and-file's main task becomes getting the party elected. However managerialism and neo-liberalism have also been embraced in Sweden. Thus while the value of the Swedish stock market grew by only 45% between 1970 and 1979, compared to GNP growth of 180%, between 1980 and 1986 while GNP grew by 100% the Swedish stock market grew by 550% (Jonnergard et al 1996). Equally, while the Swedish Employers Confederation (SAF) had been a pioneer of collaborative relationships with workers' organizations it radically changed its position in the 1980s and 1990s. Its 1996 manifesto, *The Business Sector's Joint Agenda,* repudiates its previous positions with a discourse derived directly from American management values. The document calls first for an open market economy which safeguards:

> private ownership, business freedom and contractual liberty... without barriers and distorting subsidies, even in such sectors as health and social care, education and other services that are now public monopolies. The public sector must be strong and stable, but limited to what cannot be run by private companies or individuals (SAF 1996b).

The manifesto goes on to call for low inflation and interest rates, a high return on capital, and in political terms paralleled in 1999 by the French employers' organization, Medef, for reductions in 'the overall tax *burden*' (emphasis added). Particular stress is placed on ensuring that 'wage costs in Sweden must not impair Swedish competitiveness', and on a flexible labour market to adapt pay rates, terms of employment, working hours and labour law to companies' and individuals' disparate conditions and priorities. The SAF also demands reduced regulation of business by government and an educational system more attuned to the needs of companies rather than the public services. Above all it suggests that 'Sweden must become a country where business and entrepreneurship as a lifestyle are encouraged and promoted'. These policies have also become the programme of the European-wide employers' organization, UNICE.

However, it is not inevitable that the whole managerial social stratum should identify with the new right. There remain significant differences in the degree of conservatism between managers from different sectors and countries. One British study of the political affiliations of managers in the 1980s has shown varying degrees of identification with the Conservatives ranging from 40% to 60% depending on their occupation, with 'service and leisure managers' at the low end and 'marketing mangers' and 'office managers' at the high, with public sector managers also more likely to lean leftwards (Heath and Savage 1995: 281-2). In France a study of the 1978 elections showed that while 79% of senior cadres in private industry voted for right-wing parties, 58% of senior cadres in the public sector and 75% of all teachers voted for the left (Boltanski 1987: 210). Political dissent by managers with the 'new managerialism' exists not only because managers' own origins and the extent of their exposure to American management education vary, but also because many depend for their livelihoods on jobs within Europe's welfare states. In addition, as growing numbers of managers are becoming subject to rationalization through application of new technology, work measurement, labour flexibility measures such as 'hot desking' and 'downsizing', their own jobs (particularly those of older non-senior managers) become less secure Even if they support aspects of the managerial and neo-liberal agendas many may wish to see them partially mitigated, a perspective which helps explain part of the loss of support for Europe's right parties in the mid-1990s.

7.5   CONCLUSION

While acknowledging that changing technological and competitive conditions are having significant effects, we have suggested in this chapter that the broadening scope of influence of American managerialism in Europe has been the result of a 'cultural shift' involving the mobilization of both direct and more hidden forms of power. The direct exercise has operated through the USA's 'global reach', involving a cast of American multinationals, finance markets, and nominally independent organizations like the OECD and the World Trade Organization (WTO). Within the pressures exerted by this environment, the propagation of managerial knowledge and education has formed an integral 'legitimating' feature of the broader neo-liberal project. Thus while suggesting that 'today's model business policies... tend to have transnational rather than solely US origins', Cressey and Jones (1995: 5-6) rightly describe the 'loose, but influential, paradigm of employee relations and work organization (that) is being spread by business education, consultants and multinational corporations'. It is, of course, true that after 40 years of intense multinational trading and business practice, some current managerial methods have lost their specific national origins. What is undoubtedly the case is that the managerial 'policies' making the biggest progress in Europe are those that have been 'validated' in the USA first, including apparently Japanese methods such as JIT and TQM.

American stock ownership in Europe's largest quoted companies is also now significant. Overseas institutional investors now hold between 20% and 30% of Europe's largest quoted companies, and the holding company form which used to predominate in both Europe and the USA, is now unknown among large American companies and only found among a minority of European firms (Mayer and Whittington 1996). The managers of 'European' firms with large overseas stockholdings are typically required to improve their performance or face sale or closure, and are often forced to reconstruct their business structure, accounting practices and culture in order to conform to American 'norms'. They then increasingly view former partners as competitors and state regulation as a hostile force. In Germany, where multiple shareholdings by the banks have been at the heart of a system prioritizing long-term performance above short-term profitability, shareholder pressure for higher immediate returns has mounted, persuading some banks and businesses to get rid of the cross-holdings that are illegal in Britain and the USA (Sparrow and Hiltrop 1994). There remain, of course, substantial and significant differences in the governance of large business corporations between European states and between them and America. As recently as 1996 Germany and Italy, who together provided 40% of EU GDP and 35% of EU population only provided 19% of its total stock market capitalization, whereas Britain with 11% of GDP and 15% of EU population held 35% of Europe's capitalization. But as Wymeersch's extensive review (1998: 1051-2) also suggests there is a clear trend:

> Company law has been subject to considerable re-regulation during the last thirty years... The more recent company law reforms have taken place along with or driven by substantial changes in the financial markets, among other things by the formation of a more integrated and more competitive European capital market. This explains why more recent changes are found not in the companies acts but in the 'securities regulation', often a scattered set of rules enacted by government, by government agencies, or even by self-regulatory bodies... (European) Securities directives have led to a considerable degree of harmonization, primarily in 'external' company life, such as the rules on capital, accounting, representation, mergers, and demergers.

Managers' behaviours and the bias of corporate re-regulation are going in the same direction. Thus between 1995 and 1996 new listings on the German stock market rose from 3% to 9%, on the French from 3% to 7%, and on the Spanish from 2% to 10% (*op. cit.* 1060).

In the last quarter of the twentieth century, American capitalism expanded its ambition beyond those of achieving trading advantages for its multinationals in an expanding international economy. As the dominant economic power of the late twentieth century it has increasingly sought to remodel the world in its image. An integral part of this has been the integration of American management values into other systems it can show are less profitable at running national, regional and local businesses. This extends not merely to the former Eastern Bloc regimes and those of the Asian-Pacific rim, but also to the distinctive European capitalist systems. The USA has traditionally operated a quite different model of capitalism to Europe involving low levels of state intervention and a unitary rather than 'pluralist' or power-sharing approach to management (Brewster and Hegewisch 1994). For much of the post-1945 period it accepted the distinctiveness of European forms of managerial capitalism which were even, as we saw in Chapter 4, promoted as a positive alternative to communism. With the emergence of a fiercely competitive global order in the 1980s, and the disappearance of the communist threat in the 1990s, these constraints no longer appear to operate. What is at stake between the two models are not just differences in managerial style, but whether market or political mechanisms will determine the regulation of economic life and social allocation of resources, critical issues to the kinds of lives that Europeans wish to lead. Democratically inspired constraints over managerial power are being weakened or removed, transforming the worlds of work and welfare, to which we turn in the next two chapters.

8. Work in Contemporary Western Europe

To what extent has the new managerialism and neo-liberal political economy analysed in the two previous chapters transformed work relations in Western Europe in the last two decades of the twentieth century? While significant change is undoubtedly occurring, we would caution against seeing this as evidence for a new work paradigm. This is partly because change from the old to the new has been highly uneven due to 'path dependent' economic development, influenced by the extent to which postwar settlements have been entrenched, and workers' and employers' relative mobilizing capacities. It could also be questioned whether emerging trends are entirely 'new' or rather, as Baglioni (1990: 33) puts it, represent 'a return to normalcy' as capital seeks to claw back the gains made by labour during the postwar boom.

Thus while much has changed there remain many continuities with earlier periods. Despite the shift from predominantly manual to white collar occupations, and the dramatic technological changes that have taken place at work, most of what passes as 'new', such as managerial dominance, notions of 'partnership', corporate loyalty, erosion of secure forms of employment, and so on, have long historical antecedents. Contemporary work trajectories are again starting to resemble aspects of pre-Second World War days when a minority experienced relative security but most Europeans in industrial and service occupations led lives dominated by employment insecurity and the arbitrary rule of the boss.

This chapter analyses the sources of this shift, first outlining the impact in the 1980s and 1990s of unemployment, the shift to service jobs and the new technology. Next we consider the growing labour market flexibility that has followed political pressure from ascendant neo-liberalism managerial values, and is associated with the spread of 'atypical' working patterns and payment methods. We then explore variations in these tendencies in different countries, concluding that significant numbers of Western European workers' employment experiences are beginning to approach levels of insecurity that have traditionally been more typical of the USA.

8.1 'STRUCTURAL' CHANGES IN WORK

Three major 'structural' developments have shaped the world of work in Western Europe in the 1980s and 1990s. First, there has been the creation of a European society in which one in five households have no paid work; second, those working are now increasingly in service sector jobs; and third, the introduction of new technologies have alongside other organizational changes qualitatively transformed much of the work that is done. These influences should not, however, be seen as entirely autonomous developments separate from the growing ascendancy of managerial power and neo-liberal political economy.

Unemployment

Table 8.1 Non-employment rate (NER) of working-age individuals and households within the EU, 1985-96 (ranked by their individual NER in 1996)

	Individual NER	All households non-employment rate		1996 Labour force status of multi-adult households %	
	1996	1996	% change 1985-96	*No adults with jobs*	*Two or more adults with jobs*
UK	31.3	21.6	1.8	10.9	65.3
Austria	32.7	16.8	0.9	9.0	62.3
Netherlands	34.6	19.7	-1.7	10.3	59.0
Germany	35.9	20.7	0.2	11.5	55.4
Portugal	37.7	13.3	0.6	7.1	64.8
Finland	39.5	27.1	n.a.	13.7	52.5
France	40.3	21.9	3.1	12.1	54.3
Luxembourg	40.9	16.4	1.7	8.8	46.9
Belgium	43.7	24.8	3.6	15.0	52.9
Greece	45.1	20.1	2.0	10.4	47.7
Ireland	45.1	20.4	-0.5	13.4	51.3
Italy	49.4	20.7	3.7	12.5	44.0
Spain	53.4	20.0	1.8	12.8	41.1

Source: OECD (1998: 9-11, 18, 22).

The emergence of high levels of EU unemployment over the past 20 years was described in Chapter 6. By 1998 using rates standardized according to International Labour Organization (ILO) guidelines it stood at an estimated average of 10.0% of all individuals in the EU15 labour force (OECD 1999b: 224). However these guidelines take no account of the so-called 'inactive', including those who have been discouraged from seeking work, reluctantly taken early retirement, or homemakers and carers who might like to work if opportunities presented. The broader *non-employment rate* sums those who are unemployed with those who are 'inactive', and highlight the presence of one in five working-age households where no adults at all bring in any income from paid employment. Data on 13 EU countries show that between 1985 and 1996 the entirely jobless household's average proportion of all working-age households increased by 1.5% to 20.3% (OECD 1998: 18). Column 3 of Table 8.1 indicates that only Ireland and the Netherlands, where unemployment fell and female participation rates rose significantly, bucked this trend.

In Greece, Ireland, Italy and Spain the tradition of the single, male breadwinner supporting other 'inactive' or 'unemployed' adults is still strong. Elsewhere when two adult members or more form a household, columns 4 and 5 of Table 8.1 suggest that a 'polarization' is taking place where multi-adult households are either largely jobless or largely in work (OECD 1998: 25).

Services Sector Employment

It is not only the rising proportion of workless households that has spread insecurity among the workforces of Western Europe. Work itself is now less secure partly because more of it takes place in services. Across the EU between 1985 and 1995 salaried employment rose by 3.1% a year in market services (up by 4.6 million jobs), by 2.3% in hotels and restaurants (up 0.9m), by 1% in each of retail and wholesale (up 1.5m) and financial services (up 0.4m), and by 0.9% in government services (up 2.2m). This total of 9.5 million new service jobs over ten years contrasts with falls in jobs in virtually every manufacturing industry, including a million jobs in textiles and clothing, and half a million in each of agriculture and fishing and fuel and power (EC 1997: 89).

There is certainly nothing inherent in a 'services-led' society to make work less stable than in an 'industry-led' one, but average service firm size does tend to be smaller. Though there are huge European service organizations like government-funded health, education, social and environmental services, as well as private sector banks and huge insurance companies, most private sector services are delivered 'closer to the consumer' by smaller firms, or through large firms whose employees are organized in smaller units than in comparable industrial companies. Small firms in the private service sector are associated with less employment stability because they both appear and disappear more quickly than larger firms. However, all sizes of private and public service sector firms are more likely to employ part-time workers for greater flexibility of operation.

By 1998 nearly 22.1% of EU15 service sector workers worked part-time compared to 6.6% of industrial workers (Eurostat 2000: 110). Part-time working has increased enormously in the 1980s and 1990s in every EU country except Denmark and Sweden (where it was already at a high level in the 1970s). Overall some 17.4% of all those working in the EU15 in 1998 worked part-time compared to just 10.8% of EC9 members in 1979 (Eurostat 1981: 33).

Table 8.2 EU part-time working by persons in employment, 1979-98, average part-time hours of employees (ranked by share of part-time employment 1998)

| | All part-time employment Eurostat definition (%) | | | Average P/T hours worked | Less than 30 hours OECD % |
	1979	1989	1998	1998	1998
Netherlands	11.2	30.9	38.7	18.4	30.0
UK	16.4	22.6	24.9	17.9	23.0
Sweden	23.6[a]	23.8[a]	23.2	23.8	13.5
Denmark	22.7	24.5	22.3	19.1	17.0
Germany	11.4	13.0	18.3	18.0	16.6
Finland	6.6[a]	7.4[a]	17.3	19.9	9.7
France	8.2	12.2	17.3	22.9	14.8
Austria	7.6[a]	8.8[a]	15.8	22.1	11.5
Ireland	5.1	8.0	16.7	19.0	15.2
Belgium	6.0	11.7	15.7	21.7	16.3
Portugal	-	3.7	11.1	19.8	9.9
Luxembourg	6.1	6.9	9.5	20.2	12.8
Spain	-	4.1	8.1	17.9	7.7
Italy	5.3	5.2	7.4	24.1	11.8
Greece	-	3.7	6.0	21.4	9.2

Note: [a] Data from Max-Planck-Institut (1998, Table 1.1.6).

Sources: Eurostat (1981, Table 20); Eurostat (1991, Table 38); Eurostat (2000, Tables 34 and 45); OECD (1999b, Table E).

Within this upward trend there were huge disparities between the tripling of part-timers in the Netherlands, the mere doubling of levels in France, Belgium, Ireland, Portugal and Spain and the smaller rises in Italy and Greece, as shown in Table 8.2. 'Part-time' status can be associated with considerable variations in hours, and is more likely to offer comparable conditions to full-time jobs when it is for more than 22 hours a week. Table 8.2 shows that part-time employees in the two countries, the Netherlands and Britain, with the highest level of part-time work in 1998 tended to work on average shorter hours while Italy and Greece, where the part-time proportion was lower, tended to work longer hours.

Part-time employees work overwhelmingly in low-skill occupations. Fifty-six per cent of all EU12 part-time employment occurred among service workers, agricultural workers, production workers and sales workers (De Grip *et al.* 1997: 54). These are also largely women. The 1998 Labour Force Survey reported only 6.1% of European men worked part-time, compared to 33% of women (Eurostat 2000: 106). Nevertheless the expansion of part-time employment over the last 20 years has both embraced certain highly-skilled professions and led male part-time working to increase at a faster rate than for women. In 1979, only the Netherlands and the four Scandinavian countries had more than one man in twenty-five working part-time, while by 1995 around 10% of Scandinavian and nearly 8% of British men worked part-time (OECD 1996).

Table 8.3   Occupational composition of salaried employment in EU manufacturing and services, 1995

	Manufacturing (%)	Services (%)
Managers, legislators and senior officials	4.8	8.3
Professionals	6.4	17.4
Technicians	10.2	15.9
Clerks	11.2	17.2
'White collar' occupations	*32.6*	*58.8*
Service workers	3.1	19.0
Craft and related trades	33.3	6.2
Plant and machine operators and assemblers	22.3	5.5
Elementary occupations	8.8	10.5
'Manual' occupations	*67.5*	*41.2*

Source: EC (1997: 87).

One further significant consequence of the continuing expansion of the service sector at the expense of industry was a fall in the proportion of manual jobs. Table 8.3 contrasts the occupational structures of manufacturing and services salaried employment in the EU in 1995. Services thus employ three white collar workers for every two manual workers, while manufacturing employs only one. Overall, while half of all EC12 civilian sector jobs were in services in 1975, this had risen to two-thirds by 1995 (OECD 1996: 191). By 1996 one third of all Europeans were 'skilled' white collar workers, working as trained professionals, technicians or managers. This represents a major shift towards 'knowledge-based' employment, often involving highly skilled work and requiring extensive training and professional qualifications. There were still considerable variations between different European countries. Around half of all Dutch workers have 'skilled' white collar jobs, compared to barely one quarter in Portugal and Italy.

The greater intensity of product competition and slow-down of European economic growth fed into the creation of huge numbers of jobs in product marketing, sales and advertising, retailing and finance, especially since credit became increasingly critical to sustaining current consumption. By 1994 the 8% working in public administration within the 12 European Union member states, a figure that had remained constant since 1975, were overtaken by the 9.1% working in financial intermediation, real estate and business activities (Eurostat 1996: 102).

If 'semi-skilled' white collar clerks are added to the 'skilled', three clusters of countries with different levels of white collar work appear: (1) the Netherlands, Britain and Belgium, where white collar workers make up around 70% of total employment; (2) Denmark, France, Ireland, Germany and Italy, where they are around 60%; and (3) a Southern European group, Spain, Portugal and Greece, where only 50% of all workers no longer do manual work (Eurostat 1997).

A 1994 French survey conducted by workplace-based doctors showed that 16% of service sector workers performed repetitive actions at high speed and the same proportion experienced strong noise pollution at work, compared with 24% and 43% of workers in manufacturing (Héran-Le Roy 1999: 265). The rise of Europe's service industries and the growing skill content of around half service sector jobs means that work has on the whole become both more interesting and significantly less physically arduous, though not necessarily less stressful mentally nor less exploitative than it was 20 years ago.

New Technologies

Yet Europe as whole has not become 'de-industrialized'. Industry still employs an average of 31.1% of European workers (Eurostat 2000: 86). Cars, television sets, shoes and microwave meals are still being produced on assembly lines in Europe, although they are being made by smaller numbers of manual workers working at higher levels of productivity than was the case in the 1970s. These higher levels of productivity have partly been achieved by increased use of microchip technologies, whose implementation has often involved greater worker surveillance, not just shifts in the capital-labour ratio. The third structural source of work insecurity, the rapid and widespread application of microchip technologies, thus applies to both service sector jobs and jobs in industry. Unlike previous technological transformations, this one was essentially completed within half the lifetime of a single generation, between 1980 and 1995. Exposed to international competition by government policy and driven by fear of competitive obsolescence, 'old' but often still viable products and technologies were thrown out, requiring workers to learn or train up in the new processes or risk years of unemployment. Microchip technologies became a means of destroying 'old' jobs and creating 'new' ones.

These changes enabled the greater centralization of strategic planning, at the same time as shifting responsibility downwards to subcontracted units and front-line workers. For some this involves the emergence of a post-Fordist 'second industrial divide', in which skill levels, wages and job satisfaction will rise due to 'flexible specialization' by workers as in northern Italy producing constantly changing small batches of goods for global markets (Piore and Sabel 1984). This prediction of more enriching task 'flexibility' is used to counter pessimistic notions that capitalist technological change inevitably promotes deskilling, alienation and the cheapening of labour associated with 'Fordist' mass production (Braverman 1974). The 'regulationist' perspective, however, also sees technological change as promoting 'neo-Fordism' into new areas (Aglietta 1979). In addition, small-scale production can sometimes lead back to sweated production (Pollert 1991) and may help to sustain domestic production and even child labour. In France, for example, between 1990 and 1993 the proportion of labour law infringements for attempts to operate a 'hidden economy' involving 'clandestine work' rose from 21% to 30% (*Infostat Justice*, January 1995). Regini (1995) has suggested that several varieties of both 'flexible' and mass production organizations can be identified in contemporary Europe. The shift to 'functional' flexibility, that is towards broader job responsibilities and fewer demarcations, is more likely to be a feature of high-wage sectors seeking to maintain competitive advantage by raising quality, while lower-wage sectors are more likely to turn to 'numerical' flexibility by deregulation of employment contracts and wage rates. These may not just be alternative strategies for whole sectors or economies; the two strategies may also coexist within the same 'flexible' firm (Atkinson 1984). This was also the case with large Japanese firms that managed a core of secure workers on a paternalist basis through total quality management (TQM) and 'quality circles', while still depending on an insecure, subcontracted periphery subjected to the rigours of just-in-time (JIT) (Elger and Smith 1994).

The wide variations between and within firms, sectors and countries in terms of 'flexibility' raise questions about its real purpose. Decisions to introduce new technology often both targeted higher productivity by raising the capital-labour ratio, and used new technology to ensure greater levels of surveillance and control over workers. One industrial example is the introduction of magnetic card systems by 70 Portuguese footwear manufacturers to check the amount of time their employees are spending on visits to the toilet (*EEIR*, August 1997). Its impact in the service sector is illustrated in this trade union official's account of work in a British telephone banking centre:

> People are telephone-based all day, sitting with a headset on all day... It becomes a de-skilled, de-humanizing element when you get a bleep down your ear that tells you there's another telephone call coming, and you have no control over the speed at which that call comes, and when that one's finished another one will replace it, and if you turn off someone at the gateway will remind you that you have turned off via your headset... The supervisor proudly displays on the screen the rota which everyone has been working, the speed of their calls, how much time signed on, how much signed off. Even their tea breaks are controlled... but of course they don't take them, because it's 'call rate' and all that, that's important (quoted in Thornley *et al.* 1997: 92).

While much manual work has been measured and directly controlled by management throughout the twentieth century, before the 1980s most 'semi-skilled' white collar work could only be very loosely measured and controlled indirectly, and until the 1990s even that was very difficult for most 'skilled' white collar work. Microchip technology now permits management to systematically measure and control the quantity and quality of most white collar, administrative and professional work. Thus greater employment insecurity and new forms of surveillance combine to enhance managerial power over broader layers of workers.

With greater pressure on workers to deliver higher productivity, more bullying and stress is being reported at work. In France a paperback by Marie-France Hirigoyen called *Bullying: Perverse Daily Violence* sold

125,000 copies in the first three months of 2000 (*Le Monde*, 31 March 2000). In Holland, often held up to have some of Europe's best working conditions, in the mid-1990s some 59% of the workforce were reported as complaining of 'stress' (*EEIR*, November 1997), and in 1999 nearly 900,000 working-age adults were no longer seeking work on medical grounds (*Le Monde*, 2 February 1999). The effect of changing living conditions across Europe have been monitored by two surveys in 1991 and 1996 conducted by the Dublin-based European Foundation for the Improvement of Living and Working Conditions (1996). It found that 29% of workers considered that work affects their health, with rising number complaining of back pain (30%) and stress (28%). While the proportion of their respondents who consider that they have a limited degree of autonomy has risen from 64% in 1991 to 72% in 1996, a clear majority of them also faced high-speed work and tight deadlines. The pace of work has also increased sharply at a time when expectations of 'quality' output have risen, posing demands for which people often feel inadequately trained. The source of work pressure is now more often likely to be 'clients', than machines, the boss, production norms or colleagues, consistent with the shift to services. Most blue collar workers in manufacturing still experience little sense of autonomy, and exposure to traditional hazards associated with manual work such as noise, stressful working environments and heavy loads remains widespread among them.

8.2   THE POLITICALLY INFLUENCED SHIFT TO FLEXIBLE WORK

The OECD, although geographically located in Paris, has been a key American influenced organization promoting the orthodox line that Europe's problems with relation to productivity and high unemployment have been primarily due to inflexible labour markets and over generous welfare states. The prime way that it has done this is by charting changes in a neo-liberal direction, subjecting these to some (often well-informed) analytical discussion, but then concluding that 'good practice' dictates travelling faster down the same road. Such monitoring is not an entirely neutral activity, however, especially when one is expected to think approvingly of the trends highlighted. Thus the 1994 OECD study of the relationship of labour standards to economic performance spoke with implicit approval about trends towards 'fewer governmental regulations', increased 'scope' for flexible contracts, less 'stringent' employment protection, and reduced 'incidence' of minimum wages. Its analysis concluded that these positive trends were the combined effects of trade liberalization and technological changes reducing demand for unskilled labour and increasing the need for flexible working.

Although the balance of evidence showed 'there is no simple, direct association between labour standards and trade performance' (OECD 1994: 161) this has not prevented the OECD in subsequent reports from advocating more 'reform of labour standards'. Thus a report a year later urged governments to take action to increase flexible working, to allow wages to reflect local market conditions, to reduce labour protection to encourage private sector employment growth, to enhance skills through training, and 'to reform unemployment and related benefit systems' to 'impinge far less on the efficient functioning of labour markets' (OECD 1995: 15). And governments responded. By 1999 a further study on the relationship between employment protection legislation (EPL) and labour market performance confirmed that 'between the late 1980s and the late 1990s a number of countries liberalized significantly their EPL' (OECD 1999b:50).

The OECD has thus offered academic respectability to a neo-liberal political discourse, enhancing its influence on European governments of whatever political hue. However, it is not just the force of argument that has pushed governments to act, albeit with varying degrees of enthusiasm and success. In the background lies the discipline of financial markets, with both the IMF and the OECD writing annual progress reports on governments' progress in implementing approved policies. In the 1990s this discipline was tightened by the EU's own monetarist requirements. The 1991 Maastricht Treaty and its stringent criteria for European Monetary Union (EMU) have, in fact, been a major cause of the unemployment that the OECD argues is required to secure 'supply-side' flexibility on the part of workers.

The pressure for increased flexibility was experienced by European workers in both internal and external labour markets. Thus the OECD (1999b:87) commented as follows on a 1998 survey of work organization practices conducted by the American Society for Training and Development.

It is interesting to note the similarity in the pattern of results for Europe and those for other countries. This suggests that there is a group of large firms in Europe which use flexible working practices to a roughly similar extent to large firms in North America.

We will now chart in more detail examples of this emerging labour market flexibility in the areas of working time and pay determination.

Working-time Flexibility

By the mid-1970s working time for most (male) workers had become a standard predictable five-day working week, with hours that had fallen considerably in their lifetimes as the working day got shorter and paid holidays got longer. By the 1990s, however, the century-long fall in average annual hours slowed to a halt everywhere in Western Europe except in Germany and the Netherlands. In Germany the last column of Table 8.4 shows that the cuts in working hours fought for by the metalworkers in 1983 eventually had a big knock-on effect on all full-time employees, although the fall in working hours also reflects the slow-down of the economy which led to significantly reduced overtime and in some cases the four-day week as German employers adopted the route of holding on to their employees rather than encouraging them to leave. In the Netherlands the main source of declining hours was the increased role played by part-time workers in the national labour force.

Table 8.4   Average working hours in selected European countries and the USA, 1970-97, ranked by increases in full-time workers' hours, 1983-93

	Average hours actually worked per person in full-time or part-time employment per year				Changes in hours of full-timers
	1970	1979	1990	1997	1983-1993
USA	1,836	1,905	1,943	1,966	+ 4.7
UK		1,821	1,773	1,731	+ 3.8
Sweden	1,641	1,451	1,480	1,552	+ 1.8[a]
France	1,962	1,813	1,668	1,656	+ 0.4
Netherlands[b]		1,591	1,433	1,397	0.0
Germany[b]	1,885	1,699	1,557	1,503	- 6.1

Notes:
a   1987-1994.
b   Average hours actually worked per employee per year.

Sources: OECD (1991: 258, 1998:156, 207).

It was not just that a shorter working week stopped being a regular part of full-time workers' expectations over most of Western Europe in the 1980s and 1990s. The rate of increase in holiday entitlements also ground to a halt. In most of Europe the average numbers of paid holidays doubled from about 15 in the mid-1950s to around 30 in the early 1980s, when American workers averaged only about 12 days. The advance of holiday entitlement has since been halted (OECD 1998).

As nationally driven collective improvements in hours became more rare, many workers sought individual ways of 'improving' their lives. A French study found that 'asocial' hours were increasingly being traded for extra earning opportunities and shorter hours (Thoemmes and de Terssac 1997). In a 1994 EC12 representative survey of 23,000 industrial firms (excepting Denmark), one third of workers were employed regularly on shifts, with 10% regularly working at night, 9% regularly working Saturdays and 5% regularly working Sundays (EC 1995: 106). When workers' working time from *all* sectors of the economy is examined, the numbers working 'atypical hours' jumps. The 1996 Labour Force Survey (Eurostat 1997: 142-7) demonstrates that in certain countries these 'atypical' hours are becoming the norm. As shown in Table 8.5 in Sweden and Finland around one in five of the labour force work shifts; more than a quarter in Britain work from home; in these three countries plus Ireland, Greece and Denmark a third or more work on Sundays; over half the labour force work evenings in Britain and Greece; and nearly two-thirds work on Saturdays in Italy, Britain and Greece. Six- and seven-day 24-hour production and opening, whose ending was pioneered by British craft trade unions in the late nineteenth century, has returned to large parts of Western Europe.

While the example of the Netherlands shows that shifts, night-work, Sunday working and long hours are not essential for economic 'success', atypical working is being introduced everywhere, although the rate of change is influenced by political difficulties in changing protective laws as well as European managers' reluctance to extend their own working span. Thus only 21% of French retailing firms surveyed in 1994 reported longer opening hours in the previous five years compared to 26% in the Netherlands and 39% in Germany (EC 1995: 131). It was only in 1998 and 2000 with new 35-hour week laws in France that flexible working patterns were finally placed centrally upon French collective bargaining agendas (Jefferys 2000). In Germany the 1994 working time law allowing exceptions to the maximum working day of eight hours to be negotiated at company level led to a considerable expansion of flexible working arrangements. A study comparing a sample of German workers in 1993 and 1995 found that the proportion regularly working overtime had risen from 39% to 45%, flexitime had risen from 22% to 26% and other forms of flexible working rose from 77% to 81% (EIRR, May 1996: 27). In 1997 Volkswagen negotiated an agreement with Western Europe's biggest trade union, IG Metall of Germany, to roster in Saturday as a normal working day (*EEIR*, July 1997).

Table 8.5   Europeans 'usually' or 'sometimes' working atypical working hours, %, 1996, ranked according to the proportion working shifts

	Shifts	Evenings	Nights	Saturdays	Sundays	From home
Sweden	23.7	40.0	12.3	38.6	34.0	13.5
Finland	18.8	50.0	20.7	44.9	32.9	13.0
Austria	17.9	28.8	17.8	46.0	27.1	17.8
Italy	17.5	29.1	12.9	61.8	21.8	7.1
UK	16.5	53.4	23.0	61.1	41.9	27.1
Belgium	15.2	33.3	14.4	49.4	24.5	16.6
Ireland	14.9	36.7	21.3	59.1	35.6	12.1
Greece	11.9	65.4	14.7	64.9	32.8	4.8
Germany	11.5	31.4	12.6	40.3	22.5	13.1
Luxembourg	10.1	27.2	12.7	42.7	22.1	9.4
Denmark	8.8	38.1	14.9	45.4	35.9	16.3
Netherlands	7.8	26.0	10.8	40.9	25.4	6.8
France	7.7	32.9	15.2	53.5	28.8	7.4
Spain	6.3	n.a.	10.0	43.3	18.9	1.0
Portugal	6.0	n.a.	n.a.	37.0	15.3	3.6

Source: Eurostat (1997: 142-7).

The trends towards greater flexibility in working time have been accompanied by the adoption of a 1993 EU Directive on Working Time, by a 1997 European Framework Agreement on Part-time Work, and by several important changes in national regulatory frameworks. The objectives are mixed. On the one hand they sanction greater temporal exploitation of fixed resources (shops or workplaces) by eroding norms of 'standard' working patterns. On the other hand, both to appease large employers who are not averse to seeing higher costs imposed on potential or actual competitors and to secure trade union political acquiescence to the extension of employment flexibility, they also contain very modest (and often avoidable) restraints on poor employment practices. The particular political context in each country, the balance of power between employers and the labour movement, and the differential forces of tradition mean that the regulatory details vary quite considerably. In France the 1998 law allows substantial dispensations from hours' regulations if agreed in workplace bargaining. In Austria the 1997 law permitting an averaging out of working time over longer periods and work on Sundays or public holidays 'if necessary in order to prevent economic disadvantages or to secure employment', requires that agreement is reached first in sectoral level collective bargaining. The Dutch 1995 law, by contrast, gives establishment-based works councils the discretion to conclude agreements that deviate from the industry standard on rest periods, breaks, night-work, Sunday working and, if the sectoral agreement does not cover it, on working time too (*EEIR*, June 1997, January 1996). This in a situation where a study of 50 collective agreements by the Federation of Dutch Trade Unions (FNV) had already found that 'the employers are inclined not to put into practice agreed arrangements on working time, overtime and time off' (*EEIR*, August 1997: 10).

These measures have permitted greater variations in the hours people work and encouraged the spread of other forms of 'atypical' work such as temporary, subcontract and telework. The definitions of temporary work vary considerably within Europe. In Germany, for example, it includes apprentices but excludes the agency workers who are included in France, Belgium and Britain (OECD 1996a). More women than men, but especially young people are employed on temporary contracts. In 1994 10% or more of the entire workforce in Germany, Sweden, Denmark, France, the Netherlands and Spain were on temporary contracts (OECD 1996: 8). Britain's relatively low use of temporary contracts arose out of the effective absence of employment protection of all 'permanent' workers during their first two years in a job, so the actual picture is both more 'temporary' than the statistics actually show, and it has also increased sharply by over a third from 5.5% in 1983 to 7.6% by 1998 (ONS 1998: 19).

Teleworkers are generally defined as dependent employees who spend half of their working time using a computer and telecommunications links with their employer's main premises. Teleworking is a growing and important trend which is highly significant for the future of work. Potentially it provides the worker with the 'freedom' to vary their own working routines. Yet it also undermines the dividing line between home and work that was created roughly one hundred years ago when concentrated industrialization largely ended the 'putting out' system. By the mid-1990s it has been estimated that 29% of Swedish employees work one or more hours from home and that 9% of the workforce in Finland and Norway telework occasionally. In Britain 6% of employers state that they use teleworkers and in the Netherlands and Germany 4% and 4.9% respectively of the workforce are believed to be teleworkers (*EEIR*, August 1996: 21, May 1996: 19). In France it has been estimated that there will may be as many as half a million teleworkers by 2005 (*EEIR*, June 1996: 19).

Working time flexibility is clearly making big strides in Western Europe. However, with high levels of the workless, part-timers, domestic (personal service) and home-workers, as well as a lengthening working week for many full-time workers, the picture is arguably less one of a 'transformation' and more one of a *restoration* of work experiences from the dawn of modern industrial capitalism.

Pay Flexibility

The OECD's support for greater 'wage flexibility' has also been widely echoed by many Western European governments and employers. The objective is to overturn the imposition after 1945 of a pay determination process whereby 'fair' wages were negotiated collectively according to *national* criteria of needs and skill, remote from the specific establishment or the demand for its goods or services, and independent of the level of individual worker effort. The removal of this constraint on employers has been opposed by unions in several countries. Thus even after the end of national-level LO-SAF bargaining in Sweden in 1991, the OECD, the IMF and the EU Commission have all specifically criticized the survival of centralized sectoral collective bargaining, and the LO, for its continuing support for low differentials and 'solidaristic' wage settlements (*EEIR*, July 1997). Support for decentralized collective bargaining has been less in Ireland, Portugal, the Netherlands, Denmark and Norway, the countries with the fastest-growing GDP per head in Europe between 1989 and 1994 (OECD 1996b). Governments and many employers in these countries and in Italy, preferred to generate or reinvigorate centralized 'social pacts' (vaguely reminiscent of corporatist incomes policies in the past) in order to cap pay rises. Teague (1998) has convincingly argued that far from advancing workers' economic interests, they benefited employers by helping to ensure that European increases in productivity did not release upward wage pressures.

Despite the presence of these 'new' pacts, the overall trend in Western Europe in the 1980s and 1990s has been towards policies that reduce the significance of national and/or sectoral collective bargaining, encourage levels of remuneration to be more closely related to the profitability of the individual company and the productivity of the individual worker, and permit the increase of wage differentials to allow greater 'rewards for skill and management responsibility' (Marsden and Silvestre 1992: 38). The 1992 Price Waterhouse Cranfield survey of senior European personnel managers found little importance attached to multi-employer bargaining in France and Britain, but a less marked decentralization trend in the Nordic countries, Ireland or the Netherlands. In Southern Europe some centralization of bargaining was detected, although it was not certain that this impacted on working conditions and employee pay. Throughout Europe, personnel managers reported a strong trend towards introducing variable pay and non-cash benefits (Filella and Hegewisch 1994). The ILO concluded that over the 10 years to 1996 company-level bargaining was on the increase in every EU country with the exception of Ireland where it was 'stable', but at what was already a high level (ILO 1997).

The roads taken towards this 'decentralization' could either be 'organized', where higher-level parties deliberately assigned some bargaining issues to a lower level, or 'disorganized', where the higher-level arrangements broke down (OECD 1994). If Britain is the clearest example of the latter, France, Italy and Germany exemplify the former. In 1982 the French Socialist Government introduced laws encouraging plant bargaining, and in 1986 the succeeding right administration introduced legislation to link workers' remuneration to profitability. By 1995 those French companies declaring profits paid out the equivalent of 4.1% of the total wage bill under one scheme and 2.7% under the second to roughly three million workers (*EEIR*, March 1997). In Italy in June 1997 the central bankers' association negotiated a framework agreement with the five state sector banking unions that led a month later to the Banca di Roma agreement that will permit negotiations on varying the working day to take place in individual bank branches (*EIRR*, July 1997, August 1997). In Germany, where the Federal Government has no direct legal responsibility for collective bargaining, employers and trade unions have been encouraged to introduce wage flexibility themselves. Thus the 1998 pay flexibility agreement for Germany's 590,000 chemical industry workers includes an option for employers to negotiate cuts in sectoral pay rates of up to 10% with company works councils 'if this leads to more job security and an increase in the competitiveness of the company' (*EEIR*, July 1997: 6).

The OECD's call to remove 'restrictions' on wages has also involved it in urging governments to think 'carefully' about the scope of minimum wage laws. These were introduced in Europe mainly during the two postwar shifts to the left, first in Luxembourg (1944) and France (1950), and then in the Netherlands (1968), Portugal (1974), Belgium (1975) and Spain (1976). Finally, laws were passed in Greece (1990) and Britain (1999) largely as payment of political debts to the trade unions. The only absolutely clear evidence on the impact of minimum wage laws states that 'those countries with higher minimum wage rates relative to the median have less earnings dispersion and a lower incidence of low pay', and that 'minimum wages narrow earnings differentials across demographic groups, particularly between the young and old and between men and women' (OECD 1998: 32). However this jars with the OECD's managerial project of removing such constraints on flexibility. So, although it admits that evidence on adverse employment effects was inconclusive, it nevertheless urged Britain's 1997 Labour Government to keep minimum rates low on employment grounds, especially for young workers, and not to commit itself to 'a rigid formula for regular adjustments of the minimum wage'

(OECD 1998: 57). This minimalist American approach to minimum wages was duly incorporated into British law.

Table 8.6 European trends in earnings dispersion among 'centralized' and 'decentralized' economies, 1979-1995

	D5/D1: upper limit of bottom decile to median earnings				
				Average five yearly change	
Centralized:	1980	1989	1994	1979-89	1989 only[a]
Austria	1.94	1.94	2.01	0.00	0.07
Norway	1.41	1.45[b]	1.32[c]	-	-
Sweden	1.30	1.35	1.34[d]	0.01	0.00
Denmark	1.41	1.39	-	-0.01	-
Finland	1.49	1.50	1.40	0.00	-0.10
Decentralized					
France	1.69	1.65	1.65	-0.01	0.00
UK	1.67	1.79	1.78	0.05	0.02
Italy	1.81	1.50	1.75[d]	-0.23	0.32
USA					
US men	1.85	2.05	2.13	0.11	0.07
US women	1.77	1.90	1.98	0.06	0.04

Notes:
a   From 1989 to 1995 for the UK and USA; from 1989 to 1993 for Italy and Sweden; and from 1989 to 1994 for the other countries.
b.   1987.
c.   1991.
d.   1993.

Sources: OECD (1997: 68, 1996a: 6).

The effects of the adoption by governments and employers of these 'new' flexible pay policies often take a long time to make themselves felt, and their impact depends on the underlying political economy. The OECD has acknowledged that 'more centralized/coordinated economies have significantly less earnings inequality compared with more decentralized/uncoordinated ones' and that growing inequality in parts of Western Europe, as measured by 'the rise in earnings dispersion... would appear to have been more closely associated with substantial labour and product market reform' (OECD 1997: 64, 60). This conclusion appears to confirm suspicions that the OECD's drive to flexibility involves promotion of greater inequality. Table 8.6 shows that with the exception of Austria, the European economies defined by Calmfors and Driffill (1988) as 'centralized' began the 1980s with significantly lower rates of inequality than the 'decentralized' ones, and all navigated the years since then without becoming significantly more unequal.

Nevertheless two out of the three 'decentralized' European economies for which there is evidence experienced a significant increase of inequality in either or both the 1980s and the 1990s. Only France in the bottom group of Table 8.6, with a centre-left president throughout the period covered and still expanding public sector employment, saw little change in the ratio of the median to the start of the lowest decile of earnings. In the USA, the leading exponent of flexible labour markets, by contrast, those with incomes one tenth of the way up the distribution of all earners saw the gap between their earnings and those half way up widen so that by 1994 these low-paid workers were working for less than half (men) and around half (women) of median earnings.

8.3 VARIATIONS IN WORKING PATTERNS AND WORKER MOBILIZATION ACROSS EUROPE

The removal or relaxation of constraints on employers to observe national standards or collective agreements, decentralization of bargaining systems and the individualization of pay, as well as working-time flexibility all tend to worry and weaken the individual employee. As a result, work in contemporary Western Europe is becoming a more direct market relationship between the individual worker and their employer, in which the manager increasingly has the upper hand. This claim appears to contradict fashionable human resource management theory, that the flexibility and 'flatter' hierarchies associated with the new managerialism empower individuals and workgroups who were held back by the 'rigid' hierarchies and restrictive labour markets that grew up in the post-1945 period. These are now, according to Robert Reich (1993), giving way to decentralized workplaces in which 'a web of enterprise' of horizontal coordination between 'networks' is becoming the norm in the shift from production of things to manipulation of information. Such overgeneralized 'transformation of work' paradigms are disputed by Warhurst and Thompson (1998) who point to the continuation of traditional hierarchies, and considerable diversity in the impact of change. They argue that the new forms of management, *complement* rather than replace traditional forms of control. This would certainly seem to be consistent with the evidence cited above in section 8.1 from the two European wide surveys on working conditions that a measure of increased autonomy for some workers has been associated with increased intensification of work conditions.

Beyond this it is clear that the partial decay of collective regulation of the employment contracts has empowered those 'knowledge workers' with skills in short supply, or those who have seized on opportunities presented by the expansion of middle ranking managerial positions. However for the majority, the combined effect of these changes has been more to 'empower' employers rather than workers, whether it be those in the core who must commit more of themselves to the organization, or those on the insecure periphery who must struggle harder to survive. It is also the cast that the trend towards employer empowerment varies considerably between different Western European countries, and between different sectors and occupations within countries. A great deal depends upon the extent to which workers' organizations can collectively attenuate the marked shift to enhanced employer and managerial power, their capacities to do so depending on a country's ideological traditions and institutional contexts.

Evidence of an effective mobilizing capacity that can continue to exert significant restraints upon managerial discretion should not be derived only from a country's strike rate, but also from its trade union density and collective bargaining coverage, and the broader survival of a *tripartite* corporatist culture and associated state interventionist traditions. The latter requires emphasis, as what is perceived as 'deregulation' in fact often involves a reinforcement of *bipartite* regulation between capital and the state, with labour increasingly excluded (as in Thatcher's Britain) or treated as at most a junior partner (as in Blair's Britain). Thus in some ways the relationships between capital and the state become more enmeshed in the age of neo-liberalism, as labour's influence lessons (Shutt 1998). Nevertheless, the extent to which this has happened has been affected by the relative national strength of labour movements. In addition, while we have argued that European integration has increasingly been driven by the needs of multinationals, workers' organizations have also secured some recognition of their distinct interests as 'social partners' within the EU federal state.

What evidence is there of changes affecting workers' organizations? Table 8.7 brings together some of the factors affecting workers' mobilizing capacity in Western Europe by the mid-1990s. The first column shows the extent to which within each economy employment in finance, insurance, real estate, business, community, social and personal services sector have outgrown the share of manufacturing employment since 1979. While we must remember that the white collar share of manufacturing sector employment is also rising, this index provides a useful proxy for the pressure to change faced by the employers in the different countries, and allows us to distinguish between workers' movements that have faced a greater (Portugal, UK, Finland) or lesser (Italy, France, Netherlands) structural challenge.

Table 8.7 Economic and institutional change, strikes and strike rates, 1979-1995

	Rate (%) of sectoral change 1979-96	Fall (%) in trade union density 1980-94	Change (%) in collective bargaining 1980-94	Strikes per 1,000 workers. 1990-93	Change (%) in strike rate 1980/4 to 1990/3
Italy	5.4[a]	10	-3	130	-75
France	5.4[d]	9	10	16	-41
Netherlands	5.6	9	5	6	10
Denmark	5.8	0	0	17	-28
Belgium	6.4[b]	2	0	4	-100
Germany	7.6[c]	7	1	11	14
Sweden	7.9	+11	3	8	-83
Ireland	8.5	13[f]	-	14	-57
Austria	9.8[a]	12	0	9	224
Spain	9.8	+10	2	266	2
Portugal	10.6[e]	29	1	29	-70
UK	10.8	16	-23	12	-81
Finland	10.9	+11	0	61	-67

Notes:
a   1979-1994.
b   1979-1992.
c   1980-1995.
d   1979-1989.
e   1980-1996.
f   1985-1995 in ILO (1997: 240).

Sources: Column 1: Max-Planck-Institut (1998, Tables 1.1.2.6, 1.1.2.11 and 1.1.2.12, Columns 2 and 3); OECD (1997: 71, Columns 4 and 5): Aligisakis (1997, Table 2).

In countries which faced less structural change, despite declines in trade union density, the major employers' associations chose to leave multi-employer collective bargaining pretty much in place. Strikes ebbed in Italy and France with the growth in unemployment, the decline in inflation and the decline of their communist parties, but the overall pattern of industrial relations remained generally unchanged. Strike action continued to be used essentially as a means of exercising political pressure on the state to take action on behalf of the aggrieved workers (Jefferys 1996), and huge protest strikes and demonstrations took place in Italy in 1994 and France in 1995 against proposals to introduce pension reforms. In 1997 the two new governments elected in the aftermath of these protests kept the reforms in place but 'paid' their political dues to the unions by introducing measures promising a 35-hour week from January 2000 (France) and January 2001 (Italy) - although this Italian promise appears unlikely to materialize. In both countries the employers temporarily withdrew from tripartite negotiations in protest, but their governments continue to 'modernize' labour markets by trying to exchange the shorter working week for greater flexibility. In Italy a centre-left coalition government enacted the Treu employment laws of June 1997 to legalize temporary work through employment agencies, promote part-time work and reform vocational training and apprenticeships (*EEIR*, July 1997). Overall, despite the Italian government beginning to consider limitations on the right to strike in the public services (*EEIR*, November 1997), and the February 1998 ruling by the French Supreme Court that rotating strikes in the public services were illegal (*EEIR*, March 1998), workers' mobilizing capacity, both through strikes and elections, remained relatively extensive.

In the Netherlands and Belgium below-average rates of structural change facilitated a more relaxed approach by employers. Trade union density fell further in the Netherlands than in Belgium but there was virtually no change in collective bargaining coverage. Growing numbers of employers were, however, accused of breaking the agreements reached, who in the Netherlands also opted massively for part-time working, and Belgium chose other forms of flexible working. The frequent participation of socialist parties in coalition governments in both countries over the last 20 years acted as a significant brake on radical labour reform, as for example with the 1995 proposal to abolish the Dutch government's power to declare collective agreements binding across a whole sector (*EEIR*, March 1995). Visser (1996b: 260) has suggested that:

> Belgian and Dutch corporatism has a definite tripartite nature, which is probably more a testimony of weakness, instability or one-sidedness (biased towards capital in the Netherlands and towards labour in Belgium) than anything else.

Nevertheless, while workers may not have great mobilizing capacity, their organizations remain propped up by the state which, in the absence of any acute crisis, prefers the status quo to radical change.

In Scandinavia employers had long been accustomed to working within the constraints imposed under social democratic governments. In these economies the superstructure of industrial relations also remained stable. Where structural change was slow (Denmark) there was little movement in either trade union density or the collective bargaining structure; but where it was faster (Sweden, Finland) the employers adopted a radical stance and more workers joined the trade unions for the greater protection and access to unemployment benefits they offered. By 1994 trade union density was estimated at 91% in Sweden, 81% in Finland and 76% in Denmark (OECD 1997: 71). As unemployment rose the strike rate fell, and from a significantly higher level in Finland, the only Scandinavian country to have retained an effective communist party during the postwar period. While at the margins working conditions are deteriorating, a high level of trade union coordination and effective political intervention has enabled manual and white collar workers to brake the employers' bid to see a rapid shift in their favour in the balance of power.

In Germany and Austria well-coordinated sectoral centralized bargaining has been so strongly institutionalized that despite quite rapid structural changes in Austria and the high cost of Germany reunification, trade union density in the two countries only slipped a little, and there was virtually no change in collective bargaining coverage. The lengthy periods of Christian democratic government in Germany and of social democratic and coalition government in Austria meant that despite the gathering pressures the formal structures remained intact with the continuation of the practice of extending the application of collective agreements to virtually all establishments within the relevant sector. Beneath these levels, and evidenced partially by the increase in the low level of strike frequency in both countries during the 1980s, there was growing company-level bargaining and wage drift (Traxler 1998: 216). Workers are slowly losing broad labour market strength and local enterprise bargaining is becoming more important. All the same, the strength of their economies in the contexts of rigorous legal frameworks and the mobilizing capacity of German metalworkers, have continued to severely constrain employers (OECD 1997).

Pressures on the employers to implement radical changes in the governance of work have been considerably greater in Portugal and Spain. In both Iberian countries trade union density fell precipitately after the heady period of democratic revolution and trade union-friendly laws of the mid-1970s. By 1994 trade union density stood at 32% in Portugal and 19% in Spain (OECD 1997: 71). But formal collective bargaining coverage changed little. The centralized state-directed industrial relations systems of the dictatorship periods continued to largely structure work relations, despite labour law reform in the 1990s, after which Spain saw a more than doubling between 1983 and 1994 of the proportion of the labour force on 'temporary' contracts. In part, as in Italy, France and Greece, this relative lack of change also reflects the influence of a significant-sized communist and ex-communist party presence on the national political scene, and in the trade union movements.

In both Ireland and Britain, by contrast, a high rate of structural change occurred in the absence of either legal support for union recognition or for collective bargaining, or of strong left parties capable of influencing the national political agenda. A debate is taking place about the impact in Ireland of the rapid inward investment by non-union American hi-tech companies on its trade union density. Some Irish data suggests a fall from the 1970s was followed by a recovery in the 1990s to 45% in 1993 (*EEIR*, April 1998: 22). In Britain union density has declined continuously reaching 29% in 1998 when the TUC suggested that the fall had halted or even been reversed. In both countries collective bargaining coverage and strikes also declined considerably. Under the 'exclusive' British system, where agreements are not extended to those who do not participate in the negotiations, collective bargaining coverage has been withdrawn from one in five workers since 1980. Outside its stronghold in the public sector, collective bargaining largely occurs (as in the USA) at company or individual plant level, a state of affairs 'that sets a strong incentive for employers in the organized segment (which is burdened with higher labour costs) to adopt an anti-union policy' (Traxler 1998: 216). This was facilitated by actions of British Conservative Governments from 1979-97 who introduced highly restrictive labour laws weakening trade union organization and the ability to wage effective strikes. The New Labour Government elected in 1997 introduced weak, employer-friendly recognition procedures in 2000, but did not repeal any of the plethora of anti-union laws introduced between 1980 and 1993.

The result of the interplay of all these factors is that while European workers' organizations are largely on the defensive at the close of the twentieth century, they have by no means been routed. Even in Britain, where the offensive against them was the most sustained, the resilience of shop floor organization points to a potential strength that could even prove as effective as more legally reliant trade union movements in some other parts of Europe (Traxler 1998). There has been some slippage in mobilizing capacity, particularly at the workplace level where managerial behaviours have changed most. Thus the unions still take their seats at a 'bargaining' table with the employers (and more rarely the government), but when they do so it is evident that they have considerably less power than before. The unions are less able to constrain the employers to act in the interests of their members. In the absence of effective sectoral collective bargaining, other forms of democratic employee representation in Europe such as works' councils appear at present to be rather weak instruments of employee countervailing-power (Beaupain *et al*.1999).

Nevertheless, the European Works Council directive is one example of how the EU's attempt to secure trade union commitment to the project of a (strong) Single Market and (weaker) political integration has secured a series of generally weak directives from the European Commission on 'social policy'. These will be discussed in more detail when prospects for a 'social Europe' to counter current neo-liberal tendencies are assessed in the next chapter. Here it is sufficient to observe that the much heralded Social Chapter of the 1991 Maastricht Treaty, from which the Thatcher government opted out, but to which the Labour Government subscribed from 1997, is not wholly antithetical to a modified neo-liberal political economy. The restraints on employer behaviour could be said to oblige employers to compete on the basis of certain minimum employment standards, and in many arenas such as part-timers' rights and employee representation regulations were only introduced at the 'lowest common denominator' threshold. Thus Wedderburn (1995) suggests that while the Social Chapter is not hostile to union recognition and collective bargaining, neither does it seek actively to promote it. With the Green Paper *Partnership for a new Organization of Work*, and the subsequent Title on Employment agreed at the 1997 Luxembourg Intergovernmental Conference, work flexibility is now official EU policy, albeit in terms which echo the positive spin of the post-Fordists and do not repudiate union rights (Leat 1998). So although the Chapter and other EU measures are now being used as an organizing basis for trade union action at national and international levels, they certainly do not have the significance of the national settlements of the late 1940s or the 1970s, which substantially shifted the power balance from European employers to Europe's workers.

8.4   CONCLUSION: TOWARDS A NEO-LIBERAL MODEL?

The continued variety of patterns of work relations across European societies confirms the fact that general trends are 'always refracted in nationally peculiar ways' (Lane 1995: 2-3). Thus while the influence of competitive and political pressures linked to 'globalization' and 'Europeanization' are real enough, they have relatively open outcomes whose local impact is shaped by political and cultural choices. Nevertheless there are three main conclusions to be drawn about the work trajectories that are impacting upon most Western Europeans today.

The first is that work experiences in different countries are gradually becoming less 'nationally peculiar': households throughout Europe are more likely now to experience unemployment, and to have members doing comparable sorts of white collar or service work under similarly pressured conditions. Much work has changed, in the sense that what many Western Europeans do today as 'professionals', social workers, computer programmers and technicians, and marketing consultants differs markedly from forms of work undertaken by previous generations, although there is also substantial continuity in the types of service, clerical and industrial jobs being undertaken. The second conclusion is that the forms of work relationships and regulation established during the 'exceptional' years of 1945-75 are under considerable pressure. While there has not yet been a 'fundamental' shift away from them, this is no cause for complacency as the threats are real enough (Leat 1998). The third conclusion is that the emerging model involves a gradual and variable, but definite shift towards American patterns of work relationships and labour relations. While Milkman (1998) suggests that these can sometimes involve genuine devolvement of power and freely given worker commitment, more usually management strategy follows what she calls the three-lane 'low road' in relation to trust, skills and wages. So far in Europe, Britain has been the country which has most pursued this fast track to this future. Other countries, notably Germany and Scandinavia, and official EU discourse itself have sought to combine flexibility with a high-skill strategy, with substantial emphasis on training. However, the danger is that global economic pressures can generate a 'race to the bottom' that is hard to resist (Brecher and Costello 1994).

For most of this century working conditions have changed dramatically and largely for the better. This process, combined with state welfare measures, has delivered substantial benefits to Europe's citizens. European workers are today less likely to be regarded as a 'servant' at work, and outside they more likely to enjoy decent living standards, access to forms of social provision, and an enhanced life expectancy. These gains have not been spread across the few but, despite persistent inequalities, to the many. While the rapid changes to work have involved painful transition costs, they have had beneficial or at least potentially positive, features. Much arduous and physically dangerous work, mining for example, has been largely eliminated (but also the communities associated with it), and automation has eliminated some forms of arduous alienated labour. We can produce more of quality with less effort. The shift to 'flexible' production can have benefits for workers even if these are exaggerated by those who fail sufficiently to acknowledge that they are embedded within a capitalist dynamic. In this context Danford's (1998) study of lean production among Japanese firms in South Wales shows they are organized essentially to enhance labour utilization through intense forms of 'management by detail' and cannot be claimed to have broken with Taylorism. Similarly, the growth of part-time work has enabled more women to combine work with household and caring responsibilities, and could be the basis for a more egalitarian 'social and gender contract' around work and domestic responsibilities. Thus in Holland unions have campaigned for women-friendly 'flexicurity' (Drew and Emerek 1998; O'Reilly and Spee 1998).

Our argument is that it is not necessary to dam up the flow of technical and social change, but rather to seek to divert its path in a more equitable direction. This is necessary because at the end of twentieth century there were clear signs of a reappearance of increasing disparity in work trajectories, often involving a return to forms common at that century's start. A substantial proportion of managers and professional workers appear to continue to inhabit a world of stable, secure and well-paid employment, sometimes with considerable degrees of autonomy, although often accompanied by pressure to be more productive and to work longer hours. However increasing numbers of both manual and non-manual workers are experiencing more insecure and subordinated work, and in addition a substantial and a highly vulnerable minority are experiencing extreme forms of poverty and 'social exclusion'. The 'resetting' process has not yet put the 1945 defeat of authoritarian capitalism decidedly into reverse gear. The demands of Europeans for decent working lives are too deeply embedded in expectations, in law, in trade unions and political parties, and in pluralist managerial ideology to permit any immediate reconversion to total marketization. Yet there is no mistaking which directions European employers and governments are moving, albeit within the limits set by workers' variable mobilizing capacities.

This piecemeal but continuous process is undermining the previously established West European norm of actual and 'psychological' job security associated with the 30 years before 1980, so that in 1979 labour turnover in Europe averaged only half that of the USA (OECD 1991). However by 1996 an unweighted average of 67% of EU15 workers reported feeling other than that their jobs were 'very secure', a proportion remarkably close to the 72% of American workers who answered the same question in a 1989 study (OECD 1997: 132). These feelings of greater European job insecurity flowed from a whole series of factors. There was comparatively little change in average job tenure, although in the early 1990s the less-educated and less-skilled were staying less long in their jobs than in the early 1980s (OECD 1997). However even if, on average, people tend to stay as long as they used to in their jobs, many now do so increasingly because high unemployment means they *have* to, not because they *want* to, while those staying shorter times with their firms are more likely to have left 'involuntarily' than in the 1970s. Insecurity thus depends on the degree of collective protection in work and also, of course, on the extent of social protection available to workers outside the labour market. As the OECD succinctly put it:

> Insecurity is significantly lower in countries where the unemployment benefit replacement rate is higher, where there is a higher level of collective bargaining coverage, and in countries where collective bargaining is more centralized (OECD 1997: 150).

This chapter has shown how employment 'security' has been eroded and work relations have changed since the 1970s. The next will therefore examine closely how well the postwar guarantees of wider 'social security' through state welfare have fared.

9. Welfare in Contemporary Western Europe

As Western Europe's managerial and work traditions began to swing back towards more neo-liberal positions, increasing calls have been made by the OECD and within the EU itself to bring welfare 'into line'. Welfare states remain large employers whose services 'distort' the workings of the market, with traditions of public service, trade union membership, and joint regulation of working conditions by managers and employees that are still broadly intact. Thus one aspect of the emerging welfare reform agenda is therefore to lower taxation by capping and cutting back public provision, expanding the private sector, and placing more responsibility on individuals. Yet just as important are attempts to change how welfare states operate to ensure that they are indistinguishable from other undertakings, whereas previously they set 'good examples' for the private sector to follow. Alongside this has been an attempt to shift them from a Keynesian priority to ensure high levels of demand in the economy, to one more consistent with neo-liberal emphasis upon the supply of suitably trained and motivated labour, prepared to accept work at the prevailing rates. Within Europe this has not yet eroded principles of 'citizenship' entitlements, but it has made them more conditional, with added emphasis on responsibilities.

By the end of 1970s state-delivered consumption-oriented welfare in much of Western Europe provided a degree of 'decommodification', in the sense of enabling unemployed or disabled people, single parents and pensioners to maintain a standard of living independently of the pressures of the labour market (Esping-Anderson 1990). Neo-liberal critiques saw this as undermining work incentives. and thus argued for a shift to policy regimes that actively reintegrate people into the labour market through various forms of help, incentives and penalties. In other words, in the shift to a 'supply-side' society, welfare should help to 'recommodify' labour. In addition, there were moves to radically restructure relations between the state, welfare workers and welfare's various publics according to the precepts of American managerialism, if they could not be fully privatized. A 'new public management', dominant in Britain and emerging elsewhere in Western Europe, is intent on 're-engineering' traditional relations in welfare based on citizenship, need, and professionalism, into just another service industry, where people relate as managers, producers and consumers, on the *a priori* assumption that contractual market relations provide better value for money, enhanced quality and greater consumer sensitivity (Clarke and Newman 1997).

Of course, this has been an incremental process with variable impact across Europe. Even where it has been carried furthest, in Britain, by the time of the election of the Labour Government in 1997, while social housing provision had been decimated, social security, education, health and social services remained largely intact if seriously underfunded (Lowe 1999). Nor has retrenchment been the only story, as the trend in some Southern European countries in the 1980s with the return of parliamentary democracy has until recently been towards significant welfare state expansion. Even in the developed 'North' there have been extensions of welfare in the 1990s, for example of health care in France and long-term care for older people in Germany and Scandinavia. The 'classic' welfare state undoubtedly has powerful allies. Because of the wide coverage of European welfare states, in contrast to the USA, these are first and foremost the publics who depend on its services. In addition, public health and welfare workers are a significant part of national workforces, who have maintained impressive levels of collective organization. While the new right have sought to heighten tensions between publics and providers, alliances between the two have often been successfully mobilized, and helped to check their advance. It is also the case that European governments, Britain apart, have also valued the contribution that welfare has made to social stability and cohesion, and as a contribution rather than a hindrance to international competitiveness. Thus they have moved only reluctantly down the road to retrenchment and restructuring under the impact of the constraints of recession and of monetary union in the 1990s.

Nevertheless incremental change has a significant impact over time, and welfare reform has become one of the central European political questions at the end of the twentieth century. The challenges of intensified international competition, increased unemployment (charted in previous chapters), growing numbers of older people, decay of patriarchal family forms and breadwinner models, and 'advances' in medical technology all certainly put pressures on the 'universalistic' welfare state established in the postwar period. However, as the conclusion to the chapter will argue, these need not necessarily require in a fundamental change in direction. Before that, the main trends in European welfare policy and mounting pressures upon it will be analysed, and the responses of national governments and the EU discussed.

9.1   WELFARE TRENDS AND MODELS

From the 1960s to the mid-1990s Western Europe social expenditure expanded at a significantly faster rate than in the rest of the developed world, and while it has been checked in the 1990s, it continues to grow, as illustrated by the OECD data presented in Figure 9.1. This compares expenditure on social security benefits paid for sickness, old age, family allowances, social assistance and unfunded employee welfare as a percentage of gross domestic product (GDP).

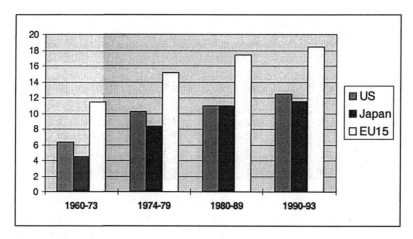

Source: OECD (1996d: 71).

Figure 9.1   Social security transfers as a % of GDP, Western Europe compared to Japan and the USA.

Thus throughout the 30 year period European social security expenditures contrast strikingly with more restrictive approaches in Japan and the USA. Nevertheless there are significant variations between European countries, which are shown in Table 9.1.

Certain trends and clusters appear. Overall both social security transfers and government expenditures rose significantly from the mid-1970s to the mid-1980s, but while the former on average continued to rise, the latter then stabilized. Above average expenditures across all three columns for the mid-1990s were recorded only by the Scandinavian countries and France, while below average expenditures were recorded by governments in the Southern and more agriculturally based societies such as Greece, Spain and Portugal. There are some major differences in trends, especially on the levels of social security transfers. Thus in the Scandinavian regimes there were large increases in transfers between 1984 and 1994, while levels fell in Ireland, Germany (very slightly), Belgium and the Netherlands. There were also considerable variations around the EU15 average of 19.3% of GDP, from a low of 12% in Portugal to a high of over 25% in the Netherlands.

Table 9.1   European social security transfers, government employment and final consumption as a % of GDP, 1974-97 (ranked by social security transfers in 1994)

	Social security transfers (% of GDP)			Government expenditures on labour market programmes (% of GDP)			Government final consumption (% of GDP)		
	1974	1984	1994	1991	1994	1996-1997	1974	1984	1994
Austria	15.5	20.0	21.8	1.4	1.9	1.7	15.8	18.6	18.8
Belgium	18.0	25.6	24.2	4.0	4.2	4.3	14.7	17.1	15.0
Denmark	12.0	17.0	22.0	6.2	7.0	5.8	23.4	25.9	25.5
Finland	7.6	14.0	25.1	3.6	6.4	4.8	15.2	19.3	22.4
France	15.5	21.8	23.3	2.8	3.2	3.1	15.4	19.6	19.6
Germany	14.6	16.5	16.1	3.1	3.9	3.8	19.8	20.5	19.6
Greece	7.1	14.0	17.0	1.0	0.7	0.7	10.0	14.1	14.0
Ireland	11.4	16.1	15.4	4.7	4.5	4.1	16.5	17.9	16.0
Italy	13.7	16.7	19.5	1.6	2.5	2.0	13.8	16.3	17.1
Netherlands	20.7	27.8	25.5	3.6	4.7	4.9	15.7	16.2	14.2
Portugal	5.3	10.9	12.4	1.2	1.8	2.0	13.1	14.0	17.2
Spain	9.5	16.0	18.2	3.6	3.7	2.4	9.9	14.3	16.9
Sweden	14.3	17.5	24.9	4.1	5.7	4.3	23.5	28.0	27.3
UK	9.2	13.5	15.4	2.0	2.2	1.5	20.5	21.9	21.6
EU15	*13.3*	*17.7*	*19.3*	-	-	-	*16.8*	*19.1*	*19.0*

Sources: OECD (1996d, 1997, 1998, 1999a).

Expenditure on unemployment benefits and other labour market measures, although the most controversial of welfare payments because of their supposed effects on work incentives, in fact represent a low and declining share of European GDP according to EU figures, with only Greece spending a lower proportion than Britain. Old age pensions represent by far the largest element in social protection expenditure in every European society, making up 67% and 64% respectively in Greece and Italy in 1994 compared to an EU12 average of 44% (*Europ News*, 2, 1997). After pensions, the next highest area of expenditure is health care which in 1992 averaged 37% of the total in the EU12, while family and maternity benefits represented around 8% of total social protection expenditure (Eurostat 1996: 135).

The solidity of welfare expenditure overall helps to put notions of a 'crisis' in European welfare states in context: they have neither 'run away out of control', nor been massively cut back. Expenditure cuts were demanded by ideological neo-liberals in pursuit of the minimalist state, but were also predicted by some Marxists (for example, O'Connor 1973). Of course, the rising levels of welfare expenditures do not give the full picture because they need to be plotted against increasing demands, and do not show the significant restructuring of provisions that has taken place. However Offe ironically points out:

> The embarrassing secret of the welfare state is that, while its impact upon capitalist accumulation may well become destructive... its abolition would be plainly disruptive... The contradiction is that while capitalism cannot coexist *with*, neither can it exist *without*, the welfare state (Offe 1984: 152-3).

Thus although it may be premature to assume the 'irreversibility' of the welfare state in the longer term due to current 'globalizing' pressures (Rhodes 1996), welfare is also difficult to cut back because it is legally and institutionally entrenched, and on the whole politically popular.

European Attitudes to Welfare

While political elites may be losing confidence in welfare states, a *Eurobarometer* review of opinion on welfare spending in 1996 found that only a small minority of people (12%) in the EU15 thought that large benefit cuts were necessary to make Europe competitive in world markets. A significant minority (26 %) did believe small cuts were necessary, but 51% thought that it was possible to maintain economic competitiveness without cutting back on benefits. Support for maintaining benefit systems was highest in Greece, Finland and France, and only in Austria did support for maintaining benefits systems fall below 40%. The same survey found that there was strong European-wide support (79%) for taking action to combat unemployment (Eurobarometer 1998). There is also strong European support for the principle of 'public services'. For example in 1996 no less than 80% and as many as 97% of Europeans polled considered health services to be a public service. On average 87% of EU15 citizens considered education to be a public service, and there was nearly as much support for regarding transport, postal services, water and electricity similarly. Another study of selected Scandinavian and Bismarckian countries also found that European attitudes on redistribution issues contrasted sharply with those in the USA, as shown in Table 9.2.

Table 9.2   European and American attitudes to redistribution, 1992

	Austria	Germany	Norway	Sweden	USA
Government has a responsibility to narrow the gap between high and low incomes	69.5	65.5	60.0	53.7	38.3
Government should provide a job for all who want one	72.1	66.3	78.3	74.1	47.1
Government should provide everyone with a guaranteed basic income	51.2	58.1	78.4	45.5	34.2

Source: Reproduced by permission of Oxford University Press from Svallfors, S. (1997: 288), 'Worlds of welfare and attitudes to redistribution: a comparison of eight western nations', *European Sociological Review*, 13 (3), 283-304.

However while a majority of Europeans believe public services improve the quality of life (57%) and provide a modern quality service (55%), a significant minority are critical of their performance. Citizens in Southern European countries are especially likely to be critical of their public services, particularly concerning the extent to which they ensure equality between users (Eurobarometer 1997). A 1990 international sociological survey pointed to stronger support for health care and pensions as 'social rights of citizenship' than for housing and unemployment benefits (Jowell *et al.* 1993: 84). The low levels of support for state housing intervention probably results from it having always been primarily a marketed 'commodity', while the less solid support for unemployment benefits suggests that neo-liberal ideology about their supposed effects on work incentives may be making inroads. Housing and unemployment benefit are also only provided to *sections* of the population, by contrast with health care and pensions, where state support tends to be *universal* in scope.

At the end of the 1990s, therefore, European support for welfare remained strong, but in certain key respects was becoming conditional. There are criticisms of the efficiency of public services, and ambivalent support for welfare for marginalized or 'socially excluded' groups. This range of views indicates that although there is little support for the wholesale dismantling of state welfare, potential constituencies do exist for the restructuring of public services and 'reform' of benefits systems.

Types of Welfare Regime

Table 9.3   European welfare state regimes following Leibfried (1993)

	Scandinavian	Bismarckian	Anglo-Saxon	Latin Rim
Type of welfare regime	Modern	Institutional	Residual	Rudimentary
Characteristics and priorities	Full employment, welfare state as employer, compensate through benefits if necessary	Economic growth, compensate first and employ if necessary as last resort	Economic growth, enforce labour discipline, compensate as last resort	Catching up, welfare state as partially institutionalized future 'promise'
Rights to:	Work	Social security	Income transfers	Work and welfare 'proclaimed'
Backed up by:	Institutionalized concept of Social Citizenship	Institutionalized concept of Social Citizenship	No such back up	Implemented only partially

Source: adapted from Leibfreid (1993: 142).

The variations in spending between capitalist countries, and among European countries themselves as identified in Table 9.1, show that differences in culture and political mobilization shape levels of welfare spending and also patterns of provision. The Scandinavian and Bismarckian countries tend to spend more on both social security and on labour market measures, while the 'Latin rim' countries and Britain tend to spend less, although Britain still has a high level of government direct expenditure on services such as health and education. In Chapter 5 Esping-Anderson's (1990) 'three worlds of welfare' model was seen as helpful in showing how national variations in social security were linked to the strength of social democracy in cementing alliances between manual and salaried groups, and in resisting religious mobilization on the right. However, equating social security with welfare states problematically excludes health care and housing and other forms of social provision, gender and 'race' are not dealt with adequately, and 'regime' theory is better at explaining welfare development than retrenchment (Sykes 1998). Another major problem is the failure to account for the development of welfare in leftist Southern European regimes, which Leibfried has sought to remedy as shown in Table 9.3.

This typology broadens Esping-Anderson's, by linking social security to the extent to which regimes prioritize full employment, and the means by which they do so. It also suggests how Scandinavian and Franco-German systems stand apart from the British Anglo-Saxon regime in terms of guarantees to citizenship rights. This suggests also that the British turn to neo-liberalism in the 1980s built on, rather than departed from its institutional traditions. Leibfried also shows how in the 'Latin Rim' countries, however, left aspirations exceeded achievements, and previous cultural features such as a strong emphasis on the roles of Church and family in welfare have not been completely transformed.

Like other typologies Leibfried's can also be faulted: there are considerable differences between Spain, Portugal and Greece, while France and Italy can be considered 'hybrids' with Southern features, and Ireland is in some senses 'Latin'. Leibfried, like Esping-Anderson, is also silent about gender issues. These have been centrally addressed by Lewis (1992) who distinguished between 'single breadwinner' welfare regimes, as in Britain and continental Europe, and 'dual breadwinner' states in Scandinavia which developed labour market and social policies (such as child care provision), which assisted women's entry into labour markets. Langan and Ostner (1991) also criticized the 'gender-blind' nature of existing typologies which ignored the hidden contribution of women's unpaid labour to welfare regimes. They sought also to develop a model encompassing Southern welfare regimes. However, their approach to the latter has been criticized by Trifiletti (1999) for its characterization of Mediteranean regimes as 'rudimentary' laggards. She suggests that the greater 'Latin' reliance on family welfare is closely linked to lower levels of economic development, arguing that substitutes for family provision are only made available in 'developed' welfare states when the wider processes of capitalist modernization make them necessary.

'Race' and Ethnic Minority Groups

The post-1945 welfare state, however, was not only constructed from discourses about work and the role of the 'breadwinner', but also on 'nationality' (Williams 1989). The result was that when Dixon and Macarov (1998) reviewed the national poverty data in 10 countries from Europe, North America and the developing world, they found considerable similarities in those likely to be identified as poor, with migrants and ethnic minority groups featured strongly everywhere. Urban exclusion and the 'deformalization' of work in Europe's underground economy particularly affects women and migrant workers of both sexes (Cross 1993).

Williams (1995) and Ginsburg (1994) analysed the evolution of different social policy approaches to postwar migrants. They found that while they were everywhere initially treated as temporary 'units' of labour with few welfare needs, as migrant communities settled permanently, different approaches emerged. From 1975 Sweden, with a small migrant population, went furthest of any country in a multicultural direction, permitting migrants full welfare and voting rights with state support for their cultural or political organizations. However, immigration rates were lower than elsewhere in Europe, probably because of the strong efforts to tap the domestic female labour reserve. In Germany, where the single breadwinner model was dominant and women's labour force participation rates were relatively low, resort to a migrant reserve . Nevertheless the Turkish and South European guest workers remained restricted to a second class status through exclusion from political citizenship, and disadvantage in the labour market and the earnings related welfare system. Lying between these two extremes, migrants from France and Britain's former colonies were provided significant political and social rights but *de facto* discrimination remained widespread in employment and social provision, and in 1981 in Britain the Nationality Act gave preferential right of entry to people from the white Commonwealth.

From the oil crisis onwards immigration was slowed to a trickle, and migrants were increasingly scapegoated by the right, including in the Scandinavian countries. Most European countries, including Sweden, have imposed restrictions on 'new' migrants, permitting only the new settlement of family members of those who had already acquired settlement rights. The 1985 Schengen Agreement allowed the removal of internal barriers to population movement within those EU countries signing up to it, in exchange for stricter controls on migrants from outside, the so-called 'Fortress Europe' policy (Read and Simpson 1991). Asylum seekers who sought refuge in Europe accordingly increasingly faced what (Mitchell and Russell (1998: 81) call a 'culture of disbelief' involving escalating demands for more proof and restrictions on eligibility of social security benefits. As *The Economist* commented aptly in 1995: 'In once-liberal countries, the gates are clanking shut'.

State targeting of migrants as labour market and welfare 'problems' has been accompanied by an alarming rise of European racism and xenophobia, often mobilized by right-wing parties (Sivanandan and Ahmad 1991). A Eurobarometer 1997 survey found that nearly one third of those questioned described themselves as 'quite racist' or 'very racist', while only another third described themselves as 'not at all racist'. There were significant variations across Europe with support for racism being lowest in Southern Europe, the Netherlands and Sweden, with Britain at the European average and the highest level (55%) found in Belgium. Everywhere beliefs were widespread that minorities claimed more in benefits than they earned (80%) and abused the benefits system (59%) (EC, 1997b). Despite state and right-wing political hostility, migration into Western Europe continues, principally across the Eastern and particularly Southern frontiers, where it is associated with the growth of a sizeable 'illegal' workforce and informal economy (Baldwin-Edwards 1991). In Italy the legalization in 1999 of nearly three-quarters of a million 'illegal' migrants (and similar moves in Greece) was in part a reflection of the left coalition government's recognition of migrants' positive social contribution, but was also an attempt to extend the state's reach for tax-raising and other purposes.

9.2   PRESSURES ON EUROPEAN WELFARE STATES

Since the mid-1970s a set of interlocking changes have put strains on Europe's postwar economies welfare systems. These include: slower economic growth, higher unemployment, an occupational shift from male-dominated manufacturing towards more feminized and 'knowledge-based' service employment, an aging population, changing family structures and declining fertility rates. Higher unemployment reduced tax and social security receipts, and increased social costs; the growth of single parenthood often left women and children poorly protected by established schemes; a decline in fertility and rising life-expectancy raised the 'dependency ratio' of older retired to employed younger people; and more insecure forms of work left growing numbers of Europeans inadequately insured by schemes based on assumptions of stable and permanent employment.

The Growth of European Poverty

Despite the major improvements in living standards in the third quarter of the century, contemporary Europe is now characterized by growing income inequalities and poverty. Overall the poorest 10% only receive 2.6% of the total income, while the richest 10% obtain nearly 25%. Such inequalities are widest in the poorer Southern countries, and narrowest in Denmark and the Netherlands whose welfare systems also involve the highest rates of social transfers from the wealthy to the poor. Germany, Austria and Belgium, by contrast, are generally prosperous countries where the poorest do relatively badly. Britain and Ireland are countries notable by the high proportions of national wealth taken by the top 20% (Eurostat 1998b).

Across Europe one in seven, or 52 million people in 17.6 million households, live below the official EU poverty line (Eurostat 1996: 212). Poverty has always been concentrated among the unemployed and low paid, single parents and children cared by them, immigrant and disabled workers. Yet the impact of higher levels of unemployment and underemployment associated with part-time work in the 1980s and 1990s has generated a growing population of working and non-working poor, as shown in Table 9.4.

This situation has put increased strain on Europe's employment-based social security systems, throwing greater numbers onto Social Assistance, which in turn has become more restrictive and rigorously means-tested (Teekens and van Praag 1990).

Table 9.4   Poverty in EU12 countries by household economic activity, 1993

Labour market status of household reference person	Distribution of poor households %	Poverty rate %
Working poor	35	10
Unemployed	13	46
Retired	33	22
Other economically inactive[a]	19	43
Total	100	-

Note: [a]Education or training, homework, looking after children, etc.

Source: Eurostat (1997), cited in Corden and Duffy (1998: 100).

Poverty increased virtually everywhere in Europe except in France and

Italy as shown in Table 9.5, whose 'household' definition underestimates the full extent of poverty, because male heads in better off families do not always share resources equitably. Particularly high increases were to be found in the Netherlands, Denmark, Britain and Belgium. The table shows a distinction North-South dimension to poverty across Europe, the exception being Britain, which had the highest absolute numbers of poor households at nearly 13 million, in which lived nearly four million children.

Of particular concern is the fact that by 1993 one in five of all European children were to be found in poor households. This trend is partly linked to failure of social protection systems based on the male breadwinner 'norm' to protect the increasing number of children growing up in single parent families.

Table 9.5   Household poverty in EU12 countries, 1993 (ranked by % of poor households)

	% of poor households 1993	Percentage increase on 1988	% of children in poor households 1993
Denmark	6.0	44.5	5.0
West Germany	11.0	23.5	13.0
Luxembourg	11.5	42.8	23.0
Belgium	13.0	38.9	15.0
Netherlands	13.0	171.9	16.0
France	14.0	-17.9	12.0
EU12 average	*17.0*	*10.0*	*20.0*
Spain	20.0	11.3	25.0
Italy	20.0	-13.7	24.0
Ireland	21.0	10.5	28.0
United Kingdom	22.0	46.8	32.0
Greece	22.0	10.1	19.0
Portugal	26.0	2.2	27.0

Source: Eurostat cited in UK Coalition Against Poverty (1998: 3).

Erosion of the Traditional Patriarchal Family?

Postwar settlements mainly gave women access to welfare through 'derived' rights associated with a male breadwinner. This in turn assumed that divorce and single-parenthood were relatively rare occurrences. However, while in 1980 one in ten European babies were born outside marriage, by the mid-1990s the figure was generally around one in four, and in Scandinavia around one in two. In most EU15 countries marriage rates are in decline, and cohabitation on the increase, particularly in Northern countries (Hantrais and Letablier 1996). Divorce rates also vary, though they are rising everywhere, with Britain and Scandinavia (Denmark excepted) leading the field with around one divorce for every two marriages (Eurostat 1998b). Single parent families, which were 9% of all families in 1983 rose to 14%, and were highest in Britain at 23% of households in 1996. The increase was lower, if still substantial, in Greece, Portugal and Spain. Throughout Europe 84% of single parent families are headed by women (Eurostat 1998c). Thus though the 'traditional' family may still be the norm, with 72% of men, women and children living within its walls, it is being rapidly eroded, especially in Northern Europe. In the South, there are more multi-generational households and children still tend to live in the parental home until they leave to form a household of their own. By contrast, in Northern Europe children leave home earlier and experience a more interrupted transition to adulthood, which may involve living alone, together and then marriage (Eurostat 1998a).

Mothers in both traditional and non-traditional families are having fewer children, and in 1995 Western Europe recorded its lowest postwar fertility levels. The most dramatic falls have occurred in Southern European countries such as Spain and Italy, whereas Scandinavian countries such as Sweden, Denmark and Finland have achieved slightly higher rates, probably because they are 'dual breadwinner societies' whose child care and benefit policies encourage women to combine work and motherhood (Ellingsæter 1998). Overall European birth rates are below replacement levels and hence population increases are now solely due to immigration, whether legal or 'illegal' (Eurostat 1996b).

Of course, many changes are responsible for Western Europe's declining fertility, but they include the continuing reverberations of the sexual revolution of the 1960s and 'second wave' feminism. Women have increasingly sought paid work, chosen to end unsatisfactory relationships or to live independently of men, and have restricted their fertility through contraception and abortion. However, one third of EU12 women in a recent survey still describe themselves as 'housewives', while only 0.8% of EU men describe themselves as being 'equivalent' to a housewife. The highest percentage of housewives are to be found in Ireland and the Latin Rim countries, who express higher levels of dissatisfaction with their situation compared to working women (Eurostat 1997).

While all European societies can be characterized as 'patriarchal', there are nevertheless important differences in the extent to which they have responded to feminist demands for disaggregated social rights to welfare as individuals, access to child benefits, child care, paid work, contraception and abortion. The most 'progressive' policies are to be found in Scandinavia, continental European countries are in the middle rank, while those of the South have conceded the least to feminist demands. By the 1990s separate taxation had been achieved in most EU countries, though 'households' are still assessed in Germany, France, Luxembourg and Portugal, and spouse allowances had not been abolished. Alongside this has been a shift to individual benefit rights. On the whole child benefits are universal but vary in the extent to which poorer families are 'targeted'. The extent to which families are expected to support each other also varies, with Southern countries and Germany defining these as obligations under law, and Scandinavian societies defining the state as responsible (Hantrais and Letablier 1996).

European welfare policies vary widely in the extent to which they make it possible for women to combine paid work and motherhood, and in encouraging sharing of child care between men and women (Schweie 1994). As far as the provision of maternity benefit is concerned, in terms of number of weeks and percentage of wages replaced, Scandinavia and Italy were the most generous, while Ireland, Greece and Britain were the most miserly. By the late 1980s, 80% and more of children from three years old and upwards in Scandinavia but also in France and Belgium received child care. In Scandinavia such provision is combined with flexible parental leave policies, which is still taken mainly by women (Singh 1998). Portugal and Britain, by contrast, provided under 50% of infants with childcare, while Germany's 'single breadwinner' society lags behind the rest of Northern Europe (Leparmentier 1999).

The disadvantage that women experience through life is particularly pronounced in old age, as women form a high proportion of the growing number of Europeans over 65 years. A key test of social policy is therefore the extent to which it can protect both men and women in their later years.

The Challenge of an 'Aging Europe'

An aging population is now often presented as a growing problem of future mammoth proportions, said to be a 'grey timebomb at the heart of the Western welfare state' as a *Guardian* headline (27 January 1996) put it, rather than celebrated as one of Western Europe's prime achievements. This results from the fact the prolongation of life well beyond the official retirement thresholds devised earlier in the century, and recent trends towards reducing unemployment through 'early retirement', put pressure on pensions systems. Additionally, as more people survive into later old age, the demands on health and social services increase. The general squeeze on social security and public provision is therefore particularly likely to impinge on the lives of older Europeans.

Portugal excepted, nearly continuous improvements in pensions have led to higher living standards for older people since the 1960s though this has slowed in the 1990s with pressures on government spending. However real pension rises have been much greater in Northern than Southern Europe, where more older people live alone (Walker and Maltby 1997). As can be seen from Table 9.6, the highest proportions of older people are to be found in Sweden, Italy and Belgium, while Ireland is by far the 'youngest' EU country.

Table 9.6 EU population (%) aged 60 and over, 1993-2020 (ranked by % of over-60s in 1993)

	1993	2020
Ireland	15.3	21.8
Netherlands	17.6	24.8
Finland	18.8	28.8
France	18.7	26.7
Luxembourg	19.2	26.3
Portugal	19.5	25.5
Spain	19.6	27.2
Austria	19.8	28.2
Denmark	20.1	24.3
Germany	20.4	27.7
UK	20.6	25.3
Greece	20.8	27.3
Belgium	21.1	28
Italy	21.3	29.9
Sweden	22.4	26.3

Source: Eurostat, cited in Walker and Maltby (1997: 10).

With the fifth of Europe's population who are elderly set to rise to one quarter over the next 20 years, the incomes and health of older people are a key touchstone of welfare policy, and are thus areas in which some of the strongest pressures towards the individualization of welfare responsibilities have been experienced in the 1980s and 1990s. Both the original level of provision and the response to these pressures has varied considerably. The Scandinavian systems traditionally differed from the rest of Europe in providing a relatively generous, universal flat rate pension without reference to people's employment records, and this therefore helped to reduce the gender inequalities of working life (Walker and Maltby 1997). There also remains extensive institutional and home-based public provision with no legal duty placed on relatives to care. Yet these services are now increasingly concentrated on those with high dependency needs, and the level of provision is being questioned as a result of fiscal pressures and of increased numbers of older people, leading to a shift in emphasis towards family (i.e. largely female) and private care (Hugman 1994). The Bismarckian welfare systems, being based on social insurance, usually reproduce the inequalities of working years through earnings-related schemes and often implicitly or explicitly expect families to provide for care, with pressures to do so growing. In Southern Europe state pensions are typically residual, covering only those excluded from occupational schemes, and there is often a statutory responsibility for families to provide care. Older people in Britain, often without family support and with a relatively ungenerous universal pension entitlement, are more likely to experience poverty than their counterparts in comparable countries (Walker and Maltby 1997).

Across Europe, however, pressures for reforming pension regimes are mounting. The publicly funded and provided 'Pay as You Go' pensions that were established after the war or earlier and which transferred wealth between the generations are now being challenged (Daly 1997). Instead variations on the 'Chilean Model' are being viewed as a possible 'stakeholder' prototype for an aging future. In this model, the state has only a residual responsibility to provide income for those in old age who will not or cannot save. Otherwise it expects that future pensions will depend on stock market earnings of privately administered funds. Inevitably such schemes will widen lifetime inequalities between the low paid and high paid, men and women, and those in secure and less secure work, as it has in Chile itself (Robinson 1997). In recent years Scandinavia and the Netherlands have shifted in this direction towards the inegalitarian earnings-related continental system (Cox 1998).

Health and Health Care

The 'success story' of an aging Europe is part of the wider narrative of improvements in health. Infant mortality per 1,000 live births within the EU12 fell from an average of 19 between 1970 and 1975 to just 8 in 1988-9 and fell further in the EU15 by 1998 to 6.6 (Noin 1995: 77; WHO 1999: 94-7). By 1998 there had been substantial gains in life expectancy, which at birth had now risen to 74.3 years for men and 80.4 years for women (WHO *ibid.*). In the process there has been considerable convergence between the richer Northern and poorer Southern countries, which can be attributed in large measure to   rising living standards and expansion of welfare states in the South, though it is clear that diet and 'social support' networks in Southern countries have positive health effects. Thus the countries with the highest male European life expectancy at 76 years are Greece and Sweden, while female life expectancy at 82 years is highest in Sweden and France. The most significant social differences in health are thus now less those between Western European countries, than the continuing gap between men and women, and the often widening gap between advantaged and disadvantaged groups (Abel Smith *et al.* 1995).

It is becoming clearer that the most important influences on good health are social and material: not just improvements in national wealth and general living standards, but also limitations on the extent of economic inequality, which impacts on both physical and emotional well-being (Wilkinson 1996). Access to health care makes some difference, but is likely to be of secondary importance. This can be seen when European experience is contrasted with that of the USA, which overall in 1998 lagged a little behind Western Europe, with an infant mortality rate of 7 years, a male life expectancy of 73 and a female one of 80 years. What this masks however is the greater significance of economic and 'race' inequalities of health which certainly are also significant within Europe, but are by no means as pronounced. Research into county variations within the US covering 1965 to 1994 shows a gap in life expectancy rates of more than 40 years, with some groups comparable to the best (Japanese women) and others to the worst (men in Sierra Leone) in the world (Murray *et al.* cited in WHO 1999: 18). Western Europe's health inequalities are not of this magnitude (though if we were to bring Eastern Europe into the picture, it would be another matter)..

American health inequalities link to wide variations in life chances, and also to access to health care, as around 15% of the population, between 40 and 45 million Americans, do not have any health insurance cover (Lassey *et al.* 1997: 27). In Western Europe access to public health care is generally regarded as a social right of citizenship, although the financial and administrative means by which this is achieved varies considerably within the two main models, taxation and social insurance based systems (Abel-Smith *et al.* 1995). Table 9.7 shows variations between European countries in overall health spending and the degree to which it is publicly financed.

While the proportion of national wealth spent on health care since 1980 fell in Ireland, Sweden and Denmark (only slightly) everywhere else it rose significantly. Ireland fell from being Europe's third highest ranking in 1980 to thirteenth by 1996, and Sweden from top to ninth place. However, except for Greece (significantly), Belgium, France and Austria, where public expenditure increased, this rise was largely financed by a rise in the share of private health expenditure.

Table 9.7 European health spending 1980-96 (ranked by GDP % spend 1996)

| | 1980 | | 1996 | |
	% GDP	% Public share in total spending	% GDP	% Public share in total spending
Austria	7.3	68.8	8.5	72.0
Belgium	6.5	83.4	7.8	87.7
Denmark	6.8	85.2	6.3	82.3
Italy	7.0	80.5	7.7	69.0
Finland	6.5	79.0	7.4	78.4
France	7.6	78.8	9.7	80.7
Germany	8.8	78.7	10.5	78.3
Greece	4.3	53.4	4.7	82.9
Ireland	8.7	81.6	5.9	74.7[a]
Netherlands	7.9	74.7	8.5	72.1
Portugal	5.8	64.3	8.3	59.8
Spain	5.6	79.9	7.4	78.7
Sweden	9.4	92.5	7.3	80.2
UK	5.6	89.4	6.9	84.5

Note: [a] 1995.

Source: OECD (1999a: 47, 50).

The rising trend in health care expenditure is due to a widening of access (especially in Southern Europe), the costs of treating more older people, and rising public expectations fed by the phenomenal growth of medical innovations. However, the general slowing down in expansion, and for some countries reductions in health care expenditure, has occurred in the 1990s as fiscal pressures have led governments to introduce or increase charges and shift to explicit rationing in order to dampen consumer demand, and market and managerial reforms intended to curtail professional power and improve utilization of available resources (Saltman *et al.* 1998). Research has confirmed that health charges deter poorer rather than better-off people (OECD 1999a). Health policy is being increasingly shaped by a more sceptical view of curative medicine which on the right is associated with attempts to limit demand and curtail producer power, is on the left more associated with   to demands to shift to a 'new public health' aimed at combatting health inequalities through more egalitarian social policies. Thus Power (1994) found that Scandinavian countries achieved the lowest European mortality and morbidity differentials and that these were due more to low levels of economic inequality than access to medical care.

Housing

Improvements in health have also been closely associated with housing improvements, and here too, postwar European welfare states have made strides that are currently threatened by welfare retrenchment. Housing and shelter have long been key concerns of European states, either through local or national government-funded building programmes or rent controls. These interventions had their roots in late nineteenth-century efforts to broaden urban policy beyond public health issues and address the wider 'social question'. The state provision of social housing, however, only became seen as a right of citizenship in the 1940s when, alongside state-assisted home-ownership, the Netherlands, Sweden, Switzerland and West Germany all put a strong emphasis on expanding social housing. Southern countries, by contrast, are less likely to define housing rights in statute (Doling 1997). Britain, consistent with what Ginsburg (1992) calls its 'liberal collectivist' regime, combined one of Europe's largest social housing sectors with a strong emphasis on home ownership. This has been dramatically cut back since the late 1970s, and the selling-off of better council houses has dramatically residualized social housing and pushed it close to the American public housing regime (Doling 1993). Alongside the general trend towards the 'commodification' of housing has been the emergence in Europe of poorer quality housing and increased homelessness. It is now estimated that 15 million EU citizens live in overcrowded and poor housing (FEANTSA 1998). Particularly worrying is the growth of homelessness in European cities. Germany, France, and Britain have by far the most homeless people than other EU15 countries with rates in excess of 10 per 1,000 inhabitants by 1991-2 (FEANTSA 1994). The low official figures in Mediterranean countries may be due to the fact that more people make private arrangements like living in tents and ramshackle dwellings (Avramov 1995, 1996).

Public housing provision became a particular target for criticism, in part because it was ripe for 'recommodification', and also because many of the mass estates built in the era of 'top-down' planning in the 1960s and 1970s offered a poor quality of life, frequently reinforcing poverty and social exclusion. Attempts were made to rescue them in the 1980s for fear of repeating the American urban scenario, as they became sites for riots and disorder (Power 1993). However these efforts have been limited by fiscal pressures, including those generated by the shift to the single currency, the prominent role of finance capital, and the declining influence of labour movements over the state ((Power 1999; Jefferys and Smith 1998).

9.3   RESTRUCTURING EUROPE'S WELFARE STATES

While European welfare states continue to provide significant protection to millions of Europeans, they have had to cope with rising social demands and an increasingly hostile neo-liberal political economy, which has not fundamentally been altered by the arrival in power of 'centre-left' governments in most of Europe from the mid-1990s onwards. This section of the chapter focuses on how neo-liberalism has led to incremental ideological and policy changes, providing greater detail for three of Europe's most developed welfare states, Sweden, the Netherlands and France. It will then consider the extent to which pressures from the global economy, as mediated by EU institutions, are starting to reshape what Leibfreid and Pierson (1995) call 'semi-sovereign welfare states'.

Ideological Challenges

Welfare has not been isolated from shifts in the ideological climate, which has been strongly encouraged by international organizations like the World Bank, IMF and OECD which have advocated a mixture of austerity and efficiency in health and welfare provision, on grounds that it enhances the powers of citizens:

> Governments can no longer be thought of as providers of largesse, but instead, as partners that enable and empower people to take initiatives on their own behalf and to exert greater control over the circumstances of their lives (OECD 1994a: 12).

In this neo-liberal approach the basic social unit becomes the individual who has been constrained or made dependant and now needs to be liberated. Gone is the social democratic and Keynesian concept of the state as having the ability and responsibility to provide welfare and ensure macroeconomic growth. In its place, neo-liberalism prioritizes wealth creation over distribution, international competitiveness over social needs, and individual responsibility before social rights. In substantive terms this involves the reining-in of universal and open-ended citizenship rights to welfare, cuts and restrictions on eligibility (Cox 1998). There is a renewed emphasis on 'targeting', a seemingly sensible method of focusing limited resources on those most in need, behind which, however, are three interlinked assumptions: First, that welfare states and workers' rights led advanced capitalist countries to under-perform economically and either socially 'flabby' or disordered; second that in the new austere and uncertain environment, risk and insecurity are something individuals must now increasingly face themselves; and third that the welfare state should serve less as a 'safety net' to prevent people's income falling below a certain level, and more as a means of encouraging self-reliance and participation in waged labour. This new liberalism is based on the view, given pseudo-academic respectability by Charles Murray (1984, 1990), that the growth of a poor 'underclass' in the USA and Europe has been encouraged by 'welfare dependency'. In the USA this is tied in with President Clinton's campaign to 'end welfare as we know it' by removing the welfare safety-net altogether after two years, in his effort to 'pioneer a welfare free world' (Bauman 1998: 92). While the USA was once seen as an 'exceptional' welfare laggard, which needed to catch up with Europe, it is now increasingly promoted as a 'new model' to be emulated (Glaser 1998).

No European government has yet sought to go as far as the USA in dismantling welfare. The notion of a right to a safety-net income has been retained but increasingly combined with stricter tests of need, for example with the introduction of the *Ingreso Minimo* in many regions of Spain in the 1980s, and a *Revenu Minimum d'Insertion* in France in 1989 (Eardley 1996). European safety-net welfare has also been increasingly combined with 'the stick' of stricter job search requirements, and in Britain there has been a shift in discourse from unemployment *benefit* to a job-seeker's *allowance*. There are still significant variations in the extent to which active job-seeking tests are applied to single parents. Before the election of the 1997 'New Labour' Government Britain did not do so, although Sweden did but in the context of widespread availability of child care. If Esping-Anderson (1990) is correct that the spread of (relatively) *unconditional* social citizenship rights helped to (partly) 'decommodify' the wage relation, then such changes aim to reassert its 'commodified' aspects, particularly by measures to reinforce participation in low-wage employment.

Privatization has also helped to 'commodify' welfare relationships themselves, as markets have emerged or extended themselves in the spaces left vacant by the state in health and welfare (Glennerster and Midgley 1991). Not surprisingly, the growth of market provision has been greatest where the political right is strongest, and more limited in countries like Sweden and Germany where it is weaker. In Italy contracting out to voluntary organizations has formed a significant route to privatization (Johnson 1995). There has been a general movement towards a 'managerial state' focusing on 'economy, efficiency and effectiveness' promoting 'marketization' of public services, with the state increasingly retreating to a strategic and regulatory role (Clarke and Newman 1997). These changes have been partly stimulated by professional dominance and inefficiency within the welfare state but they have also been fuelled by the search for new sources of profit in an era of slower growth, especially finance capital in areas like pensions and health care, often operating across national boundaries. The commodification process has been carried furthest in Britain, but is increasingly emulated elsewhere in Europe (Lane 1997). With the separation of central policy and contracting from operational functions, public providers increasingly have to compete for business in 'quasi-markets' alongside commercial and voluntary suppliers and 'contracting out' becomes more common (Le Grand and Bartlett 1993). Another significant British innovation is the Private Finance Initiative (PFI) under which the private sector agree, say, to build a hospital in return for a subsequent stream of operating receipts from the public purse.

Social discipline has always been a dimension of welfare citizenship, in that 'rights' implied individual 'responsibilities'. However in neo-liberal welfare ideology, the balance shifts much more to the latter. This is also associated with a more coercive approach towards socially excluded people, not just towards more disciplinary welfare but also from welfare to punishment, which is particularly prominent in the 'American model'. Russia apart, the USA has the highest imprisonment rate in the world, at 615 per 100,000 in 1996. Much of this is recent, having tripled since 1980 to now stand at nearly 1.6 million, at a huge cost to the public purse. Stern (1998) argues that imprisonment is now seen as a desirable measure in itself, as a way of dealing with an 'irredeemable' underclass, the most dangerous elements of whom need to be 'weeded out' from society. This is strongly linked to racism in that a black male now has a higher chance of going to prison than entering higher education (Stern 1998). With the exception of Portugal, Britain's rate of imprisonment is the highest in Western Europe (127 in Scotland and 120 per 100,000 in England and Wales) and has been rising rapidly in the 1980s and 1990s as American approaches have been imitated by successive governments.

The more restrictive approaches and commodification of provision are being pursued not just by the right, but with varying degrees of enthusiasm by the centre-left governments now in power across most of Western Europe, as now illustrated more concretely by analysis of three of Europe's more developed welfare states.

Crisis in Sweden, the Netherlands and France

The current malaise in the Swedish welfare state essentially reflects the reversal of trends that had encouraged the earlier national compromise between business and labour. The 'Swedish model' of free enterprise, high consumption, taxes and social benefits established after the social democrats came to power in the 1930s, showed strains in the 1970s when there was a 'labour offensive' against it on both work and welfare fronts. Olsen (1996) argues that this soon gave way to a 'capital offensive' in the 1980s when the employers retreated from centralized collective bargaining. The relaxation of controls on outward investment further exposed the Swedish economy to the rigors of the global economy, as did strategic mistakes by government and business that over priced Swedish goods (Stephens 1996). The flight of capital led in 1988 to 1991 to inegalitarian tax cuts which proportionately favored higher income groups. Welfare provision started to be cut and steps taken down the road of privatization. The first 'real' Conservative Government since the 1930s accelerated market reforms and introduced 'a revolution of free choice in health and welfare'. It also initiated austerity measures and significant benefit cuts in the international currency crisis of 1992 (Gynnerstedt 1997), by which time poverty rates rose to 7.2% and unemployment to double figures. While it is possible to dispute the extent to which the Swedish model traditionally benefited labour against capital, it has been claimed that by the early 1990s the advantage had tilted strongly towards capital (Pontusson 1997). With the abandonment of centralized collective bargaining, wage differentials have increased. The 1990 decision to apply for EU membership underlined the power of multinational businesses and locked Sweden on a neo-liberal trajectory. Nevertheless the basic elements of the welfare system and the corporatist approach to politics have been preserved, which may help the Swedish system to adapt rather than totally perish.

In the Netherlands, by contrast, the welfare state has undergone more dramatic change. Judged by Esping-Anderson (1990) to be have been one of the most highly 'decommodified' in Europe in 1980, van Oorschot (1998) suggests that it has now shifted from solidaristic to selectivist principles. The original growth of the patchwork system involved the extension of solidaristic 'people's insurances' from 1945. With the growth in numbers of claimants, and in response to the severe economic difficulties of the early 1980s, the system underwent continuous reconstruction to counter its supposed welfare dependency effects. Paradoxically, since the greater individualization of welfare with means testing and reductions in benefit levels was accompanied by equal treatment, the reforms partly benefited women. In 1987 stringent work tests were introduced for unemployment benefit and wage related payments were limited to 18 months, forcing long-term unemployed people to turn to social assistance. Eligibility rules were further tightened in 1995, and social assistance itself was rationalized with strong compulsions to take either paid or voluntary work. With the numbers receiving disability benefit rising to 900,000 in 1998, these too have been targeted for cuts and tighter definitions. The Netherlands was the first European health care system to experience significant marketization (the 'Dekker' reforms) from 1987 (Robinson 1998) and, as we have already seen (Table 9.5), the numbers of Dutch households living in poverty increased 172% between 1988 and 1993. Despite this, the Dutch system has been held up by some as a 'model' of 'third way' social policy between American deregulation and continental 'bloated' welfare. It is held up as a small open economy where the trade unions have cooperated with efforts to keep wage rises below those in Germany and to raise profitability levels and enforce work incentives, and it is claimed these policies reduced its unemployment levels. Often ignored but at least as important in its success, however, has been the Netherlands' location as a key inward investor location for multinationals seeking to get a foothold in Europe's Single Market. Even so, the 'social compact' has been severely tested at times, as in 1991 with the largest demonstration since the Second World War in opposition to cuts in disability benefit when Prime Minister Kok's slogan was 'work, work, and again work' (van Oorschot 1998). The workers relented only when the government threatened to break with corporatism and expel both unions and employers from the administration of the social security system (Hemerijck 1997).

France provides the most dramatic European example of the social pressures that can be released when governments attempt significant welfare reform. As Ambler (1991) observes, almost without noticing it France became one of the most developed welfare states in the world and costs accelerated. In 1995 the Juppé Plan for Reform of Social Security sought to achieve savings in social security, especially the health budget and public sector pensions, but was also an attempt to shift from corporatism, in which unions had a strong voice, to a system more firmly under state control. Another goal was to reduce the latitude given to welfare state professionals and to bring them to heel through capping expenditures (Spicker 1998). Reform of public sector pensions and management of pension funds were however quickly abandoned in the face of massive union-led strikes and street protests on a scale not seen since May 1968 (Jefferys 1996). The French experiences shows that Bismarckian 'stakeholder' systems of social insurance are sometimes harder to reform than universalistic tax-funded ones. Although often inegalitarian in their effects they are deeply rooted because workers' organizations collectively participate in their administration and individuals experience a strong sense of entitlement because they feel they are paying directly rather than receiving 'largesse' from the state. This has helped to protect them from the kinds of cuts that have occurred in Britain (Hirsch 1997). Ironically, therefore, the state-run welfare systems of Britain and Sweden have been more susceptible to cost control and managerial rationalization than some other regimes where control is more dispersed or shared.

Although contested, the cumulative effect of the ideological reorientation and policy changes that have been described are changing the nature of European welfare states, even if their institutional edifices and expenditure levels have generally been maintained. The direction is slowly being turned back towards neo-liberalism, the full consequences of which will be felt by future generations. While this chapter has so far examined these processes at the national level, a crucial question is the extent to which the emerging structures and policies of the EU are acting as either a brake or accelerator upon them.

9.4   A SOCIAL OR NEO-LIBERAL EUROPE?

Europe's nation states' location within the global economy is increasingly mediated by the 'emergent multi-tiered system of governance' or 'thin federal state' that is the European Union (Leibfried and Pierson 1995). The EU does not operate in purely in neo-liberal ways, but neither should it be either welcomed, or feared as was the case with Margaret Thatcher, as 'socialism by the back door'.

The European Economic Community was conceived primarily as a political and customs union and its 'social dimension' did not achieve any real prominence until the late-1980s. The 1957 Treaty of Rome gave no clear competence in the social field, although Articles 117-127 enabled it to promote 'improved working conditions and an improved living standard of living for workers', by fostering cooperation rather than through legislation. In 1960 the European Social Fund was created to assist the retraining of redundant workers in anticipation of the effects of accelerating economic integration (Leat 1998). In the 1970s the social dimension 'proper' emerged as a product of left political pressure, notably from the German Social Democrat Willy Brandt, who saw harmonization of national social policies as simply a first step towards a European welfare state (George 1996). As a result a first Social Action Programme was adopted by Council in 1974 and in 1975 the European Regional Development Fund (ERDF) was created to deal with the effects that economic integration was having on the poor. Equal Treatment of men and women had been inserted as Article 119 of the Treaty of Rome at France's insistence, concerned that its recent ratification of the International Labour Organization (ILO) equality convention would otherwise put it at a competitive disadvantage with the rest of Europe.

Feminist pressure in the 1970s turned this into the 1975 Equal Pay Directive, the 1976 Equal Treatment Directive on education and training, and the 1978 Social Security Directive (George 1996).

Table 9.8   Summary of the Social Chapter of the Maastricht Treaty (the Protocol on Social Policy)

1	Freedom of movement and recognition of qualifications
2	Fair and equitable wages
3	Improvement of living and working conditions
4	Social protection
5	Freedom to join or not join unions and associations
6	Access to vocational training through life
7	Equal treatment for men and women
8	Information, consultation and participation of workers
9	Health and safety in the workplace
10	Protection of children and adolescents
11	Decent standard of living in retirement
12	Rights for disabled persons.

However the impact of recession and the political stalling of the integration process blunted the impact of these attempts to give Europe a 'social dimension'. It returned to prominence only when it was hitched to renewed efforts to achieve economic union through the 1986 Single European Act (SEA). As we saw in Chapter 6, this project was particularly associated with the former French Socialist Finance Minister, Jacques Delors, who served as President of the European Commission from 1985 to 1995. The SEA committed the EU to the establishment of the free movement of labour, and a free market in goods and services by 1993. It was stimulated by perceptions of 'Eurosclerosis' that economically Europe was not doing as well as it might in the context of increased global competition from Japan and the emergent Asian 'Tigers'. Delors insisted that 'social cohesion' in Europe was essential to the economic success of this project and he found allies in trade unionists from the wealthier Northern countries who were concerned that 'social dumping' or 'regime shopping' through less restrictive labour laws or lower wage and social costs, might give poorer countries an unfair economic advantage (Abrahamson 1991). The major outcome was the launch of a Social Charter of Workers' Rights, which was eventually endorsed by the European Council of heads of government in Strasbourg in 1989, with Britain dissenting. A watered down version of this charter (summarized in Table 9.8) became the 'Social Chapter' or protocol annexed to the 1992

Maastricht Treaty, and was eventually subscribed to by the new British government in the Amsterdam Treaty of 1997.

The European Commission also launched 'Poverty 3' in 1990 as a community action programme to combat 'social exclusion' and promote the economic and social integration of the least privileged groups, recognizing that poverty denied people access to social participation as well as to material resources.

In the mid-1980s there thus were high hopes (or fears) that the first steps were being taken towards the creation of a pan-European welfare state to parallel that of the Single Market (Ross 1995). By the early 1990s, however, Europe's 'social' dimension had largely become an adjunct to a market building exercise, constrained through the whole of the 1990s by the determination to impose budgetary discipline as the framework for launching a 'hard' European currency. Under Delors' influence, the social or 'structural' budget doubled from 18% to 31%, and the cost of the Common Agriculture Policy (CAP) - the farmers' welfare state - was cut back from 59% to 48% of the Community's budget. Yet since the EU's budget was only 1.26% of member states' GDP, this meant that 'Social Europe' only amounted to around 0.5% of the community's total measured production (Amin 1997). This does not seem much to combat the inegalitarian pressures unleashed by the single market (Baine, *et al.* 1992). In any case EU social expenditure was not primarily welfare-oriented but essentially involved supply-side measures to enhance the ability of regions and individuals, particularly the long-term unemployed, to compete in the marketplace. Thus the Cohesion Fund provided resources on top of structural funds of £1.7 billion in 1993, rising to £2.1 billion in 1999 to the four poorest EU countries, to be spent on transport infrastructure and environmental protection. These were poor alternatives to proper social policy measures (Anderson 1995). The main policy weight is towards integration into low-paid work without significant alterations to fundamental economic and social inequalities or recognition of the value of unpaid work of women in the community (Levitas 1996). Wise and Gibb (1992) therefore argued that the EU's social measures were largely 'cosmetic'.

The neo-liberal emphasis of EU social policy heightened after Maastricht with moves towards monetary union leading up to the launch of the Euro in 1999. The strict criteria imposed for joining inevitably put pressure on welfare across Europe. The first goal was price stability, with inflation rates of no higher than 1.5% above the average of the 'best' three countries in the EU. Annual government borrowing had to be no more than 3%, and the total borrowed no more than 60% of GDP. The 'Stability Pact for Europe' proposed by Germany in 1995 and adopted in 1996 imposed still stricter budgetary constraints in the longer term, with automatic heavy fines for economic 'indiscipline', thereby ensuring no relaxation after monetary union. Policy documents have also increasingly highlighted welfare provision and labour market regulation as 'problems'. This was particularly the case with Delors' 1993 *Growth, Competitiveness and Employment* White Paper. The 1994 *European Social Policy* White Paper did, by contrast, endorse 'the European social model' as a 'unique blend of economic well-being, social cohesiveness and high overall quality of life'. However job creation and competitiveness were emphasized with the need to invest in human capital rather than simply provide unconditional benefits, while 'social exclusion' was to be tackled primarily through integration into the labour market.

In 1997 the Commission produced a Communication on *Modernization and Social Protection* which represents a further shift in a neo-liberal direction. Strongly reminiscent of previous OECD documents, it calls for a shift in the balance from collective to greater individual responsibility in welfare. It argues the need for reform to provide protection in response to the 'flexible working patterns', which are themselves simply seen as a necessary and unalterable feature of the landscape, and suggests that unemployment insurance needed to become 'employability insurance'. It argues for policies to address the needs of increasing numbers of older people at the same time as containing costs. It views pensions reform as urgent, involving shifts from pensions based on wages to prices, which will inevitably widen the gap between the retired and those in work. It criticizes the increasing resort to early retirement and argues for the raising of retirement ages and for measures to prevent exit of older workers from the labour market. On health care it calls for greater efficiency and reducing costs and the extension of market mechanisms without 'jeopardizing the principle of universal access to optimum care', but does not suggest how this circle will be squared.

Ginsburg (1998) sees these changes as indicative of the abandonment of the goal of a supranational welfare state and as marking the ascendancy of a neo-liberal agenda around monetary union, though with some nods in the direction of creating a more 'woman-friendly' welfare state, and to tackling exclusion experienced by black and disabled people. While emerging EU discourse argues for the need to protect European welfare systems by 'modernizing' them, the shift flagged up is clear enough away from the policy presumptions of the mid-1980s when a social democratic welfare state was seen as a necessity to economic success.

9.5 CONCLUSION

Neither the resilience of welfare state expenditure nor the appearance of resistance to the welfare state restructuring should lead to a sense of complacency. As Bonoli and Palier (1998) point out substantial 'innovative' reform has occurred which has placed European welfare states along neo-liberal pathways. The political-economic conditions of the late 1990s specifically threaten Europe's welfare states as they face American capitalism's global dominance and renewed competitive pressures (Rhodes 1996). There is a danger, however, that the power of the global economy and the weakness of national or regional institutions in the face of it can be exaggerated, especially since the vast bulk of European economic investment and activity still occurs between European countries (Hirst and Thompson 1996; Mayne 1998: 25). States remain important actors within global economies, but as their economic and military decision making becomes somewhat attenuated by supranational insititutions, the welfare state becomes even more of a core area of responsibility. They ensure some degree of equity in access to the market (through education and training), participation in it (through anti-discriminatory, minimum wage and health and safety laws) and enforced exit from it (through unemployment, health and pension provisions). There remain pressures to respond to socially defined 'needs' by offering equal access to health and social service provision to all citizens. They also remain bastions of public service and pluralist managerial traditions and the stronger they are, the less inequality and poverty there tends to be in society.

A danger of 'strong' globalization theories is that by arguing that the welfare state was merely a by-product of the 'mass production' era, then its attenuation can be seen as necessary or inevitable under 'lean production' and 'flexible accumulation'. Jessop (1994) thus argues that the nation state is being 'hollowed out' from above and below, undermining national markets and full employment on which welfare states were based. In a related vein Hoggett (1994) argues that the managerial reorganization of the welfare state has emulated the more efficient flexible capitalist strategies of coordinated central and decentralized responsibility. As this chapter has shown, some of these changes are occurring, but rather than simply reflecting 'productive needs' they can also be seen as politically influenced responses of Europe's ruling groups to the mounting challenges by the 1970s. These were not just the decline in capitalist profitability and tighter competitive conditions but also the emergence of broad democratic challenges from below. The response to this was not just investment in ideological and political argument to combat collectivism and promote individualism in all areas of social life, but also a shift to material conditions of heightened insecurity and fear aimed at reinforcing discipline and lowering collective expectations (Navarro 1991; Elliott and Atkinson 1998; Bauman 1999).

In any case, as has been emphasized throughout this book, the global international order is not just an autonomously generated and immutable economic 'structure', but also a political and military construction (Held *et al.* 1999). It is in principle capable of being reformed and redirected, and in the context of deepening instability and crisis in the world economy, the European 'social' model of capitalism offers potential ways of stabilizing an 'order' that seems chronically prone to crisis. There is thus nothing inevitable about the current primacy of markets, and European attachments to social protection and resistance to the market have blunted some of the effects of monetary union (Teague 1998). The argument that 'times have changed' could foster a radical recognition that new technology could enable us to reduce working time, maintain living standards, expand leisure and improve welfare. However, unless there is a significant change in direction, European welfare, like management and work processes, appears to be travelling towards national variants of 'an American future' (Singer 1995).

10. The Future of European Management, Work and Welfare

This book has reviewed developments in European management, work and welfare from a long historical approach. The aim was to underline the point that within a framework of constraints given by existing social arrangements, possibilities were relatively open, shaped by uncertain events, and political mobilizations and choices. We want to conclude by applying this to the future. Although Europe is currently travelling at some speed towards a neo-liberal future and associated forms of employment and welfare relations, this is not predestined and possibilities do exist for substantially altering course.

10.1 THE UNLIKELY ORIGINS OF EUROPEAN WELFARE CAPITALISM

The early chapters sought to show that European traditions of management, work and welfare are historically rooted in changing *political*-economic frameworks. The roots of 'the modern' were traced first to the emergence of town-based economies in the 'high' and later Middle Ages, and then to the accelerating decay of feudal relationships in the shift to nation-based trading economies in the run-up to the modern period. These societies were dramatically transformed in the nineteenth century by the rise of modern capitalist societies in Northernern Europe based on the economic power and political enfranchisement of the industrial and commercial middle classes. However these societies proved internally unstable in that the aristocracy sought to hang on to power as much as it could, the working classes demanded more of the economic spoils and their own political enfranchisement, and women also started to demand social and political emancipation. We showed how patterns of management, work and welfare were shaped in various ways by emerging settlements between these social groups in the late nineteenth- and early twentieth-centuries, and how these occurred in the context of nationally competitive imperialisms that eventually caused a destructive war between European powers in 1914. This was only eventually settled in favour of the Allies by the military intervention of the USA, which signalled its own arrival as a major industrial and military power and the launching of the 'American century'. However the USA largely retreated into itself in the interwar period, and it can truly be said that Europe imploded under the weight of its own internal problems. After the rise of fascism, and the depression of the 1930s, by 1940 'liberal' capitalism had been all but extinguished from continental Europe.

The social creation of 'welfare capitalism' therefore only emerged due to a politically fortuitous combination of circumstances in 1945 associated with what we have called the 'American-European compromise', the essential elements of which were the military defeat of fascism by the combined American and Soviet military machines, the division of Europe into 'East' and 'West' sides of the Cold War, and the USA's reconstruction of an expansionist world market. Within this framework the improbable happened: European economies were revived, 'modern' patterns of management and pluralist industrial relations systems were established, living standards rose and 'citizenship' welfare states were conjured out of prewar social insurance roots. It was a European achievement, but one facilitated and endorsed by the USA who encouraged both European nation-based welfare capitalisms and the shifts to greater economic and political integration at the European level. Western Europe was at one and the same time dependent on, and relatively autonomous from the USA.

Thus within an American dominated capitalist political economy and NATO military alliance, European and American forms of capitalism continued to diverge after the Second World War, with significant implications for their patterns of management, work and welfare. It is true to say that the USA had itself been partly 'Europeanized', as a result of the shock-waves caused by the Great Depression and the resulting New Deal. It adopted a more active form of state planning that caused it to seek closer alliances with both big business and representatives of labour. In 1935 it brought in union recognition and adopted German-style social insurance. Even so it remained a more 'liberal' form of capitalism, which had resulted from a combination of Protestant ideology, the lack of an aristocratic class, and the weakness of labour due to waves of immigration and 'race' divisions. After 1945, it failed to build on its prewar welfare settlement and partially withdrew the union rights achieved during the New Deal. It was in this period that it assumed its world role. Early in the century it had become the world's largest industrial power, and by the late 1940s it had saved Europe (twice), underwritten the expansion of the world economy, and now turned its mind towards 'making the world safe for democracy', replacing Britain as the chief international power and competing with the USSR for global dominance.

10.2   THE ROAD TO NEO-LIBERALISM

By the end of the 1960s we saw that Europe had partly 'Americanized': there had been a definite if uneven shift to American methods of mass production and consumerism. However Europe remained wedded to its more interventionist state traditions, joint regulation of working conditions and extensive forms of welfare capitalism. By the 1970s the economic gap was closing between the USA and Europe, and Japanese capitalism was rising on the horizon. There was a world-wide challenge to USA power as the 'new imperialists' and the postwar settlements in Europe started to fray as the long postwar economic boom came to end. It is undoubtedly the case that the collapse of the Bretton Woods monetary system in 1973 signalled the end of an international economy so directly controlled by the USA. Neverthless it was suggested that it is mistaken to see the ensuing years simply as a shift towards deregulation and dispersion of power in the world economy, and a international financial system out of the control of any system of political regulation. The American influence may not be so direct and obvious but, as Strange (1997) put it, its 'global reach' has been impressive, as its political morale and economic confidence recovered from the setbacks of the 1970s, boosted by the collapse of the communist threat by 1989.

Thus the neo-liberal challenge to European political economies charted in Chapters 6 to 9 of this book was not seen as due to the autonomous workings of a world economy that has moved from one 'Fordist' to another 'post-Fordist' and 'flexible' system of capitalist accumulation. Rather the global shift towards neo-liberalism was seen as politically constructed, with direct and indirect forms of American influence giving it a strong impetus. However, in the 1990s the EU itself and the monetarist policies associated with the single market in 1993, and moves towards a single currency, were also portrayed as a significant influence eroding distinctly European systems of management, work and welfare. Of course, these processes are uneven in their effects: they are leading not so much to convergence as to nationally distinct variants of the American 'model' of contractural capitalism.

Thus 'political choice' was emphasized both in the emergence and expansion of European welfare capitalisms after 1945 and the response to their difficulties since the 1970s. Emphasis on the political-military context in relation to post-1945 developments disputes the notion that the forms of management, work and welfare associated with European welfare capitalisms, were regulatory forms necessarily tied to a particular form of capitalist accumulation. Therefore the problems now experienced are less the result of their economic but political viability. Externally, there has undoubtedly been a shift from national to international levels of power which presents significant obstacles in the way of attempts to use nation states as bases from which seek to democratize the market. Internally, there has been an expansion of the managerial classes which, until recently at least, has been on the whole favourable to the spread of neo-liberal politics and American managerialism, and served to weaken alliances between salaried groups and the traditional batallions of labour. Undoubtedly technological developments have played a significant role. Microcomputing has had a profound effect on productive processes, has permitted the integration of the world's financial markets, enabled the decentralization of functional responsibilities, and promoted forms of networking through email and other means. Innovations in transportation have also been influential. Nevertheless while technology has an impact on social life, it is also a product of it, and both its centralizing and decentralizing effects result in part from the search for more effective forms of social control to deal with the challenges of the 1960s and 1970s.

10.3   ALTERNATIVE FUTURES FOR MANAGEMENT, WORK AND WELFARE

Will the combined social weight of markets, neo-liberal ideology and new technology therefore sweep everything before them? The 1990s started with 'triumphalism' in honour of market liberalism, as represented notably by Fukuyama's (1989) proclamation, as advisor to the RAND corporation that 'the end of history' (i.e. of alternatives to Amercian liberal capitalism) had arrived in the wake of the collapse of Soviet communism. A decade further on, the mood is not quite as euphoric. Capitalism can scarcely be said to have been a success in Russia and much of Eastern Europe, Africa's economies remain burdened with massive poverty and mountains of debt which two decades of neoliberal medicine has not remedied, and in 1998 even the successful Far-Eastern 'Tiger' economies were threatened with economic meltdown as the world's financial markets lurched into crisis. As George Soros, the renowned international speculator, put it in conversation with Anthony Giddens:

> I'm afraid that the prevailing view, which is one of extending the market mechanism to all domains, has the potential of destroying society. Unless we review our concepts of markets... they will collapse... We have this false theory that markets, left to their own devices, tend towards equilibrium (Soros and Giddens 1997: 25)

Soros went on to state that the system 'has survived only with intervention:

the authorities have come to the rescue' (*ibid.*: 25). Certainly intervention, internationally by the IMF, and nationally by the American government when domestic financial interests were threatened, helped to check the 1998-9 crisis.

The defence of a social sphere from incursion by the market, and a positive view of state regulation as a means of promoting social cohesion and combatting the destructive instabilities of amoral market liberalism, is leading to something of a revival in reformist sentiment and politics. Even the World Bank, which played a key role in arguing for and implementing the neo-liberal revolution of the 1980s and 1990s, has recently modified its line, its 1997 Report grudgingly acknowledging that an 'effective state' is an essential element of sustainable social and economic development (World Bank 1997). In Europe, this new mood has led to the election of centre-left governments in Europe, and crystallized around advocacy of a so-called 'third way' between unrestrained neo-liberalism and traditional social democracy, of which Giddens (1998) is a leading advocate. These have been particularly reinforced by the election of the Blair Government in 1997 and the German Social Democrats under Chancellor Schröder in 1998. During the European elections of 1999, the two leaders launched a joint Labour/SPD policy document *Europe: the Third Way/Die Neue Mitte* whose aim is to break away from 'tax and spend' traditions, to:

> give Europe a chance to catch up with the USA. We must combine the economic dynamism that Europe desperately needs with the commitment to social justice that remains at the core of our beliefs (cited in White 1999).

What this means in practical terms however is limited intervention to complement an unregulated global economy with some 'supply side' investment. This aims to ensure that individuals can be self-reliant and compete in flexibile labour markets, stimulated by reforms to shift the 'welfare system from a safety net of entitlements into a springboard to personal responsibility'.

While portrayed as 'modernizing', the heightened emphasis on the 'work ethic', and on shoring up traditional gender relations, locates this approach in the eyes of some firmly in the past. The demands of feminists that housework and care be recognized as socially valuable, the Green critique that much so-called 'productive' labour is environmentally damaging, and the emergence of a 'post-industrial' society, might all create possibilities for devising strategies to share paid work and allow people to combine it with family responsibilities or voluntary work (Bauman 1998). This might be facilitated by a citizenship right to a Basic Income Guarantee (BIG) paid to all adult individuals which, if set at a realistic level, would radically alter the contours between paid work and other forms of social activity (Jordan

1998, Pierson 1998).

The third way's attempt to tackle globalization by measures to enhance individual adaptability to its dictates represents one vision of the future. Though it is gaining ground in Europe, and increasingly shapes EU discourse, there is less popular enthusiasm for it outside Britain. Right-wing British newspapers like the *Daily Telegraph* (9 June 1999) for example noted that the joint Labour/SPD document was being launched at the same time when a law was being implemented in France to cut the working week to 35 hours, Italy was threatening to breach the 'stability pact' and raise its deficit, and German Social Democrats were in fact devising new taxes on businesses. Of course, what they bemoan as a continued commitment to interventionism across the English Channel, might give others cause for hope that European social democracy, though moribund, is not yet quite dead. On the other hand, the scope for this remains severely limited by the dominance of what Luttwak (1997) calls the EU's 'central bankism', which prioritizes the control of inflation and monetary stability over measures that might seek to combat unemployment and tackle growing poverty and widening inequality. Opinion is divided about whether the project of a European single currency itself dictates that the European future will be a monetarist one. Certainly the evidence to date is that it has steered Europe in that direction, although others would argue that it is necessary to create a political-economic arena in which the European social model might be able to withstand the pressure of global economic forces. Gray (1998) has argued that while not rendering Europe immune from international pressures, its success would help to establish a more equal trading position with the USA. Others have argued that there needs to be a revival of Keynesian strategies at the European level to deal particularly with the problem of unemployment. Thus Lipietz (1996) has called for a more concerted shift to a 'social Europe' aided by a Keynesian economic 'recovery programme' to increase employment while at the same time (inspired by the European Greens) seeking to direct them in an ecologically sustainable direction.

In practice, the feasibility of a solely European solution might be seen as debatable, or even ethically suspect as a 'Fortress Europe' policy intended to protect European advantages. It could be argued that action needs also to be focused at the global level, because only then could the rest of the world start to be brought up to European levels of labour and social protection, rather than Europe levelled down. Thus Brecher and Costello (1994) have argued for a global and not just a European 'Social Charter' as a framework of rights for workers and citizens. It might be that this could be constructed in stages, for example, as some have advocated by the insertion of a 'social clause' of minimum labour standards enforced by the World Trade Organization (WTO). The International Confederation of Free Trade Trade

Unions (ICFTU) have argued these should be based on International Labour Organization (ILO) conventions, who could be given an enhanced role to monitor and judge when these have been enfringed (Mayne 1998). Since the ILO is unique as a tripartite supranational organization of governments, employers and workers' organizations, such a reform would represent a significant shift to global corporatism. Another proposal that has attracted a great deal of interest has been the 'Tobin Tax', named after the economist who first proposed it (Tobin 1978). This would involve levying a small tax of 1% on international money transactions, discouraging excessive speculation and bringing an element of stability to the world financial system. Even if it reduced transactions by three-quarters it is estimated that it would produce between $150 to $720 billion that could provide the tax base for a system of global governance to promote greater international social justice (Martin and Schumann 1997: 83). Critics of the tax do not fault it on theoretical as much as practical grounds. Arguing that it must be introduced globally or not at all, it is portrayed as a non-starter that would inevitably be blocked by financial interests in New York and London. In response, Tobin suggested that individual countries and the EU itself could act alone in implementing such a tax (Eichengreen etal. 1995; Stecher and Bailey 1999).

The presentation of these two policy proposals is merely meant to illustrate the point that a global future gives rise to a *range* of possible political-economic frameworks for the development of management, work and welfare. These might come about partly through the strength of reasoned argument, and appeals to 'human rights' rather than the sanctity of market forces. However there is also a need to address questions of power and agency: where will the democratic pressure come from for change that we argued was key to the emergence of European welfare capitalism? The answer is that it is already there in well-developed proposals to democratize the UN's system of global governance and attenuate the power of the USA and allied institutions like the IMF and World Bank (e.g. Commission on Global Governance 1995). At European level, campaigns to democratize EU institutions might make them more sensitive to people's needs. While such proposals seek to change global institutions, there are also a multiplicity of specific campaigns, such as those to cancel Third World debt, to combat child labour, and so on, which Brecher and Costello (1994) see optimistically as a people-centred process of 'globalization from below'. Moody (1997) has argued for a more activist 'movement unionism' at national and international level that links with such campaigns, spanning worker, consumer and human rights concerns.

It is of course possible to have a negative view of the effects of global neo-liberalism, while also being pessimistic about the immediate possibility of achieving any significant change. Gray (1998) argues that any shift to a managed international economy will be vetoed by the USA until its economic bubble bursts and there is a crisis of major proportions such as the Great Depression of the 1930s that forces a painful rethink. While he may well be right, an alternative to waiting for disaster might be to act at the European level, not just to preserve and improve its own systems of management, work and welfare, but also facing outwards as a force for change in the world. Martin and Schumann (1997) argue that the European trade union movement could help this process, by acting more effectively in concert at the European level. Despite its obvious shortcomings and imperfections, there is still a social dimension to the EU, it is an association of relatively equal partners and has a democratic system of governance, all of which mark it out as radically different from the North American Free Trade Association (NAFTA). It might therefore be commended as a workable starting point for future forms of transnational governance (Mayne 1998).

In the final analysis, the ultimate political choice is one of optimism or pessimism itself. This is because neo-liberalism fundamentally rests upon an *a priori* pessimism that selfish humans 'need' the external strictures of the market, managerial or state compulsion, which must not be 'interfered with' by democratic political processes. However we continue to draw a sense of optimism from the fact that in 1945 flourishing European welfare capitalisms were constructed from far less promising political circumstances and economic and technological resources than exist today. Despite their problems and contradictions Western Europe's systems of pluralist employment relations and welfare states remains a viable framework on which to build for the future, rather than outmoded institutions which economic logic dictates must now be abandoned.

Bibliography

Abel-Smith, B. *et al* (1995), *Choices in Health Policy*, Aldershot: Dartmouth.

Abrahamson, P. E. (1991), 'Welfare and poverty in the Europe of the 1990s: social progress or social dumping?', *International Journal of Health Services*, **21** (2), 237-64.

Addison, P. (1977), *The Road to 1945*, London: Quartet.

Aglietta, M. (1979), *A Theory of Capitalist Regulation*, London: New Left Books.

Alber, J. (1983), 'Social security expenditure in Western Europe', 1949-77', in M. Loney, D. Boswell, and J. Clarke (eds), *Social Policy and Social Welfare*, Milton Keynes: Open University Press, 156-70.

Albert, M. (1991), *Capitalisme contre Capitalisme*, Paris: Editions de Seuil.

Aldcroft, D. (1993), *The European Economy 1914-1990*, London and New York: Routledge, Third Edition.

Aligisakis, M. (1997), 'Labour disputes in Western Europe: typology and tendencies', in *International Labour Review*, **136** (1), 73-94.

Allum, P. (1995), *State and Society In Western Europe*, Cambridge: Polity.

Ambler, J. S. (1991), 'Preface', in J. S. Ambler (ed.), *The French Welfare State: Surviving Social and Ideological Change*, New York and London: New York University Press, vii-viii.

Ambrose, S. E. (1988), *Rise to Globalism: American Foreign Policy Since 1938*, London: Penguin, fifth edition.

Amin, A. (1997), 'Tackling regional inequality in Europe', in S. Hall, D. Massey and M. Rustin (eds), *Soundings: The Next Ten Years*, London: Lawrence and Wishart, 53-67.

Anderson, B. and J. P. Zinsser (1988), *A History of Their Own: Women in Europe From Prehistory to the Present*, vol. 2, Harmondsworth: Penguin.

Anderson, J. J. (1995), 'Structural funds and the social dimension of EU policy: springboard or stumbling block?', in S. Leibfried and P. Pierson (eds), *European Social Policy: Between Fragmentation and Integration*, Washington, DC: The Brookings Institution, 123-58.

Anderson, M. (1980), *Approaches to the History of the Western Family, 1500-1914*, London: Macmillan.

Anderson, M. (ed.) (1996), *British Population History: From the Black Death to the Present Day*, Cambridge: Cambridge University Press.

Anderson, P. (1979), *Lineages of the Absolutist State*, London: Verso.

Anderson, P. (1980), *Arguments Within English Marxism*, London: Verso.

Anderson, P. (1997), 'Under the sign of the interim', in P. Gowan and P. Anderson (eds), *The Question of Europe*, London and New York: Verso, 51-71.

Armengaud, A. (1973), 'Population in Europe 1700-1914', in C. M. Cippola (ed.), *The Fonatana Economic History of Europe: The Industrial Revolution*, vol. 3, London: Collins/Fontana, 22-76.

Armstrong, C. (1997), 'Thousands of women sterilized in Sweden without consent',

British Medical Journal, **315**, 563.

Armstrong, G., Glyn, A. and J. Harrison (1991), *Capitalism Since 1945*, Oxford: Basil Blackwell.

Armstrong, P. (1988), 'The personnel profession in the age of management accountacy', *Personnel Review*, **17** (1), 25-31.

Arrighi, G. (1994), *The Long Twentieth Century: Money, Power and the Origins of Our Times*, London: Verso.

Atkinson, J. (1984), 'Manpower strategies for the flexible organization', *Personnel Management*, August, 28-31.

Avramov, D. (1995), *Homelessness in the European Union: Social and Legal Context of Housing Exlusion in the 1990s*, Fourth Research Report of the European Observatory on Homelessness. Brussels: FEANTSA.

Avramov, D. (1996), *The Invisible Hand of the Housing Market: A Study of Effects and Changes in the Housing Market on Homeless in the European Union*, Fifth Research Report of the European Observatory on Homelessness, Brussels: FEANTSA.

Baglioni, G. (1990), 'Industrial relations in Europe in the 1980s', in G. Baglioni and C. Crouch (eds), *European Industrial Relations: The Challenge of Flexibility*, London: Sage, 1-41.

Baine, S., Beninton, J. and J. Russell (1992), *Changing Europe: Challenges Facing the Voluntary and Community Sectors in the 1990s*, London: National Council of Voluntary Organizations.

Balanyá, B., O. Hoedeman, A. Ma'anit and E. Wesselius (2000), *Europe Inc.: Regional and Global Restructuring and the Rise of Corporate Power*, London: Pluto.

Baldwin, P. (1990), *The Politics of Social Solidarity*, Cambridge: Cambridge University Press.

Baldwin-Edwards, M. (1991), 'The socio-political rights of migrants in the European community', in G. Room (ed.), *Towards A European Welfare State?*, Bristol: SAUS Publications, 189-234.

Bartolini, S. and P. Mair (1990), *Identity, Competition and Electoral Availability: The Stabilisation of European Electorates 1885-1985*, Cambridge: Cambridge University Press.

Baruel, J. (1996), 'Spain the context of European human resource management', in T. Clark (ed.), *European Human Resource Management*, Oxford: Blackwell, 93-117.

Bauman, Z. (1998), *Work, Consumerism and the New Poor*, Buckingham and Philadelphia: Open University Press.

Bauman, Z. (1999), 'The burning of popular fear', *New Internationalist*, March, 20-23.

Beaupain, T., S. Jefferys, and G. Lanotte (1999), 'European works councils: a step towards European industrial relations? Preliminary findings from some Belgian case studies', *IREC Conference*, Aix-en-Provence, France:19-21 May.

Beck, U. (1992) *Risk Society: Towards a New Modernity*, London: Sage.

Bell, D. (1973), *The Coming of Post-Industrial Society*, New York: Basic Books.

Berg, M. (ed.) (1983), *Manufacture in Town and Country Before the Factory*, Cambridge: Cambridge University Press.

Berggren, C. (1993), *The Volvo Experience: Alternatives to Lean Production in the Swedish Auto Industry*, Basingstoke: Macmillan.

Bergier, J.F. (1973), 'The industrial bourgeoisie and the rise of the working class

1700-1914', in C. M. Cippola (ed.), *The Fonatana Economic History of Europe: The Industrial Revolution*, vol. 3, London: Collins/Fontana, 22-76.

Berstein, S. and P. Milza (1990), *Histoire de la France au XXe Siècle, 1900-1930*, Paris: Editions Complexe.

Black, B.(1999), *Industrial Relations Regulation: A Product of and Constrained by National Culture*, IREC: Aix-en-Provence, 20-22 May.

Blair, T. (1998), *The Third Way*, London: The Fabian Society.

Bloch, M. (1962), *Feudal Society*, vols 1 and 2, London: Routledge and Kegan Paul.

Bobbio, N. (1987), *The Future of Democracy: A Defense of the Rules of the Game*, Minneapolis: University of Minnesota Press.

Bock, G. and P. Thane. (1991), *Maternity and Gender Policies: Women and the Rise of the European Welfare States, 1880s-1950s*, London and New York: Routledge.

Boltanski, L. (1987), *The Making of a Class: Cadres in French Society*, Cambridge: Cambridge University Press.

Bonoli, G. and B. Palier (1998), 'Changing the politics of social programmes: innovative change in British and French welfare reforms', *Journal of European Social Policy*, **8** (4), 317-30.

Boreus, K. (1992), 'The shift to the right: neo-liberalism in argumentation and language in the Swedish public debate since 1969'. *European Journal of Political Research*, **31** (3), 257-286.

Bourke, J. (1994), *Working-Class Cultures in Britain 1890-1960*, London and New York: Routledge.

Bradley, H. (1996), *Fractured Identities: Changing Patterns of Inequality*, Cambridge: Polity Press.

Braudel, F. (1982) *Civilisation and Capitalism, 15th-18th Century*, vols 1, 2 and 3, London: Collins.

Braudel, F. (1993), *A History of Civilizations*, Harmondsworth, Middlesex: Penguin.

Braverman, H. (1974), *Labor and Monopoly Capital*, New York: Monthly Review Press.

Brecher, J. and T. Costello (1994), *Global Village or Global Pillage: Economic Restructuring from the Bottom Up*, Boston: South End Press.

Brewster, C. and A. Hegewisch. (1994), 'Human resource management in Europe: issues and opportunities', in C. Brewster and A. Hegewisch (eds.), *Policy and Practice in European Human Resource Management*, London: Routledge, 1-21.

Brewster, C., A. Hegewisch, L. Mayne and O. Tregaskis (1994), 'Employee communication and participation' in C. Brewster and A. Hegewisch (eds.), *Policy and Practice in European Human Resource Management*, London: Routledge, 154-68.

Bridgford, J. and J. Stirling (1994), *Employee Relations in Europe*, Oxford: Blackwell.

Briggs, A., and P. Clavin (1997), *Modern Europe 1789-1989*, London and New York: Longman.

Brooke, M. A. and H. L. Remmers (1978), *International Management and Business Policy*, Boston, MA: Houghton-Mifflin.

Burnham, J. (1945), *The Managerial Revolution*, Harmondsworth: Penguin.

Butera, F. (1985), 'Italy', in B. C. Roberts (ed.), *Industrial Relations in Europe: The Imperatives of Change*, London: Croom Helm, 137-58.

Butler, T. and M. Savage (eds) (1995). *Social Change and the Middle Classes*, London: UCL Press.

Calmfors, L. and J. Driffill. (1988), 'Bargaining structure, corporatism and macroeconomic performance'. *Economic Policy*, April, 1-41.

Calori, R. (1994), 'The diversity of management systems', in R. Calori and P. de Woot (eds), *A European Management Model: Beyond Diversity*, London: Prentice Hall, 11-30.

Cardwell, D. (1994), *The Fontana History of Technology*, London: Fontana.

Carew, A. (1987), *Labour Under the Marshall Plan: The Politics of Productivity and the Marketing of Management Science*, Manchester: Manchester University Press.

Carlin, M. (1989), 'Medieval English hospitals', in Granshaw, L. and R. Porter (eds), *The Hospital in History*, London and New York: Routledge, 21-39.

Carpenter, M. (1994), *Normality is Hard Work: Trade Unions and the Politics of Community Care*, London: Lawrence and Wishart.

Cassis, Y. (1997), *Big Business: The European Experience in the Twentieth Century*, Oxford: Oxford University Press.

Castel, R. (1995), *Les Métamorphoses de la Quesiton Sociale: Une Chronique du Salariat*, Paris: Fayard.

Castells, M. (1989), *The Informational City*, Oxford: Blackwell.

Castles, F. G. (ed.) (1993), *Families of Nations: Patterns of Public Policy in Western Democracies*, Aldershot: Dartmouth.

Castles, F. G., and D. Mitchell. (1993), 'Worlds of welfare and families of nations', in F. G. Castles (ed.), *Families of Nations: Patterns of Public Policy in Western Democracies*, Aldershot: Dartmouth, 93-128.

Castles, S., H. Booth and T. Wallace. (1987), *Here for Good: Western Europe's New Ethnic Minorities*, London: Pluto.

Cerny, P. G. (1997), 'International finance and the erosion of capitalist diversity', in C. Crouch and W. Streeck (eds), *Political Economy of Modern Capitalism: Mapping Convergence and Diversity*, London: Sage, 173-81.

Champion, A. (1993), 'Geographical distribution and urbanization', in D. Noin and R. Woods (eds) *The Changing Population of Europe*, Oxford: Basil Blackwell, 23-37.

Chandler, A. (1977), *The Visible Hand: The Managerial Revolution in American Business*, Cambridge, MA: Belknap Press.

Chandler, A. (1988), 'Scale, scope and organizational capabilities', in T. McCraw (ed.), *The Essential Alfred Chandler: Essays Toward a Historical Theory of Big Business*, Boston: Harvard Business School Press, 472-504.

Chandler, A. (1990), *Scale and Scope*, Cambridge, MA: Harvard University Press.

Cippola, C. M. (1976), *Before the Industrial Revolution: European Society and Economy, 1000-1700*, London: Methuen, second edition.

Clarke, J., A. Cochrane and E. McLaughlin. (1994), *Managing Social Policy*, London, Sage.

Clarke, J. and J. Newman (1997), *The Managerial State: Power, Politics and Ideology in the Remaking of Social Welfare*, London: Sage.

Clarke, S. (1992), 'What in the f---'s name is Fordism?', in N. Gilbert, R. Burrows and A. Pollert (eds), *Fordism and Flexibility: Divisions and Change*, 13-30.

Cole, J. and F. Cole (1997), *The Geography of the European Community*, London and New York: Routledge.

Commision on Global Governance (1995), *Our Global Neighbourhood*, Oxford:

Oxford University Press.

Cook, C. and J. Stevenson (1998), *The Longman Handbook of Modern European History 1763-1997*, London and New York: Longman, Third Edition.

Cooper, C., R. Cooper and L. Eaker (1988), *Living With Stress*, Harmondsworth: Penguin.

Corden, A. and K. Duffy (1998), 'Human dignity and social exclusion', in R. Sykes and P. Alcock (eds), *Developments in European Social Policy: Convergence and Diversity*, Bristol: The Policy Press, 95-124.

Cox, R. H. (1998), 'The consequences of welfare reform: how conceptions of welfare rights are changing', *Journal of Social Policy*, **27** (1), 1-16.

Crafts, N. (1999), 'The Great Boom 1950-73', in M.-S. Schulze (ed.), *Western Europe: Economic and Social Change since 1945*, London: Longman, 42-62.

Cressey, P. and B. Jones. (1995), *Work and Employment in Europe: A New Convergence?* London: Routledge.

Cross, M. (1993), 'Generating the "new poverty": a European comparison', in R. Simpson and R. Walker (eds), *Europe: For Richer or Poorer?*, London: Child Poverty Action Group, 5-24.

Crouch, C. (1986). 'Sharing public space: states and organized interests in western Europe', in J. A. Hall (ed.), *States in History*, Oxford: Basil Blackwell, 177-210.

Crouch, C. (1993), *Industrial Relations and European State Traditions*, Oxford: Clarendon Press.

Crouch, C. and W. Streeck (1997), 'Introduction: the future of capitalist diversity', in C. Crouch and W. Streeck (eds), *Political Economy of Modern Capitalism: Mapping Convergence and Diversity*, London: Sage, 1-18.

Crouch, C. (1999), 'Employment, industrial relations and social policy: new life in an old connection', *Social Policy and Administration*, **33** (4), 437-57.

Daly, M. (1997), 'Cash benefits in European welfare states', *Journal of European Social Policy*, **7** (2), 129-46.

Danford, A. (1998), 'Work organization inside Japanese firms in south Wales: a break with Taylorism?', in P. Thompson and C. Warhurst (eds), *Workplaces of the Future*, Basingstoke: Macmillan, 40-64.

Daniels, J. D. and L. H. Radebaugh (1995), *International Business: Environments and Operations*, Reading, MA: Addison-Wesley.

Dany, F. and V. Torchy (1994), 'Recruitment and selection in Europe: policies, practices and methods', in C. Brewster and A. Hegewisch (eds.), *Policy and Practice in European Human Resource Management*, London: Routledge, 68-88.

De Grip, A., J. Hoevenberg and E. Willems. (1997), 'Atypical employment in the European union', *International Labour Review*, **136** (1), 49-71.

Deaton, A. S. (1976), 'The structure of demand in Europe 1920-1970', in C. M. Cippola (ed.), *The Fonatana Economic History of Europe: The Twentieth Century*, vol. 5, Part 1, London: Collins/Fontana, 89-131.

Den Boer, P. (1993), 'Europe to 1914: the making of an idea', in in K Wilson and J. van der Dussen (eds). *The History of the Idea of Europe*, London and New York: Routledge, 13-82.

Dicken, P. (1998), *Global Shift: Transforming the World Economy*, London: Paul Chapman, third edition.

Dixon, J. and D. Macarov (eds) (1998), *Poverty: A Persistent Global Reality*, London and New York: Routledge.

Doling, J. (1993), 'Encouraging home ownership: trends and prospects', in C. Jones (ed.), *New Perspectives on the Welfare State in Europe*, London and New York:

Routledge, 64-83.

Doling, J. (1997), *Comparative Housing: Government and Housing in Advanced Industrialized Countries*, Basingstoke: Macmillan.

Donzelot, J. (1979), *The Policing of Families: Welfare Versus the State*, London: Hutchinson.

Dore, R. (1972), *British Factory-Japanese Factory: The Origins of National Diversity in Industrial Relations*, London: Allen and Unwin.

Doyal, L., G. Hunt and J. Mellor (1981), 'Your life in their hands: migrant workers in the National Health Service', *Critical Social Policy*, **1** (2), 54-71.

Doyal, L. and S. Epstein (1983), *Cancer in Britain: The Politics of Prevention*, London: Pluto.

Drew, E. and R. Emerek (1998), 'Employment, flexibility and gender', in E. Drew, R. Emerek and E. Mahon (eds), *Women, Work and the Family in Europe*, London and New York: Routledge, 89-99.

Droz, J, (ed.) (1977), *Histoire Générale du Socialisme, Tome 3: 1919-1945*, Paris: PUF.

Duby, G. (1980), *The Three Orders: Feudal Society Imagined*, Chicago: University of Chicago Press.

Eardley, T. (1996), 'From safety nets to springboards? Social assistance and work incentives in the OECD countries', in M. May, E. Brunsdon and G. Craig (eds), *Social Policy Review*, **8**, London: Social Policy Association, 247-85.

EC (1991), *Panorama of EC Industry, 1991-1992*, Luxembourg: European Commission.

EC (1995), *European Economy: Performance of the European Union Labour Market*, Luxembourg: European Commission.

EC (1997), *Panorama of EU Industry, 1997*, Luxembourg: European Commission.

EC (1997a), *Employment in Europe 1997*, Luxembourg: Office for Official Publications of the European Communities.

EC (1997b), *Racism and Xenophobia in Europe: Eurobarometer Opinion Poll, No. 47.1, First Results*, Luxembourg: European Commission.

Economist (1995), 'No room at Europe's inn', *The Economist*, 9 December.

Economist (1999a), 'Fruitless but not harmless', *The Economist*, 10 April.

Economist (1999b), 'Glittering economic prizes', *The Economist*, 10 April.

Eichengreen, B., J. Tobin, and C. Wyplosz (1995), 'Two cases for sand in the wheels of international finance', *Economic Journal*, **105** (428), 162-172.

EIRR (various dates), *European Industrial Relations Review*.

Elger, T. and C. Smith (eds) (1994), *Global Japanization? The Transnational Transformation of the Labour Process*, London: Routledge.

Ellingsæter, A. L. (1998), 'Dual breadwinner societies: provider models in the Scandinavian welfare states', *Acta Sociologica*, **43** (1), 59-73.

Elliott, L. and D. Atkinson (1998), *The Age of Insecurity*, London and New York: Verso.

Ellwood, D. W. (1998), '"You too can be like us": selling the Marshall plan', *History Today*, October, 33-39.

Esping-Anderson, G. (1990), *The Three Worlds of Welfare Capitalism*, Cambridge: Polity.

Esping-Anderson, G. (1993), 'The comparative macro-sociology of welfare states', in L. Moreno (ed.), *Social Exchange and Welfare Development*, Madrid: C.S.I.C, 123-36.

Eurobarometer (1997), *The Opinions of Europeans on Public Services*,

Luxembourg: Office for Official Publications of the European Communities.

Eurobarometer (1998), *Citizens and Health Systems: Main Results From a Eurobarometer Survey,* Luxembourg: Office for Official Publications of the European Communities.

European Foundation for the Improvement of Living and Working Conditions (1996), *Working Conditions in the European Union,* Luxembourg: Office for Official Publications of the European Communities.

Eurostat (1977), *Labour Force Survey,* Luxembourg: EC.

Eurostat (1981), *Labour Force Survey, Results 1979,* Luxembourg: EC.

Eurostat (1996), *Labour Force Survey: Results 1994,* Luxembourg: EC.

Eurostat (1996b), *Eurostat News Release,* No. 63, Luxembourg: Office for Official Publications of the European Communities.

Eurostat (1997), *Labour Force Survey: Results 1996,* Luxembourg: EC.

Eurostat (1998a), *Eurostat News Release,* No. 58, Luxembourg: Office for Official Publications of the European Communities.

Eurostat (1998b), *Eurostat News Release,* No. 60, Luxembourg: Office for Official Publications of the European Communities.

Eurostat (1998c), *Eurostat News Release,* No. 77, Luxembourg: Office for Official Publications of the European Communities.

Eurostat (2000), *Enquête sur les Forces de Travail: Résultats 1998,* Luxembourg: Office for Official Publications of the European Communities.

Fajertag, G. and P. Pochet (eds) (1997), *Social Pacts in Europe,* Brussels: European Trade Union Institute (ETUI).

FEANTSA (1994), *Abandoned: Profile of Europe's Homeless People,* Brussels: European Federation of National Organisations Working with the Homeless.

FEANTSA (1998), *Message to the European Union - Housing: Essential for Building a Social Europe,* Brussels: European Federation of National Organisations Working with the Homeless.

Filella, J. and A. Hegewisch (1994), 'European experiments with pay and benefits policies', in C. Brewster and A. Hegewisch (eds.), *Policy and Practice in European Human Resource Management,* London: Routledge, 89-107.

Fligstein, N. (1985), 'the spread of the multidivisional form', *American Sociological Review,* **50,** 377-91.

Flora, P., F. Kraus and W. Pfenning, (1983), *State, Economy and Society in Western Europe, 1815-1975: A Data Handbook,* Frankfurt, London and Chicago: Campus Verlag, Macmillan and St. James Press.

Foreman-Peck, J. (1995), *A History of the World Economy: International Economic Relations Since 1850,* Hemel Hempstead: Harvester Wheatsheaf, second edition.

Foucault, M. (1967), *Madness and Civilization: A History of Insanity in the Age of Reason,* London: Tavistock.

Foucault, M. (1977), *Discipline and Punish,* Harmondsworth: Penguin.

Fraser, D. (1973), *The Evolution of the British Welfare State,* London: Macmillan.

Freidmann, A.L. (1977), *Industry and Labour: Class Struggle at Work and Monopoly Capitalism,* London: Macmillan.

Fukuyama, F (1989), 'The end of history?', *National Interest,* No. 16, 3-18.

Gamble, A. (1988), *The Free Economy and the Strong State,* Basingstoke: Macmillan.

Garrison, T. (1994), 'Managing people across Europe: an introductory framework', in T. Garrison and D. Rees (eds), *Managing People Across Europe,* London: Butterworth-Heinemann, 1-24.

Garson, R. and C. J. Bailey (1990), *The Uncertain Power: A Political History of the United States Since 1929*, Manchester and New York: Manchester University Press.

Geary, D. (1981), *European Labour Protest 1848-1939*, New York: St. Martin's Press.

George, C. S. (1972), *The History of Management Thought*, Englewood Cliffs, NJ: Prentice-Hall.

George, S. (1988), *A Fate Worse Than Debt*, New York: Grove Press.

George, S. (1996), *Politics and Policy in the European Union*, Oxford: Oxford University Press, third edition.

George, V. and P. Wilding (1985), *Ideology and Social Welfare*, London: Routledge.

Gerschenkron, A. (1962), *Economic Backwardness in Historical Perspective*, Cambridge, MA: Harvard University Press.

Giddens, A. (1984), *The Constitution of Society: Outline of the Theory of Structuration*, Cambridge: Polity Press.

Giddens, A. (1998), *The Third Way: The Renewal of Social Democracy*, Cambridge: Polity.

Ginsburg, N. (1992), *Divisions of Welfare*, London: Sage.

Ginsburg, N. (1994), '"Race", racism and social policy in western Europe', in J. Ferris and R. Page (eds), *Social Policy in Transition*, Aldershot: Avebury, 165-86.

Ginsburg, N. (1998), 'Postmodernity and social Europe', in J. Carter (ed.), *Postmodernity and the Fragmentation of Welfare*, London and New York: Routledge, 267-77.

Glaser, N. (1998), 'The American welfare state: exceptional no longer?', in H. Cavanna (ed.), *Challenges to the Welfare State*, Cheltenham UK and Northampton, USA: Edward Elgar, 7-20.

Glass, D.V. and E. Grebenik (1941-78), 'World population, 1800-1950', in *The Cambridge Economic History of Europe, 7 Vols*, Cambridge: Cambridge University Press, 6: 68-9.

Glennerster, H. and J. Midgley (eds) (1991), *The Radical Right and the Welfare State: An International Assessment*, Hemel Hempstead: Harvester Wheatsheaf.

Glyn, A. and R. Sutcliffe (1972), *British Capitalism, Workers and the Profits Squeeze*, London: Penguin.

Goldthorpe, J. (1995), 'The service class revisited', in T. Butler and M. Savage (eds), *Social Change and the Middle Classes*, London: UCL Press, 313-29.

Goodman, J. and K. Honeyman (1988), *Gainful Pursuits: The Making of Industrial Europe 1600-1914*, London: Edward Arnold.

Gough, I. (1979), *The Political Economy of the Welfare State*, London: Macmillan.

Grahl, J. (1997), *After Maastricht: A Guide to European Monetary Union*, London: Lawrence and Wishart.

Gray, J. (1998), *False Dawn: The Delusions of Global Capitalism*, London: Granta.

Guillén, M. (1994), *Models of Management: Work, Authority and Organization in a Comparative Perspective*, Chicago: University of Chicago Press.

Gustaffson, B. (1996), 'The industrial revolution in Sweden', in M. Teich and R. Porter (eds), *The Industrial Revolution in National Context: Europe and the USA*, Cambridge: Cambridge University Press, 201-25.

Gynnerstedt, K. (1997), 'Social policy in Sweden: current crises and future prospects', in M. Mullard and S. Lee (eds), *The Politics of Social Policy in*

Europe, Cheltenham UK, and Lyme, USA: Edward Elgar, 188-206.

Hall, S. and M. Jacques, (eds) (1989), *New Times: The Changing Face of Politics in the 1990s*, London: Lawrence and Wishart.

Hamerow, T. S. (1983), *The Birth of a New Europe: State and Society in the Nineteenth Century*, Chapel Hill and London: University of North Carolina Press.

Hampden-Turner, C. and F. Trompenaars (1994), *The Seven Cultures of Capitalism: Value Systems for Creating Value Systems for Creating Wealth in the United States, Britain, Japan, Germany, France, Sweden, and the Netherlands*, London: Piatkus.

Hantrais, L. and M. T. Letablier (1996), *Families and Family Policies in Europe*, London: Longman.

Harbison, F. and C. Myers (1959), *Management in the Industrial World*, New York: McGraw-Hill.

Hartwell, R. M. (1973), 'The service revolution: the growth of services in the modern economy', in C. M. Cippola (ed.), *The Fontana Economic History of Europe: The Industrial Revolution*, vol. 3, London: Collins/Fontana, 358-96.

Hayek, F. (1944), *The road to Serfdom*, London: Routledge and Sons.

Health and Safety Executive (1991), *Workplace Health and Safety in Europe*, London: HMSO.

Heath, A. and M. Savage. (1995), 'Political alignment within the middle classes, 1972-89', in T. Butler and M. Savage (eds), *Social Change and the Middle Classes*, London: UCL Press, 275-92.

Heer, F. (1962), *The Medieval World: Europe 1100-1350*, London: Weidenfeld and Nicholson.

Held, D. A. McGrew, D. Goldblatt and J. Perraton (1999), *Global Transformations: Politics, Economics and Culture*, Cambridge: Polity.

Hemerijck, A. (1997), 'Let's go dutch on the welfare bill', *New Statesman*, 19 December.

Henderson, D. (1998), *The Changing Fortunes of Economic Liberalism: Yesterday, Today and Tomorrow*, Occasional Paper 108, London: Institute of Economic Affairs.

Henderson, J. and R. Wall (eds) (1994), *Poor Women and Children in the European Past*, London: Routledge.

Henderson, W. O. (1969), *The Industrialization of Europe 1780-1914*, London: Thames and Hudson.

Héran-Le Roy, O. (1999), 'Les risques professionnels pour la santé', in P. Champsaur (ed.), *Données sociales: La société française*, Paris: INSEE, 264-70.

Hilton, R. (1969), *The Decline of Serfdom in Medieval England*, London: Macmillan.

Hiltrop, J-M. (1991), 'Human resource practices of multinational organizations in Belgium', *European Management Journal*, 9 (4), 404-11.

Hirsch, D. (1997), 'Solidarity: the missing link in the UK's welfare chain', *New Statesman*, 19 December.

Hirst, P. and G. Thompson. (1996), *Globalization in Question: The International Economy and the Possibilities of Governance*, Cambridge: Polity.

HMSO (1981), *Labour Force Survey 1979*, London: Stationary Office.

HMSO (1991), *Labour Force Survey 1988-1989*, London: Stationary Office.

Hobsbawm, E. (1962), *The Age of Capital 1848-1875*, London: Weidenfeld and Nicholson.

Hobsbawm, E. (1975), *The Age of Revolution: Europe 1789-1848*, London: Weidenfeld and Nicholson.

Hobsbawm, E. (1987), *The Age of Empire 1875-1914*, London: Weidenfeld and Nicholson.

Hobsbawm, E. (1994), *Age of Extremes: The Short Twentieth Century, 1914-1991*, London: Michael Joseph.

Hochschild, A. (1983), *The Managed Heart: Commercialization of Human Feeling*, Berkeley, CA: University of California Press.

Hofstede, G. (1980), *Culture's Consequences: International Differences in Work Related Values*, Beverly Hills, CA: Sage.

Hogan, M. J. (1987), *The Marshall Plan: America, Britain and the Reconstruction of Western Europe, 1947-1952*, Cambridge: Cambridge University Press.

Hoggett, P. (1994), 'The politics of the modernisation of the UK welfare state', in R. Burrows and B. Loader (eds), *Towards a Post-Fordist Welfare State?* London: Routledge, 38-48.

Holzer, (1989), *Management Education for Small and Medium-sized Enterprises in the European Communities*, Luxembourg: Office for Official Publications of the European Communities.

Hugman, R. (1994), *Ageing and the Care of Older People in Europe*, London: Macmillan.

Humes, S. (1993), *Managing the Multinational: Confronting the Global-Local Dilemma*, New York: Prentice Hall.

Hunt, E. H. (1981), *British Labour History, 1815-1914*, London: Weidenfeld and Nicholson.

Hutton, W. (1995), *The State We're In*, London: Jonathan Cape.

Hyman, R. (1996), 'Union identities and ideologies in Europe', in P. Pasture, J. Verberckmoes and H. de Witte (eds), *The Lost Perspective? Trade Unions Between Ideology and Social Action in the New Europe: Vol. 2, Significance of Ideology in European Trade Unionism*, Aldershot: Avebury, 60-89.

Ikeda, S. (1996), 'World production', in T. Hopkins and I. Wallerstein (eds), *The Age of Transition: Trajectory of the World-System 1945-2025*, London and New Jersey: Zed Books, 338-86.

ILO (1997), *World Labour Report: Industrial Relations, Democracy and Social Stability*, Geneva: International Labour Office.

Jacques, R. (1996), *Manufacturing the Employee: Management Knowledge From the 19th to the 21st Centuries*, London, Thousand Oaks and New Delhi: Sage.

Jefferys, S. (1986), *Management and Managed: Fifty Years of Crisis at Chrysler*, Cambridge: Cambridge University Press.

Jefferys, S. (1995), 'European industrial relations and welfare states', *European Journal of Industrial Relations*, **1** (3), 317-340.

Jefferys S. (1996), 'France 1995: the backward march of labour halted?', *Capital and Class*, No. 59, 6-21.

Jefferys, S. (1997), 'The exceptional centenary of the confédération générale du travail', *Historical Studies in Industrial Relations*, **3**, 123-42.

Jefferys, S. (2000), 'A "Copernican" revolution in French industrial relations: are the time a'changing?', *British Journal of Industrial Relations*, **38** (2) 241-60.

Jefferys, S. and J. Smith (1998), '"If you want to be happy - hang your landlord": housing welfare, industrial relations and political economy in France and Britain', unpublished paper to *Varieties of Capitalism in Europe, North America and Japan Conference*, Cologne: Max Planck Institute for the Study of Society.

Jessop, B. (1990), *State Theory: Putting Capitalist States in Their Place*, Oxford: Polity Press.

Jessop, B. (1994), 'The transition to post-Fordism and the Schumpeterian welfare state', in R. Burrows and B. Loader (eds), *Towards a Post-Fordist Welfare State?*, London and New York: Routledge, 13-37.

John, P. (1998), *Analysing Public Policy*, London: Pinter.

Johnson, N. (ed.) (1995), *Private Markets in Health and Welfare: An International Perspective*, Oxford: Berg.

Jones, B. and P. Cressey (1995), '"Europeanisation": motor or mirage for employment systems', in P. Cressey and B. Jones (eds), *Work and Employment in Europe: A New Convergence?* London: Routledge, 1-27.

Jonnergard, K., C. Svensson and M. Karreman (1996), 'Short-termism and corporate board orientation: the Swedish context', *Advances in International Comparative Management*, **11**, 143-163.

Jordan, B. (1998), *The New Politics of Welfare: Social Justice in a Global Context*, London: Sage.

Jowell, R., L. Brook and L. Dowds (1993), *International Social Attitudes: The Tenth BSA Report*, Aldershot: Dartmouth Publishers.

Jütte, R. (1994), *Poverty and Deviance in Early Modern Europe*, Cambridge: Cambridge University Press.

Kamen, H. (1984), *European Society 1500-1700*, London: Routledge.

Kaplan, G. (1992), *Contemporary Western European Feminism*, London: UCL Press.

Keating, M. (1993), *The Politics of Modern Europe: The State and Political Authority in the Major Democracies*, Aldershot: Edward Elgar.

Kelly, J. (1998), *Rethinking Industrial Relations: Mobilization, Collectivism and Long Waves*, London: Routledge.

Keman, H. (1996), 'The low countries: confrontation and coalition in segmented societies', in J. M. Colomer (ed.), *Political Institutions in Europe*, London: Routledge, 211-53.

Kerr, C., J. T. Dunlop, F. H. Harbison and C. A. Myers (1973), *Industrialism and Industrial Man*, Harmondsworth: Penguin.

Kochan, T.A., H. C. Katz and R.B. McKersie (1994), *The Transformation of American Industrial Relations*, Ithaca, NY: ILR Press.

Koven, S. and S. Michel (eds) (1993), *Mothers of a New World: Maternalist Politics and the Origins of Welfare States*, London and New York: Routledge.

Kranzberg, M. and J. Gies (1975), *By the Sweat of Thy Brow: Work in the Western World*, New York: G. P. Putnam and Sons.

Kriesi, K., R. Koopmans, J. W. Duyvendak and M. G. Guigni (1995), *New Social Movements in Western Europe: A Comparative Analysis*, London: UCL Press.

Kristantonis, N.D. (1998), 'Greece: the maturing of the system', in A. Ferner and R. Hyman (eds), *Changing Industrial Relations in Europe*, Oxford: Basil Blackwell, second edition, 504-28.

Kumar, K. (1978), *Prophecy and Progress: The Sociology of Industrial and Post-Industrial Society*, Harmondsworth: Penguin.

Kvinder, O. M. (1995), *Danmarks Statistike*, Copenhagen.

Labbé, D. (1994), *Les Élections aux Comités d'Enterprise (1945-1993)*, Grenoble: Centre de Recherche sur la Politique, L'Administration et le Territoire.

Lane, C. (1989), *Management and Labour in Europe: The Industrial Enterprise in Germany, Britain and France*, Aldershot: Edward Elgar.

Lane, C. (1995), *Industry and Society in Europe: Stability and Change in Britain, Germany and France*, Aldershot: Edward Elgar.

Lane, J. E. (1997), *Public Sector Reform: Rationale, Trends and Problems*, London: Sage.

Landes, D. (1969), *The Unbound Prometheus*, Cambridge: Cambridge University Press.

Langan, M. and I. Ostner (1991), 'Gender and welfare: towards a comparative framework', in G. Room (ed.), *Towards a European Welfare State?* Bristol: SAUS, 127-50.

Laqueur, W. (1992), *Europe in Our Time: A History 1945-1992*, Harmondsworth: Penguin.

Lash, S. and J. Urry (1987), *The End of Organized Capitalism*, Cambridge: Polity Press.

Lassey, M., W. Lassey and M. Jinks (1997), *Health Care Systems Around the World: Characteristics, Issues, Reforms*, New Jersey: Prentice Hall.

Lawrence, P. A. (1980), *Managers and Management in West Germany*, New York: St. Martins Press.

Lawrence, P. A. and T. Spybey (1986), *Management and Society in Sweden*, London: Routledge and Kegan Paul.

Leat, M. (1998), *Human Resource Issues of the European Union*, London: Financial Times Management.

Le Grand, J. and W. Bartlett (eds) (1993), *Quasi-Markets and Social Policy*, Basingstoke: Macmillan.

Le Grand, J. and R. Goodin (eds) (1987), *Not Only the Poor: The Middle Classes and the Welfare State*, London: Allen and Unwin.

Leibfried, S. (1993), 'Towards a European welfare state? On integrating poverty regimes in the European community', in C. Jones (ed.), *New Perspectives on the Welfare State in Europe*, London and New York: Routledge, 133-56

Leibfried, S. and P. Pierson, (1995), 'Semi-sovereign welfare states: social policy in a multi-tiered Europe', in S. Leibfried and P. Pierson (eds), *European Social Policy: Between Fragmentation and Integration*, Washington, DC: The Brookings Institution, 43-77.

Leion, A. (1985), 'Sweden', in B. C. Roberts (ed.), *Industrial Relations in Europe: The Imperatives of Change*, London: Croom Helm, 204-21.

Leparmentier A. (1999), 'Le système fiscal et social incite les Allemandes à rester chez elles', *Le Monde,* 6 February.

Levitas, R. (1996), 'The concept of social exclusion and the new Durkheimian hegemony', *Critical Social Policy,* **16**, 5-20.

Lewis, J. (1992), 'Gender and the development of welfare regimes', *Journal of European Social Policy,* **2** (3), 159-73.

Lewis, J. (1993), 'Introduction: women, work, family and social policies in Europe', in J. Lewis (ed.), *Women and Social Policies in Europe: Work, Family and the State*, Aldershot: Edward Elgar, 1-24.

Lipietz, A. (1987), *Mirages and Miracles: The Crises of Global Fordism*, London: Verso.

Lipietz, A. (1996), 'Social Europe, the post-Maastricht challenge', *Review of International Political Economy,* **3** (3), 369-79.

Lis, C. and H. Soly (1979), *Poverty and Capitalism in Pre-industrial Europe*, New Jersey: Humanities Press.

Lis, C., J. Lucassen, and H. Soly, (1994), 'Introduction', *International Review of*

Social History, **39**, Supplement, 'Before the Unions: Wage Earners and Collective Action in Europe, 1300-1850'.

Littler, C. R. (1982), *The Development of the Labour Process in Capitalist Societies*, London: Heinemann.

Locke, R., T. Kochan and M. Piore (1995), *Employment Relations in a Changing World Economy*, Cambridge, MA: London: MIT Press.

Locke, R. (1996), *The Collapse of the American Management Mystique*, Oxford Oxford University Press.

Lowe, R. (1999), *The Welfare State in Britain Since 1945*, Basingstoke: Macmillan, ssecond edition.

Luttwak, E. (1997), 'Central bankism', in P. Gowan and P. Anderson (eds.), *The Question of Europe*, London and New York: Verso, 220-33.

Maddison, A. (1987), 'Origins and impact of the welfare state', *Banca Nazionale de Lavoro, Quarterly Review*, **37** (148), 55-87.

Maddison, A. (1989), *The World Economy in the Twentieth Century*, Paris: OECD.

Maier, C. S. (1981), 'The two postwar eras and the conditions for stability in twentieth-century western Europe', *American Historical Review*, 86: 327-52.

Mann, M. (1995), 'Sources of variation in working class movements in twentieth century Europe', *New Left Review*, No. 212, July/August, 14-54.

Marchand, O. and C. Thélot (1991), *Deux Siècles de Travail en France*, Paris: INSEE.

Marcuse, H. (1961), *Soviet Marxism: A Critical Analysis*, New York: Columbia University Press.

Marglin, S. (1976), 'What do bosses do?', in A. Gorz (ed.), *The Division of Labour: the Labour Process and Class Struggle in Modern Capitalism*, Brighton: Harvester, 13-54.

Marsden, D. and J-J. Silvestre (1992), 'Pay and European integration', in D. Marsden (ed.), *Pay and Employment in the New Europe*, Aldershot: Edward Elgar, 1-41.

Marshall (1950), *Citizenship and Social Class and Other Essays*, Cambridge: Cambridge University Press.

Martin, H.-P. and H. Schumann (1997), *The Global Trap: Globalization and the Assault on Democracy and Prosperity*, London and New York: Zed.

Max-Planck-Institut für Gesellschaftforschung (1998), *Adjustment Data Base Structure*, Cologne.

Mayer, M. and R Whittington 1996, 'The survival of the European holding company: institutional choice and contingency', in R. Whitley and P. H. Kristensen (eds),   Kristensen, *The Changing European Firm: Limits to Convergence,* London: Routledge, 87-112.

Mayne, R. (1998), *The International Dimensions of Work: Some Implications for the UK*, Oxford: Oxfam.

McCraw, T. K. (ed.) (1988), *The Essential Alfred Chandler*, Boston, MA: Harvard Business School Press, 472-504.

McGivering, I. C., D. G. J. Matthews and W. H. Scott (1960), *Management in Britain: A General Characterisation*, Liverpool: Liverpool University Press.

McNeill, W. H. (1983), *The Pursuit of Power*, Oxford: Basil Blackwell.

Meer, M. van der (1996), 'Aspiring corporatism? Industrial relations in Spain', in J. van Ruyssevedelt and J. Visser (eds), *Industrial Relations in Europe*, London: Sage, 310-36.

Merriman, J. (1996), *A History of Modern Europe: From the Renaissance to the*

Present, New York and London: W. W. Norton.

Miliband, R. (1972), *Parliamentary Socialism: A Study: The Politics of Labour*, London: Merlin Press, second edition.

Milkman, R. (1998), 'The new American workplace: high road or low road', in P. Thompson and C. Warhurst (eds), *Workplaces of the Future*, Basingstoke: Macmillan, 25-39.

Millward, A. S. (1997), 'The springs of integration', in P. Gowan and P. Anderson (eds), *The Question of Europe*, London and New York: Verso, 5-20.

Mintzberg, H. and J.B. Quinn (1996), *The Strategy Process: Concepts, Contexts, Cases*, London: Prentice Hall International.

Mitchell, M. and D. Russell (1998), 'Immigration, citizenship and social exclusion in the new Europe', in R. Sykes and P. Alcock (eds), *Developments in European Social Policy: Convergence and Diversity*, Bristol: The Policy Press, 75-94.

Mollat, M. (1986), *The Poor in the Middle Ages: An Essay in Social History*, New Haven, CT and London, UK: Yale University Press.

Moody, K. (1997), *Workers in a Lean World: Unions in the International Economy*, London: Verso.

Mosson, T. M. (1965), *Management Education in Five European Countries*, London: Business Publications.

Mundy, J. H. (1991), *Europe in the High Middle Ages: 1150-1309*, London and New York: Longman, second edition.

Murray, C. (1984), *Losing Ground: American Social Policy 1950-1980*, New York: Basic Books.

Murray, C. (1990), *The Emerging British Underclass*, London: Institute of Economic Affairs.

Navarro, V. (1989), 'Why some countries have national health insurance, others have national health services, and the US has neither', *Social Science and Medicine*, **28** (9), 887-98.

Navarro, V. (1991), 'Production and the welfare state: the political context of reforms', *International Journal of Health Services*, **21** (4), 585-614.

Noin, D. (1995), 'Spatial inequalities of mortality in the European Union', in R. Hall and P. White (eds.), *Europe's Population: Towards the Next Century*, London: UCL Press.

Noiriel, G. (1986), *Les ouvriers dans la société française*, Paris: Éditions du Seuil.

Norberg, K. (1993), 'Prostitutes', in N. Z. Davis and A. Farge (eds), *A History of Women in the West: vol. 3. Renaissance and Enlightenment Paradoxes*, Cambridge, MA.; London: Harvard University Press, 458-74.

North, D. (1965), 'Industrialization in the United States', in H. J. Habakkuk and M. Postan (eds), *The Cambridge Economic History of Europe*, vol. 6, Part 2, Cambridge: Cambridge University Press, 673-705.

O'Connor, J. (1973), *The Fiscal Crisis of the State*, New York: St. James's Press.

OECD (1989), 'Occupational accidents in OECD countries', *Employment Outlook*, Organization for Economic Cooperation and Development, July, 133-59.

OECD (1991), *Employment Outlook*, Paris: Organization for Economic Cooperation and Development.

OECD (1994), *Employment Outlook*, Paris: Organization for Economic Cooperation and Development, July.

OECD (1994a), *New Orientations in Social Policy*, Paris: Organization for Economic Cooperation and Development, Social Policy Studies No. 12.

OECD (1995), *The OECD Jobs Study: Implementing the Strategy*, Paris:

Organization for Economic Cooperation and Development.

OECD (1996a), *OECD Jobs Study: Evidence and Explanations*, Paris: Organization for Economic Cooperation and Development.

OECD (1996b), *OECD Jobs Study: Taxation, Employment and Unemployment*, Paris: Organization for Economic Cooperation and Development.

OECD (1996c), *OECD Health Data 96*, Paris: Organization for Economic Cooperation and Development.

OECD (1996d), *Historical Statistics 1960-1994*, Paris: Organization for Economic Cooperation and Development.

OECD (1997), *Employment Outlook*, Paris: Organization for Economic Cooperation and Development.

OECD (1998), *Employment Outlook*, Paris: Organization for Economic Cooperation and Development.

OECD (1999a), *A Caring World: The New Social Policy Agenda*, Paris: Organization for Economic Cooperation and Development.

OECD (1999b), *Employment Outlook*, Paris: Organization for Economic Cooperation and Development.

Offe, C. (1984), *Contradictions of the Welfare State*, London: Hutchinson.

Olsen, G. M. (1996), 'Re-modeling Sweden: the rise and demise of the compromise in a global economy', *Social Problems*, 43 (1), 1-17.

Olson, M. (1982), *The Rise and Decline of Nations*, New Haven, CT: Yale University Press.

ONS (1998), *Labour Force Survey Quarterly Supplement*, 2, HMSO: London.

O'Reilly, J. and C. Spee (1998), 'The future regulation of work and welfare: time for a revised social and gender contract?', *European Journal of Industrial Relations*, 4 (3), 259-81.

Padgett, S. and W. E. Paterson (1991), *A History of Social Democracy in Postwar Europe*, London and New York: Longman.

Park, K. (1992), 'Medicine and society in medieval Europe, 500-1500', in A. Wear (ed.), *Medicine in Society: Historical Essays*, Cambridge: Cambridge University Press, 59-90.

Parker, W. (1996), 'Revolutions and continuities in American development', in M. Tech and R. Porter (eds), *The Industrial Revolution in National Context: Europe and the USA*, Cambridge: Cambridge University Press, 350-70.

Pellicelli, G. (1976), 'Management 1920-1970', C. M. Cippola (ed.), *The Fonatana Economic History of Europe: The Twentieth Century*, vol. 5, Part 1, London: Collins/Fontana, 184-216.

Peters, T. and R. Waterman (1982), *In Search of Excellence: Lessons from America's Best-run Companies*, New York: Harper and Row.

Pierson, C. (1998), *Beyond the Welfare State? The New Political Economy of Welfare*, Cambridge: Polity, second edition.

Piore, M. and C. Sabel (1984), *The Second Industrial Divide*, New York: Basic Books.

Pollard, S. (1965), *The Genesis of Modern Management: A Study of the Industrial Revolution in Great Britain*, London: Edward Arnold.

Pollard, S. (1982), *Peaceful Conquest: The Industrialization of Europe 1760-1970*, Oxford: Oxford University Press.

Pollard, S. (1996), 'The industrial revolution - an overview', in M. Teich and R. Porter, (eds), *The Industrial Revolution in National Context: Europe and the USA*, Cambridge: Cambridge University Press, 371-88.

Pollard, S. (1997), *The International Economy Since 1945*, London and New York: Routledge.

Pollert, A. (ed.) (1991), *Farewell to Flexibility?* Oxford: Basil Blackwell.

Pollitt, C. (1990), *Managerialism and the Public Services: The Anglo-American Experience*, Oxford: Basil Blackwell.

Polyani, K. (1944), *The Great Transformation: The Political and Economic Origins of Our Time*, Boston: Beacon Press.

Poni, C. and G. Mori (1996), 'Italy in the longue dureé: the return of an old first-comer', in M. Teich and R. Porter (eds), *The Industrial Revolution in National Context: Europe and the USA*, Cambridge: Cambridge University Press, 149-83.

Pontusson, J. (1997), 'Between neo-liberalism and the German model: Swedish capitalism in transition', in C. Crouch and W. Streeck (eds), *Political Economy of Modern Capitalism: Mapping Convergence and Diversity*, London: Sage, 55-70.

Porter, A. (1994), *European Imperialism 1860-1914*, London: Macmillan.

Porter, M. E. (1985), *Competitive Advantage: Creating and Sustaining Superior Performance*, New York: Free Press.

Power, A. (1993), *Hovels to High Rise: State Housing in Europe Since 1850*, London and New York: Routledge.

Power, A. (1999), 'High-rise estates in Europe: is rescue possible?', *Journal of European Social Policy*, 9 (2), 139-63.

Power, C. (1994), 'Health and social inequality in Europe', *British Medical Journal*, 308, 1153-6.

Prasad, S. and D. Sprague (1996), 'Is TWM a global paradigm?' *Advances in International Comparative Management*, 11, 69-85.

PSPRU (1996), *The Privatisation Network - The Multinationals' Bid for Public Services*, London: Public Services Privatisation Research Unit.

Quine, M. S. (1996), *Population Politics in Twentieth-Century Europe*, London and New York: Routledge.

Read, M. and A. Simpson (1991), *Against A Rising Tide: Racism, Europe and 1992*, Nottingham: Spokesman.

Regini, M. (1995), 'Firms and institutions: the demand for skills and their social production in Europe', *European Journal of Industrial Relations*, 1 (2), 191-202.

Reich, R. (1993), *The Work of Nations*, London: Simon and Schuster.

Rhodes, M. (1996), 'Globalization and west European welfare states: a critical review of recent debates', *Journal of European Social Policy*, 6 (4), 305-27.

Rimlinger, G. (1971), *Welfare Policy and Industrialization in Europe, America and Russia*, New York: John Wiley.

Ritter, G. (1983), *Social Welfare in Germany and Britain: Origins and Development*, Leamington Spa and New York: Berg.

Ritzer, G. (1996), *The McDonaldization of Society: An Investigation into the Changing Character of Contemporary Social Life*, Thousand Oaks: Pine Forge Press, second edition.

Robinson, A. (1997), 'Why a Chile pension is not so hot after all', *The Guardian*, 14 July.

Robinson, R. (1998), 'Managed competition: health care reform in the Netherlands', in W. Renade (ed.), *Markets and Health Care: A Comparative Analysis*, London and New York: Longman, 147-63.

Rokkan, S. (1972), 'Nation building: a review of models and approaches', *Current Sociology*, 3, 7-38.

Ronan, S. and O. Shenkar (1985), 'Clustering countries on attitudinal dimensions: a review and synthesis', *Academy of Management Journal*, **10** (3), 435-54.

Rose, M. (1986), *Industrial Behaviour*, Harmondsworth: Penguin, second edition.

Rose, R. (1996), *What is Europe? A Dynamic Perspective*, New York: HarperCollins.

Ross, G. (1995), 'Assessing the Delors era and social policy', in S. Leibfried and P. Pierson (eds), *European Social Policy*, Washington, DC: The Brookings Institution, 357-88.

Ruggie, J. G. (1982), 'International regimes, transactions and change: embedded liberalism in the postwar economic order', *International Organization*, **36** (2), 379-416.

Ruggie, J. G. (1994), 'Trade, protectionism and the future of welfare capitalism', *Journal of International Affairs*, 48, Summer, 1-11.

Rule, J. (1986), *The Labouring Classes in Early Industrial England, 1750-1850*, London and New York: Longman.

Rustin, M. (1989), 'The politics of post-Fordism: or, the trouble with "New Times"', *New Left Review*, No. 175, 54-77.

Ruysseveldt, J. Van. and J. Visser (1996), 'Weak corporatism going different ways? Industrial Relations in the Netherlands and Belgium', in J. van Ruysseveldt and J. Visser (eds), *Industrial Relations in Europe*, London: Sage, 205-64.

SAF (1996a), *Membership Statistics*, Stockholm: Swedish Employers' Association.

SAF (1996b), *The Business Sector's Joint Agenda*, Stockholm: Swedish Employers' Association.

Sallmann, J-M. (1993), 'Witches', in N. Z. Davis and A. Farge (eds), *A History of Women in the West: Vol. 3. Renaissance and Enlightenment Paradoxes*, Cambridge, MA and London: Harvard University Press, 444-57.

Saltman, R., J. Figueras and C. Sakellarides (1998), *Critical Challenges for Health Care Reform in Europe*, Buckingham and Philadelphia: Open University Press.

Sampson, A. (1968), *The New Europeans: A Guide to the Workings, Institutions and Character of Contemporary Western Europe*, London: Hodder and Stoughton.

Samuel, R. (1977), 'Workshop of the world: steam power and hand technology in mid-Victorian Britain', *History Workshop Journal*, No. 3, 6-72.

Sassoon, D. (1996), *One Hundred Years of Socialism: The West European Left in the Twentieth Century*, London: Fontana Press.

Schumpeter, J. (1943), *Capitalism, Socialism and Democracy*, London: Allen and Unwin.

Schulze, M.-S. (1999), 'Conclusion: the postwar European economy in long term perspective, in M.-S. Schulze (ed.), *Western Europe: Economic and Social Change since 1945*, London: Longman, 372-87.

Schweie, K. (1994), 'Labour market, welfare state and family institutions: the links to mothers' poverty risks', *Journal of European Social Policy*, **4** (3), 201-24.

Scott, J. W. (1988), *Gender and the Politics of History*, New York: Columbia University Press.

Servan-Schreiber, J.-J. (1968), *The American Challenge*, London: Hamish Hamilton.

Shorter, E. and C. Tilly (1974), *Strikes in France, 1830-1968*, Cambridge: Cambridge University Press.

Shutt, H. (1998), *The Trouble with Capitalism*, London: Zed.

Siaroff, A. (1994), 'Work, welfare and gender equality: a new typology', in D.

Sainsbury (ed.), *Gendering Welfare States*, London, Thousand Oaks, New Delhi: Sage.

Singer, D. (1995), 'Europe in search of a future', in L. Panitch (ed.) *The Socialist Register*, London: Merlin, 117-28.

Singh, R. (1998), *Gender Autonomy in Western Europe: An Imprecise Revolution*, London: Macmillan.

Sivanandan, A. and E. Ahmad (1991), 'Europe: variations on a theme of racism', *Race and Class*, **32** (3), (whole issue).

Smith, C. and T. Elger (1995), 'International competition, inward investment and the restructuring of European work and industrial relations', *European Journal of Industrial Relations*, **3** (3), 279-304.

Soros, G., and A. Giddens (1997), 'Beyond chaos and dogma...', *New Statesman*, 31 October, 24-7.

Sparrow, P. and J.M. Hiltrop (1994), *European Human Resource Management in Transition*, New York: Prentice Hall.

Spicker, P. (1998), *'Le Trou de la Sécu*: Social Security in France', in E. Brunsdon, H. Dean and R. Woods (eds), *Social Policy Review*, **10**, 203-16.

Sretzer, S. R. S. (1988), 'The importance of social intervention in Britain's mortality decline c. 1850-1914: a reinterpretation of the role of public health', *Social History of Medicine*, **1**, 1-38.

Standing, G. (1997), 'Globalization, labour flexibility and insecurity: the era of market regulation', *European Journal of Industrial Relations*, **3** (1), 7-37.

Stecher, H. and M. Bailey (1999), *Time for a Tobin Tax? Some Practical and Political Arguments*, Oxford: Oxfam UK.

Stephens, J. D. (1996), 'The Scandinavian welfare states: achievements, crisis and prospects', *Welfare States in Transition: National Adaptations in Global Economies*, London: Sage, 32-65

Stern, V. (1998), *A Sin Against the Future: Imprisonment in the World*, Harmondsworth: Penguin.

Strange, S. (1997), 'The future of global capitalism; or, will divergence persist forever?', in C. Crouch and W. Streeck (eds), *Political Economy of Modern Capitalism: Mapping Convergence and Diversity*, London: Sage, 182-91.

Supple, B. (1973), 'The state and the industrial revolution 1700-1914', in C. M. Cippola (ed.), *The Fonatana Economic History of Europe: The Industrial Revolution*, vol. 3, London: Collins/Fontana, 301-57.

Svallfors, S. (1997), 'Worlds of welfare and attitudes to redistribution: a comparison of eight western nations', *European Sociological Review*, **13** (3), 283-304.

Sykes, R. (1998), 'Studying European social policy: issues and perspectives', in R. Sykes and P. Alcock (eds), *Developments in European Social Policy: Covergence and Diversity*, Bristol: The Policy Press, 7-26.

Teague, P. (1998), 'Monetary union and social Europe', *Journal of European Social Policy*, **8** (2), 117-37.

Teekens, R. and B. M. S. van Praag (1990), *Analszing Poverty in the European Community: Policy Issues, Research Options and Data Sources*, Luxembourg: Office for Official Publications of the European Community.

Thane, P. (1996), *Foundations of the Welfare State*, London and New York: Longman, second edition.

Therborn, G. (1995), *European Modernity and Beyond: The Trajectory of European Societies 1945-2000*, London: Sage.

Thoemmes, J. and G. de Terssac (1997), 'La construction des arrangements temporels: Une étude de cas sur 11 ans', in G. Bosch, D. Meulders and F. Michon (eds), *Le Temps de Travail: Nouveaux Enjeux, Nouvelles Normes, Nouvelles Mesures*, Paris: Editions du Dulbea, 217-45.

Thompson, E. P. (1967), 'Time, work-discipline and industrial capitalism', *Past and Present*, **38**, 56-97.

Thompson, E. P. (1968), *The Making of the English Working Class*, Harmondsworth, Middlesex: Penguin (first edition, London: Victor Gollancz, 1963).

Thompson, P. and D. McHugh (1995), *Work Organizations: A Critical Introduction*, London: Macmillan.

Thornley, C., S. Contrepois, and S. Jefferys (1997), 'Trade unions, restructuring and individualization in French and British banks', *European Journal of Industrial Relations*, **3** (1), 83-105.

Tilly, C. (1992), *Coercion, Capital and European States, AD 900-1990*, Oxford: Blackwell.

Tilly, R. (1996), 'German industrialization', in M. Teich and R. Porter (eds), *The Industrial Revolution in National Context: Europe and the USA*, Cambridge: Cambridge University Press, 95-125.

Timmins, N. (1995), *The Five Giants: A Biography of the Welfare State*, London: HarperCollins.

Tipton, F. and R. Aldrich (1987), *An Economic and Social History of Europe From 1939 to the Present*, Basingstoke: Macmillan.

Tobin, J. (1978), 'A proposal for international monetary reform', *Eastern Economic Journal*, July-October, 153-9.

Touraine, A. (1966), *La Conscience Ouvrière*, Paris: Editions de Seuil.

Traxler, F. (1998), 'Collective bargaining in the OECD: developments, preconditions and effects', *European Journal of Industrial Relations*, **4** (2), 207-26.

Trempe, R. (1995), 'Luttes, practiques syndicales et progrés social, relations professionnelles et institutions sociales', *Colloque Centenaire de la Confederation Generale du Travail*, Paris: CNAM.

Trifiletti, R. (1999), 'Southern European regimes and the worsening position of women', *Journal of European Social Policy*, **9** (1), 49-64.

UK Coalition Against Poverty (1998), *Fighting Poverty and Social Exclusion: The European Experience*, London: UK Coalition Against Poverty and European Anti Poverty Network.

Urwin, D. W. (1997), *A Political History of Western Europe Since 1945*, London and New York: Longman, fifth edition.

Van der Pijl, K. (1989), 'The international level', in Bottomore, T. and R. J. Brym (eds), *The Capitalist Class: An International Study*, London: Harvester Wheatsheaf.

Van Kersbergen, K. (1995), *Social Capitalism: A Study of Christian Democracy and the Welfare State*, London and New York: Routledge.

Van Oorschot, W. (1998), 'From solidarity to selectivity: the reconstruction of the Dutch social security system 1998-2000', in E. Brunsdon, H. Dean, H. and R. Woods (eds), *Social Policy Review*, **10**, 183-202.

Van Zweeden, A. F. (1985), 'The Netherlands', in B. C. Roberts (ed.), *Industrial Relations in Europe: The Imperatives of Change*, London: Croom Helm, 159-79.

Visser, J. (1996), 'A truly mixed case: industrial relations in Italy', in J. van

Ruysseveldt and J. Visser (eds), *Industrial Relations in Europe: Traditions and Transitions*, London: Sage, 265-309.

Visser, J. (1996a), 'Traditions and transitions in industrial relations: a European view', in J. van Ruyssevedelt and J. Visser. (eds), *Industrial Relations in Europe: Traditions and Transitions*, London: Sage, 1-41.

Visser, J. (1996b), 'Weak corporatisms going different ways? Industrial relations in the Netherlands and Belgium', in J. van Ruyssevedelt and J. Visser. (eds), *Industrial Relations in Europe: Traditions and Transitions*, London: Sage, 205-64.

Walker, A. and T. Maltby (1997), *Ageing Europe*, Buckingham: Open University Press.

Walkowitz, J. R. (1980), *Prostitution and Victorian Society: Women, Class and the State*, Cambridge: Cambridge University Press.

Wallace, W. (1997), 'Rescue or retreat? The nation state in western Europe, 1945-93', in P. Gowan and P. Anderson (eds), *The Question of Europe*, London and New York: Verso, 21-50.

Warhurst, C. and P. Thompson, (1998), 'Hands, hearts and minds: changing work and workers at the end of the century', in P. Thompson and C. Warhurst (eds), *Workplaces of the Future*, Basingstoke: Macmillan, 1-24.

Watts, S. (1997), *Epidemics: Disease, Power and Imperialism*, New Haven, CT and London: Harvard University Press.

Wedderburn, B. (1995), 'European Community law and workers' rights after 1992: fact or fake?', in B. Wedderburn (ed.), *Labour Law and Freedom: Further Essays in Labour Law*, London: Lawrence and Wishart, 247-85.

Wegs, J. R. and R. Ladrech (1996), *Europe Since 1945: A Concise History*, New York: St. Martin's Press, fourth edition.

Weir, M. and T. Skocpol (1985), 'State structures and the possibilities of "Keynsian" responses to the great depression in Sweden, Britain and the U.S.', in P. B. Evans, D. Rueschemeyer and T. Skocpol (eds), *Bringing the State Back In*, Cambridge: Cambridge University Press, 107-63.

Weisner, M. E. (1993), *Women and Gender in Early Modern Europe*, Cambridge: Cambridge University Press.

Western, B. (1998), *Between Class and Market: Postwar Unionization in the Capitalist Democracies*, Princeton: Princeton University Press.

White, M. (1999), 'Blair and Schröder share a vision', *The Guardian*, 9 June.

Whiteside, N. (1987), 'Social Welfare and Industrial Relations', in C. J. Wrigley (ed.), *A History of British Industrial Relations, Volume 2: 1914-1939*, Brighton: Harvester, 211-42.

Whitley, R. (ed.) (1992), *European Business Systems: Firms and Markets in their National Contexts*, London: Sage.

Whitley, R. (1999), *Divergent Capitalisms: The Social Structuring and Change of Business Systems*, Oxford: Oxford University Press.

WHO (1999), *The World Health Report 1999: Making a Difference*, Geneva: World Health Organization..

Wilensky, H. L. and C. N. Lebeaux (1965), *Industrial Society and Social Welfare*, New York: Free Press.

Wilkinson, R. (1996), *Unhealthy Societies: From Inequality to Well-Being*, London: Routledge.

Williams, A. M. (1994), *The European Community*, Oxford: Basil Blackwell, second edition.

Williams, F. (1989), *Social Policy: A Critical Introduction*, Cambridge: Polity Press.

Williams, F. (1995), 'Race/ethnicity, gender, and class in welfare states: a framework for comparative analysis', *Social Politics*, 127-59.

Williams, R. (1973), 'Base and superstructure', *New Left Review*, No 82, 3-16.

Williams, R. (1976), *Keywords: A Vocabulary of Culture and Society*, London: Fontana.

Williamson, O. (1975), *Markets and Hierarchies*, New York: The Free Press.

Wilson, K. and J van der Dussen (1995), *The History of the Idea of Europe*, London: Routledge.

Wise, M. and R. Gibb (1992), *Single Market to Social Europe: The European Community in the 1990s*, Harlow: Longman.

Woolf, S. J. (1986), *The Poor in Western Europe in the Eighteenth and Nineteenth Centuries*, London: Methuen.

World Bank (1997), *The State in a Changing World: World Development Report 1997*, Oxford: Oxford University Press.

Woronoff, J. (1996), *Japan as Anything but Number One*, Basingstoke: Macmillan, second edition.

Wymeersch, E. (1998), 'A status report on corporate governance rules and practices in some continental European states', in K. Hopts, H. Kanda, M. Roe, E. Wymeersch and S. Prigge (eds), *Comparative Corporate Governance: The State of the Art and Emerging Research*, Oxford: Clarendon, 1045-1209.

Zeitlin, J. (1999), 'Americanization and its limits: the reconstruction of Britain's engineering industries, 1945-55', in N. Whiteside and R. Salais (eds), *Governance, Industry and Labour Markets in Britain and France: The Modernizing State in the Mid-twentieth Century*, London: Routledge, 101-22.

Zöllner, D. (1982), 'Germany: characteristics and special features of social legislation in Germany', in P. Köhler and H. Zacher (eds), *The Evolution of Social Insurance 1881-1981: Studies of Germany, France, Great Britain, Austria and Switzerland*, London: Frances Pinter, 1-92.

Index

agency, European tradition 7–11
aging Europe 208–10
agriculture 14, 17, 39, 85–6, 221
American Management Society 74
American National Association of
    Manufacturers 76
American National Management Council
    76
Americanism 38
Americanization 63, 78, 107–39, 142
ancien régimes 18–19
Anglo-American cluster, managerial
    systems 83
Anglo-American Council on Productivity
    (AACP) 75
Anglo-Saxon model, welfare 201–2
Arkwright, Richard 23
artisans 19, 24
asylum seekers 203–4
attitudes, to welfare 199–201
atypical hours 179, 180t
Austria
    flexible work 180
    postwar recovery 59
    public health care 211
    trade unionism 189
authority relations, at work 94–5
autonomy, of managers 146

Babbage, Charles 23
banking mergers 115–16
Basic Income Guarantee (BIG) 229
BAT, merger with Zurich Group 116
Bayer, Frederick 30
Belgium
    childcare 208
    management training 77–8
    minimum wage laws 183
    part-time employment 172
    public health care 211
    social expenditure 198

    structural change 188
    temporary work 181
    white collar workers 173
    women in workforce 87
Benelux Countries 57
best practice, acceptance of 159–60
Beveridge Report 52, 97–8, 101
bilateral agreements, American 76
birth rates 207
Bismarck, Chancellor 46
Bismarckian welfare 98–9, 201, 202, 218
Black Death 17
black workers, in management 146
Blair, Tony 129
Bolshevik revolution (1917) 27, 33
Bon Marché 33
bourgeoisie 29
Brandt, Willy 219
Bretton Woods system 53, 66, 113
Britain
    childcare 208
    collective savings 114t, 115
    flexible work 179, 181
    imprisonment 216
    labour legislation 89
    management positions 73
    management training 76–7, 78
    maternity benefit 208
    minimum wage laws 183
    neo-liberalism 5
    new political right 125–6
    political party system 18
    postwar economic growth 60
    postwar political right 65
    resurgent managerialism 163, 164
    single parent families 207
    structural change 190
    unionism 91, 92
    white collar workers 173
British Institute of Economics 124
British Institute of Management (BIM) 79